Alfresco

Enterprise Content Management Implementation

How to install, use, and customize this powerful, free,
Open-Source Java-based Enterprise CMS

Author

Munwar Shariff

Editor

Mike W. Walker

BIRMINGHAM - MUMBAI

Alfresco

Enterprise Content Management Implementation

First published: December 2006

Production Reference: 1121206

Published by Packt Publishing Ltd.
32 Lincoln Road
Olton
Birmingham, B27 6PA, UK.

ISBN 1-904811-11-6

www.packtpub.com

Cover Image by www.visionwt.com

Credits

Author

Munwar Shariff

Editor

Mike W. Walker

Reviewer

Mike W. Walker

Development Editor

David Barnes

Technical Editors

Rashmi Phadnis

Saurabh Singh

Viraj Joshi

Editorial Manager

Dipali Chittar

Project Manager

Patricia Weir

Project Coordinator

Suneet Amrute

Indexer

Bhushan Pangaonkar

Proofreader

Chris Smith

Layouts and Illustrations

Shantanu Zagade

Cover Designer

Shantanu Zagade

Foreword

Dear Reader,

By picking up this book you have joined a growing band of people, who will benefit from the power of the open-source movement to create great software, a system that is free to all. Alfresco is unique and different. It is the first new Enterprise Content Management system built, in over five years, based on Open Source and Open Standards.

Late in 2004, it struck John Newton (Alfresco's CTO) and me that all the fastest growing software companies were open source. It was particularly clear to us that the operating system, database, and application server market were being consolidated by open source.

There are literally hundreds of open-source content management systems on the market, but none address the requirement of small, medium, and large enterprises to manage, share, control, and reuse content across the company. So we asked ourselves: "Why would anyone care about another open-source CMS?" The answer to this question was deceptively simple. John Newton was the co-founder of Documentum, which makes him probably the single most influential person in the history of ECMS, as he invented many of the concepts we take for granted today. He said to me in November 2004, "What if we had a real open-source ECMS that was ten times faster, and free?" ECMS was a well defined software category (around $4billion), with no credible open-source enterprise-scale projects, and dominated by expensive, complex, and hard-to-deploy products. Despite the exponential growth in the volume of content, the ECMS market was growing at only 15% per year, and over 50% of that revenue was in maintenance. There were few new customers for the closed-source ECMS vendors.

Within John Newton's simple question, we also had the specification:

- Enterprise features (scalability, security, and failsafe plus the power to manage any form of unstructured data, not just web content)

- Super fast
- Simple (to install, to use, and to customize)
- With low costs

It was now clear that the market was looking for an open-source alternative to monolithic, legacy stack vendors. In order to succeed, we needed to have a product that was not just free, but also demonstrably better.

John Newton and I, along with an exceptionally experienced team of ECM engineers, started Alfresco in January 2005. After six months of hard work, we had created a completely new content management system, based on modern, advanced open-source architecture. The big question was: would anyone care? With a great deal of trepidation we loaded the code to SourceForge, and waited. We thought we could get a couple of hundred downloads rapidly, but on a long term basis we simply hoped for maybe 10,000 in the first year. In fact, we had 10,000 in the first week. At that point we knew our original hunch was right: there were thousands of people out there searching for easier content management solutions.

In June 2005 we announced the preview release, and received $2 million in new development funding. In January 2006 we went GA with version 1.1. We had our first production release, our first six subscribing customers and $8 million to secure the permanent future of Alfresco. On the publication of this book we now have 500,000 downloads, 5,000 community sites running on Alfresco and hundreds of subscribers to the Enterprise Network.

With customers such as NASA, the American Stock Exchange, Davis Polk Wardwell LLP, H&R Block, the UK Ministry of Defence, the EU Commission, McGraw Hill, Boise Cascade, and three top-ten global investment banks—spread across the US, France, Australia, Venezuela and the UK—Alfresco is now justifiably a major force in the ECMS market.

After it reached 30,000 downloads a month, publisher David Barnes spotted Alfresco, and was surprised to pick up the phone to another Englishman (and one who knows Birmingham well, having been to University there). We quickly agreed that a book on Alfresco would be a great way to provide our community with the team's expertise at a very low cost of delivery. I was impressed that Packt as a publisher had a track record in open-source publishing. Importantly, we agreed that the book should be written by someone independent of the company, who had the book writing experience, which our team lacked! It took another four months to find the right person, but I'm pleased to see that Munwar has more that stepped up to the challenge. The task has been complex given that Munwar has had to juggle his full-time role as CTO at CIGNEX, a dynamic US-based systems integrator, with racing against the speed of evolution within the Alfresco community. I hope that you will agree this is a great result.

So what is better about Alfresco?

Alfresco solves the two key problems in implementing ECMS:

1. How do I get users to use the system (and become contributors)?
2. How do I customize the system to meet my business needs?

We solved the first problem by enabling Alfresco to run inside the file system. We figured that if the user could use the Windows Explorer/File Manager, he or she could become a content contributor. This was done by providing the ability to mount Alfresco as a shared drive. The result is that the system can implement any content behavior (versioning, transformation, workflow) by the user just dropping the file into the shared drive folder, from any PC (or Mac) on the planet with no training, and no client software installed. Sounds magic? Well, actually it is the CIFS protocol as a Java Server.

We solved the second problem with the help of Rod Johnson, and the Spring Project. Rod's team has created Spring: the most popular open-source framework, implementing Aspect-Oriented Programming (AOP). AOP comes from Xerox Park; the birthplace of object-oriented programming, and solves a key problem for any widely deployed 'horizontal' application. It allows systems to get flexibility and extensibility without imposing on all users the burden of all functionality (whether it is used or not). This enables the Alfresco Community and customers to innovate and add capabilities with ease while retaining a fast and easy upgrade path.

So in two years Alfresco has evolved to cover the four major pieces of Enterprise Content Management—record management, document management, image management, and now web content management. At the time of writing, Alfresco is the fastest JSR-170 repository on the market today. I hope this book will enable you to participate in the open-source community, and the Alfresco journey. There is still much more to do.

John Powell

CEO, Alfresco

About the Author

Munwar Shariff is the CTO and VP of Business Development at CIGNEX. CIGNEX is the leading provider of open-source Enterprise Content Management (ECM) solutions for businesses and government agencies.

He has worked as the chief architect and manager of engineering teams for 15 years in the areas of system software, Internet applications, and mobile commerce applications for customers in the United States, Japan, Germany, and India.

He is an expert in Content Management Systems (CMS). Since co-founding CIGNEX in late 2000, he has successfully delivered more than 50 CMS applications using various open-source technologies. He has written a number of articles on open-source CMS; he is an experienced trainer and a frequent speaker at conferences related to this topic.

Munwar earned his MS in Digital Electronics and Advanced Communications from REC Surathkal, India. Munwar is the co-author of the book on the Plone Open Source Content Management System called *Plone Live*.

I would like to thank John Powell, CEO of Alfresco for introducing me to the publishers, and for writing the foreword. Thanks to John Newton, Ian Howells, Paul Holmes-Higgin, David Caruana, and Kevin Cochrane of Alfresco for providing me with valuable information. Thanks to Alfresco USA team Matt Asay, Jason Hardin, Martin Musierowicz, Luis Sala, and Michael Uzquiano for all the support. They are great partners to work with.

My special thanks to all my team members at CIGNEX for making this book a reality. I would like to thank Navin Nagiah, CEO of CIGNEX for his encouragement and great support; without him, this book would not have existed. My sales and presales team at CIGNEX, Amit, Candace, Harish, and Jarred helped me understand what customers are looking for. I have learnt a lot through numerous discussions with them. I owe them a party, and a special thanks. Our consulting team at CIGNEX presented me with various flavors of Alfresco implementations that I would not have imagined possible, with real-life examples as they work on Production projects. I am thankful to them too.

I sincerely thank and appreciate David Barnes, Development Editor at Packt Publishing for criticizing and fixing my writing style. He claims to be a non-technical person but provides very valuable feedback on technical documentation. Thanks to the entire team at Packt Publishing and it is really joyful to work with them.

Never attempt to write a book when you have a 3-year old and 1-year old at home. You always feel guilty of not spending time with them. Thanks to my wonderful and understanding kids Amaan and Muskaan. I would like to thank my wife Nafeesa, who encouraged and supported me throughout this book. My special thanks to my younger brother Shahin, he is my best friend and supporter.

And finally thanks to all my buddies here in Santa Clara, California, who tolerated my absence in all the social functions for the past six months.

This book is dedicated to my loving parents whose care, unconditional love and sacrifice resulted in where I stand today – Munwar Shariff

About the Editor

Mike W. Walker is a Vice President, in-charge of consulting at CIGNEX (http://www.cignex.com). He has over 16 years of progressive consulting experience with world class consulting firms, including KPMG, Accenture, and Ernst & Young Cap Gemini America.

Mike's organization at CIGNEX is among the very first to successfully deliver ECM projects using Alfresco. He is currently engaged in very complex ECM projects based on Alfresco. Mike has deep expertise both in Alfresco technical architecture and in creating Content Management solution architectures containing Alfresco. Mike's main areas of interest include consulting services delivery processes and methodologies development.

Table of Contents

Preface

Looking at the title of this book, most people may think, "Another book on an open-source CMS?" It's a natural reaction as there are about 1700 content management systems out there in the market.

For the past ten years, I have been implementing various content management systems. I started with multi-million dollar implementations of proprietary software, and faced all kinds of challenges including vendor lock-in, rigid code base, and expensive upgrades. At CIGNEX, our focus has been proving value to our customers using open-source alternatives to commercial CMS products. We research on various open-source products, and propose the most suitable product, which satisfies our customers' requirements over a long period of time.

Unlike most other open-source CMSes, which offered only web content management, Alfresco provided a wide range of solutions to Enterprise customers with an impressive roadmap. And most importantly, it is created using completely open standards. This excited us a lot, and we started implementing Alfresco in many enterprises. As part of our implementation, we also train our customers, so that they are equipped with all the information required to manage their systems. I have trained many users, administrators, and developers in Alfresco and many other systems. This book distils the hands-on approach of my training courses into a concise, practical book.

The book focuses on business needs rather than technical syntax. I started by showing the reader how to do something — a step by step example. I explained how that process worked. Then, I explained what other options are available, and how they fit into the overall picture. I hope this helps the reader "generalize" from such examples. I hope that you take advantage of this book by setting up a flexible enterprise content management system for your company and customers.

Your feedback is very valuable to me. You can contribute by reporting any errors you find in the book, making suggestions for new content that you'd like to see in future updates, commenting, and blogging about it.

What This Book Covers

This book will take you through the complete cycle of planning, implementing, and customizing your ECM installation. The topics that this book covers are:

Chapter 1 includes an overview of Alfresco architecture and key features of the software. This chapter also includes using Alfresco for your document management, records management, web content management, and collaboration requirements and also a future roadmap.

Chapter 2 includes tips to choose the right installation for you, and also installation of the software and start using it.

Chapter 3 includes basic planning and configuring your Alfresco installation.

Chapter 4 includes working with users, and membership accounts, including LDAP integration.

Chapter 5 includes using Alfresco as a smart document repository; working with automatic version tracking and control, and accessing the repository from the Web, shared network folders, or FTP.

Chapter 6 includes automating document management tasks with business rules and complete workflows.

Chapter 7 includes designing custom content types.

Chapter 8 includes making content easy to find using search, content categorization, and metadata.

Chapter 9 includes enhancing automated document management tasks with business rules, and complete workflows.

Chapter 10 includes working together using Alfresco's collaboration and syndication features to create effective working groups.

Chapter 11 includes customizing the user interface and creating your own dashboard layouts, presenting content in custom ways relevant to your business.

Chapter 12 includes maintaining your system including exporting data and upgrading your system to newer versions.

Chapter 13 includes collecting paper documents and forms, transforming them into accurate, retrievable information, and delivering the content into an organization's business applications.

What You Need for This Book

The default installation of Alfresco software requires installing the Windows community version `alfresco-<version>-windows-community.exe` downloaded from the SourceForge project location (`http://sourceforge.net/projects/alfresco`). At the time of writing this book the latest version was 1.4 and the installer file `alfresco-1.4-windows-community.exe` is approximately 183 MB in size.

This installer will install:

- Java Development Kit (JDK), version 5.0
- MySQL database, version 4.1.16
- Apache Tomcat, version 5.5.12
- Portable Open Office, version 2.0.3
- Alfresco, version 1.4, which is packaged as a Web Archive (WAR) file and deployed on the Tomcat server

To install and run Alfresco, you need at least 500 MB disk space and at least 512 MB RAM on the desktop or server.

Who is This Book for

This book is designed for system administrators, experienced users or developers who want to install and use Alfresco in their teams or businesses. Because Alfresco is free many teams can install and experiment with its ECM features without any upfront cost, often without management approval. The book assumes a degree of technical confidence but does not require specialist system administration or developer skills to get a basic system up and running.

Alfresco is particularly suitable for IT consultants who want or need to set up a flexible enterprise content management system for their clients, be that for demonstration, development, or as a mission-critical platform. This book gets you to that result quickly and effectively.

This book also helps business users to make decisions to migrate from the existing proprietary ECM to standards based open source ECM.

This book is not targeted at developers who want to change the core code structure of Alfresco. Although no knowledge of Alfresco is presumed, exposure to HTML, XML, JavaScript and related web technologies will help to get the most from this book.

Conventions

In this book, you will find a number of styles of text that distinguish between different kinds of information. Here are some examples of these styles, and an explanation of their meaning.

There are three styles for code. Code words in text are shown as follows: "Note that the `scheduled-action-services-context.xml` file has two blocks of XML configuration."

A block of code will be set as follows:

```
<cm:person view:childName="cm:person">
<cm:userName>fredb</cm:userName>
<cm:firstName>Fred</cm:firstName>
<cm:lastName>Bloggs</cm:lastName>
<cm:email>fredb@alfresco.org</cm:email>
```

When we wish to draw your attention to a particular part of a code block, the relevant lines or items will be made bold:

```
</property>
<property name="stores">
    <list>
        <value>workspace://SpacesStore</value>
    </list>
</property>
<property name="queryTemplate">
    <value>PATH:"/app:company_home"</value>
</property>
<property name="cronExpression">
    <value>0 0/15 * * * ?</value>
</property>
<property name="jobName">
    <value>jobD</value>
</property>
<property name="jobGroup">
    <value>jobGroup</value>
</property>
```

Any command-line input and output is written as follows:

```
> chmod a+x ./alfresco-<version>-linux-community.bin
```

New terms and **important words** are introduced in a bold-type font. Words that you see on the screen, in menus or dialog boxes for example, appear in our text like this: "Go to a space and add a file by clicking on the **Add Content** link."

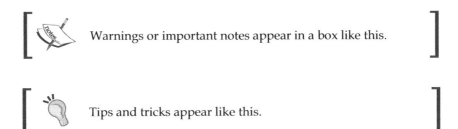

Warnings or important notes appear in a box like this.

Tips and tricks appear like this.

Reader Feedback

Feedback from our readers is always welcome. Let us know what you think about this book, what you liked or may have disliked. Reader feedback is important for us to develop titles that you really get the most out of.

To send us general feedback, simply drop an email to feedback@packtpub.com, making sure to mention the book title in the subject of your message.

If there is a book that you need and would like to see us publish, please send us a note in the **SUGGEST A TITLE** form on www.packtpub.com or email suggest@packtpub.com.

If there is a topic that you have expertise in and you are interested in either writing or contributing to a book, see our author guide on www.packtpub.com/authors.

Customer Support

Now that you are the proud owner of a Packt book, we have a number of things to help you to get the most from your purchase.

Downloading the Example Code for the Book

Various sample scripts, images, and content files are used in each chapter of this book. In some of the chapters you will also find information to edit various configuration files. All the files required for you to try out the examples used in the book are provided as downloads.

Also, you can download the files required to bring up the complete final demo site as per this book.

Visit http://www.packtpub.com/support, and select this book from the list of titles to download any example code or extra resources for this book. The files available for download will then be displayed.

The downloadable files contain instructions on how to use them.

Errata

Although we have taken every care to ensure the accuracy of our contents, mistakes do happen. If you find a mistake in one of our books—maybe a mistake in text or code—we would be grateful if you would report this to us. By doing this you can save other readers from frustration, and help to improve subsequent versions of this book. If you find any errata, report them by visiting http://www.packtpub.com/support, selecting your book, clicking on the **Submit Errata** link, and entering the details of your errata. Once your errata have been verified, your submission will be accepted and the errata added to the list of existing errata. The existing errata can be viewed by selecting your title from http://www.packtpub.com/support.

Questions

You can contact us at questions@packtpub.com if you are having a problem with some aspect of the book, and we will do our best to address it.

1
Introduction to Alfresco

Enterprise Content Management (**ECM**) is the fastest growing category of enterprise software. Customers who are implementing or upgrading ECM systems are facing issues such as vendor lock-in, high maintenance costs, and lack of standardization. Open-source technologies and open standards are becoming powerful alternatives to commercial closed-source ECM software. Alfresco, a new player in this market, is gaining a lot of momentum by providing content management solutions to enterprises using state-of-the-art open-source technologies and open standards. This chapter provides an introduction to Alfresco and outlines the benefits of using it for your enterprise's content management requirements.

By the end of this chapter you will have learned about:

- An overview of Alfresco architecture
- Key features of Alfresco software
- Using Alfresco for your document management, records management, web content management, and collaboration requirements
- The future roadmap

Overview of Alfresco

Alfresco was founded in 2005 by John Newton, co-founder of Documentum, and John Powell, former COO of Business Objects. Its investors include the leading investment firms Accel Partners and Mayfield Fund. The proven track record of its leaders, the features in the technology, the open-source business model, and good venture capital backing of the team, as a combination makes Alfresco different.

Leverage the Benefits of Open Source

Enterprise customers can reduce costs, minimize business risks, and get competitive advantage by adopting the right open-source-based business software solutions. You can reduce the cost of software solution acquisition, deployment, and maintenance by brining the community into the development, support, and service process.

Alfresco is the leading open-source alternative for enterprise content management. It couples the innovation of open source with the stability of a true enterprise-class platform. The open-source model allows Alfresco to use the best-of-breed open-source technologies and contributions from the open-source community to get higher quality software produced more quickly and at a much lower cost.

State-of-the-Art Content Repository

The following diagram shows an overview of Alfresco content repository and its integration with external systems such as Virtual File Systems, Web Applications, Knowledge Portals, and Web Services:

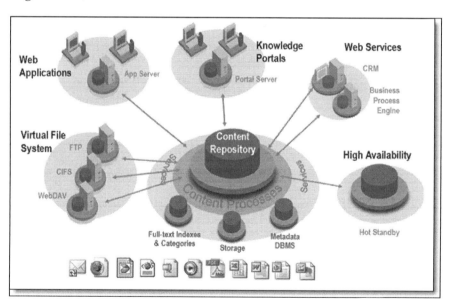

A content repository is a server or a set of services used to store, search, access, and control content. The content repository provides these services to specialist content applications such as document management, web content management systems, image storage and retrieval systems, records management, or other applications that require the storage and retrieval of large amounts of content. The repository provides content services such as content storage or import, content classification, security on content objects, control through content check-in and check-out, and content query services to these applications.

What distinguishes content management from other typical database applications is the level of control exercised over individual content objects and the ability to search content. Access to these services requires wrapping the calls in security to prevent unauthorized access or changes to content or its metadata. The finer granularity of this security and its complex relationship with other objects such as people and folders requires a more sophisticated mechanism than provided by traditional database security.

The complex requirements of these services imply that often the business logic of the content repository can be as large as or larger than the database itself. Almost all the content repository vendors provide proprietary service interfaces to encapsulate the breadth of functionality required. Despite attempts over the last ten years to standardize these interfaces, it is only over the last two years that any progress has been made. In 2005, the Java community adopted the JSR-170 standard interface and Alfresco's content repository is based on this and related standards.

Scalable Architecture

The single most important aspect of any ECM system is the underlying architecture. Alfresco supports pluggable aspect-oriented architecture out of the box by leveraging the open-source standards such as Spring, Hibernate, Lucene, MyFaces, JSR 168, JSR 170, and JSE5.

The Alfresco architecture supports high availability for mission-critical applications using clustering, fully distributed caching, and replication support across multiple servers. The functionality and the various architectural layers are shown in the following figure:

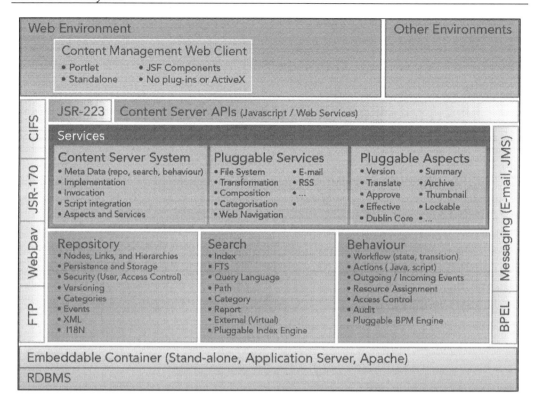

The architecture is based on open standards, hence the applications built using Alfresco can be deployed on any environment such as Windows, Linux, Mac, etc., can use any relational database such as MySQL, Oracle, etc., can run on various application servers such as JBoss Application Server, Apache Tomcat, etc., can work with any Browser such as Mozilla Firefox, Microsoft Internet Explorer, etc., and can integrate with any portal such as JBoss Portal, Liferay Portal, etc.

In any enterprise, the amount of content you will manage will keep on increasing. In some organizations such as media, pharmaceutical, healthcare, etc., the content increases exponentially every year. Hence scalability is a critical issue when evaluating ECM solutions.

Due to its modular and light-weight architecture, Alfresco is highly scalable. Alfresco provides horizontal scalability by having each tier in the architecture deployed on multiple servers. Similarly Alfresco can scale vertically by partitioning and load balancing in a multi-server environment.

Alfresco server can scale in information using complex search, structure, and classification of information. Alfresco server can scale in activity using complex information per activity with dynamic views and with full object-level security.

Open Standards-based Underlying Components

Open standards protect enterprise investment, promote innovation, and make it easier for IT departments to support the software. By adopting open standards for their ECM requirements, enterprises can lower the risk of incompatibilities with existing technologies. Enterprise application integration becomes easier with open standards.

Alfresco is completely built on the following open standards:

- Java 1.5
- JSR 170—Java Content Repository API
- JSR-168 Java Portlet Integration
- Spring 1.2 Aspect-Oriented Framework
- ACEGI Aspect-Oriented Security Framework
- MyFaces 1.0.9 JSF Implementation
- Hibernate 3.0 ORM Persistence
- Lucene 1.4 Text Search Engine
- JLAN—Java-based File Server supporting Windows Files sharing (SMB/CIFS), NFS, FTP
- WebDAV/DeltaV
- JBoss App Server 4.0
- JBoss Portal 2.0
- Jakartha POI—Java API to Access Microsoft File formats
- PDFBox—Open Source Java PDF Library
- Open Office 2.0
- JSR-223 Java Language Integration—Scripting for Java Platform

Globalization Support

If your enterprise has a global business model, it is very important for you to provide content in multiple languages. Most enterprises look beyond their geographic borders for new markets. The majority of the web users speak little or no English. Hence ECM systems should be designed with globalization in mind.

Out of the box Alfresco supports major languages including Chinese, Dutch, English, French, German, Italian, Russian, and Spanish.

Security and Access Control

Protecting against unauthorized access to the content is the key requirement for enterprises. This is true for corporate websites, intranets, extranets, front office, and back-office applications.

Nice thing about Alfresco is that the permissions can be applied at a space (folder) level or can be set for each individual content item. Out of the box, Alfresco supports a relational database-based membership system and also supports external identity management systems such as LDAP, NTLM, Kerberos, and Active Directory.

Essential Library Services

Library services are required if you want to manage, leverage, modify, and control the content in an ECM system. Alfresco provides library services such as Check-in/Check-out, version control, auditing information, and content streaming.

Using Alfresco, you can define the library services to be executed automatically based on the business rules. For example, every edit to the content can version the content automatically. Or every check-out can move the content to a specific location based on the business rules.

Alfresco provides additional intelligence to the content by adding metadata (data about data), business rules, security rules, and collaboration rules dynamically, using aspect-oriented programming. Alfresco also provides features such as content metadata extractors, content transformers, translations, and auto-categorization to make the content intelligent.

Business-Process Automation

Business-process automation increases productivity, reduces costs, streamlines processes, and shortens operation cycles. Alfresco includes **JBoss Business Process Manager (JBPM)** as a business process management and automation solution. This helps to manage document life-cycle with security and audit trails capabilities.

Enterprise Integrations

No application is an island. Alfresco provides Web Services and the **Java Content Repository Application Programming Interface (JCR API)** to integrate with external applications.

Alfresco integrates with Kofax Ascent Capture and offers customers access to a comprehensive production capture solution, including automatic document classification, data extraction, and validation for both Internet-based distributed capture and centralized environments.

Alfresco integrates with an open-source J2EE-based leading portal framework called Liferay. The Alfresco-Liferay bundle is an out-of-the-box solution, which provides an excellent portal-based ECM solution.

Alfresco integrates with external identity management systems such as LDAP and Active Directory and supports centralized security and single sign-on.

How You Can Benefit from Alfresco

Alfresco offers Enterprise Content Management (ECM) such as *document management, collaboration, records management, knowledge management, web content management,* and *imaging.* You can configure and customize Alfresco to address your business requirements. Some of them are listed here for your reference.

Using Alfresco for Document Management

Using Alfresco you can implement document management solutions such as *enterprise document management, Digital Asset Management,* and *contracts management.*

Alfresco document management features provide organizations with all the services necessary for creating, converting, managing, and sharing electronic documents. Built on industry-standard open-source platforms, Alfresco provides version management, search capabilities, and visualization showing relationships and dependencies.

It uses full Service-Oriented Architecture using industry standards such as Spring, Hibernate, Lucene, MyFaces, JSR 168, JSR 170, and JSE5. Its architecture includes high availability using Master/Slave Distributed Synchronization within a Data Center through 2-phase commit or remotely between sites through replication. Its architecture supports zero-footprint clients to easily access the server via standard Windows Network File Share.

Document management administrator interface allows you to *import/export workspaces* and *documents,* define security, and manage users with *users, groups* and *roles.* Cost-effective upgrades and data migration administration are some of the key benefits.

Built-in data management and transformation engine enables you to transform the data into required formats based on the business rules. Integrated workflow provides you with full control over the document lifecycle, management, and process flow.

Presentation templates and *dashboard* views provide you with a personalized and real-time reporting of your content. The *Preview* feature is useful to view the content in combination with other content elements. Similarly the *composite document* feature helps you to logically group the documents and digital assets for your marketing projects.

Digital Asset Management provides a single access point for all your rich digital media and its underlying metadata information throughout the extended enterprise. Alfresco centralizes storage and provides easy, efficient, enterprise access to digital assets, and allows them to be quickly repurposed, which streamlines processes and saves money.

Whether it's an employment contract, purchase agreement, maintenance contract, or collaboration agreement with a business partner, completeness, validity, traceability, and inalterability must be guaranteed if a company is to protect its commercial interests. Alfresco's document lifecycle management features ensure that people in various company departments, divisions, and regions can work together to support all processes relating to a contract throughout its lifecycle—from creation through fulfillment and modification to termination.

Key features include:

- Flexible metadata management
- Full audit control
- Transformation of data
- Security and version control
- Indexing and full-text search
- Locking, check-in/check-out
- Offline briefcase synchronization to access content offline
- Taxonomy and categorization of content
- Advanced search with combined metadata, location, and multi-category search
- Advanced reporting and dashboards
- Document composition by logically grouping various content
- Preview feature with presentation templates
- Soft deletes and deleted document recovery support
- Scheduled jobs and actions
- Management of web assets
- Brand management
- Digital image library

Using Alfresco for Records Management

Using Alfresco you can implement records management solutions such as enterprise records management, compliance, imaging, forms management, and business process management.

Alfresco records management features provide a secure, auditable environment for creating, declaring, classifying, retaining, and destroying records. Organizations can ensure compliance by defining and enforcing policies for records use, storage, and disposition, with a legally defensible audit trail.

Records management capabilities are modeled to support the US Department of Defense 5015.2 Records Management standards. Alfresco provides file plan templates for numbering, classification, disposition, and other metadata population of records. Disposition includes the transfer of records and/or the ultimate destruction of the record.

Predefined reports will provide you with information about recent records, records due for cutoff, records retention due for expiry, records due for transfer, and records due for destruction.

The lifecycle determines the disposition of the record including when the records will be cutoff or grouped together, how long the records will be held, and what happens to the records after the hold period expires—whether they are transferred to a records holding area or whether they should be destroyed.

By integrating with scanning and OCR technologies, Alfresco provides an end-to-end solution by collecting paper documents and forms; transforming them into accurate, retrievable information; and delivering the content into an organization's business applications. The information is then full-text searchable and goes through various lifecycles based on the organization's defined business process management.

Emails are considered as records in some organizations. Alfresco enables you to drag and drop emails from Microsoft Outlook into the file plan space. The system will extract the metadata from email files and populate information such as whom the e-mail is from, who the recipients are, and the subject of the email. Email content is stored in a secure and scalable repository and is full-text searchable.

Key features include:

- Record plans
- Automatic conversion from proprietary office formats to long-term vendor-neutral formats such as **Open Document Format (ODF)** and **Portable Document Format (PDF)**
- Vital records information management

- Record cutoff information management
- Record holding and retention management
- Record transfer process
- Record destruction management
- Record lifecycle management
- Archival policies
- Disposition schedules
- Restriction of user functions
- Audit trails

Using Alfresco for Web Content Management

Using Alfresco you can implement web content management solutions with a scalable content repository, web 2.0 AJAX-based user interface, flexible workflow, multi-language support, and a robust search engine.

Alfresco web content management features provide a rich environment for creating, managing, and publishing web content, and an infrastructure for supporting multiple sites. The content managed can include text, HTML, XML files, graphics and photos, video or audio, and specialized programming for user interaction. Through this solution, organizations can integrate multiple disparate sites and data formats, and give users (often sales people, partners, and customers) rapid access to timely information. Since, Alfresco web content management is built on open-source platforms, supporting, managing, and expanding these systems is straightforward and cost-effective.

Alfresco supports a wide range of protocols such as HTTP, HTTPS, WebDAV, web services, XML-RPC, FTP, and RMI to exchange content with external systems. With the help of technologies such as RSS syndication and web services the content is delivered to various channels such as public internet sites, internal marketing sites, or portals.

Alfresco leverages the existing infrastructure for membership such as LDAP, Active Directory, or a relational database. Its fine granular level of security enables content authors to secure a web page and also the files, embedded images, and videos within a web page.

Users of Alfresco web content management systems are mostly non-technical business users or subject matter experts who do not understand HTML syntax. Alfresco includes inline editors to edit text, HTML, and XML content, and connectors to edit Office documents using desktop tools of your choice. The transformation engine is used to transform content from one form to another. For example, all the incoming images of various types and sizes can be transformed to a standard format and size.

Drag-and-drop layout lets users customize the look and feel of websites without waiting for assistance from developers. Alfresco speaks your language and supports multilingual content management.

A robust full-text search engine lets you search your web content (HTML, PDF, MS-Word, PowerPoint slides, etc.) based on your security access permissions. Advanced search features enable you to search the web content based on the metadata and keyword values.

Key features include:

- Contextual delivery of information based on community intelligence
- Standards-based forms to create pages
- Email-based workflow and approval process
- In context review: View changes in the context of a live site with no broken URLs
- Manage branches: Parallel branching and merging
- Dependency management: Impact management and automatic updates
- Pre-built templates: Websites and website components
- Integration of enterprise systems
- Re-use existing sites: Easily reuse existing look and feel
- High-availability, fault tolerance, and scalability: Any number of sites, auto failover, and clustering
- Multi-site change set management: Support for projects, sandboxes, change sets, layers, and snapshots
- Multi-site transactional publishing: Guaranteed delivery to multiple run-time sites
- Virtualization server: Preview web 2.0 site updates in context, view the site in the past, present, or future
- Business process-driven web content management

Using Alfresco for Collaboration Management

Using Alfresco you can implement collaboration solutions such as corporate and departmental intranets, knowledge management, and client and project extranets.

Alfresco collaboration features provide the infrastructure, integration points, and tools required for accessing, sharing, and distributing content among users or systems. Built upon industry-standard, open-source platforms, Alfresco helps you to quickly define and develop environments for teams (project teams, associations, research, etc.) that will streamline processes, reduce costs, and improve time to market. Users can manage and collaborate on documents, web information, and forms within a single system through a consistent user interface.

A comprehensive security model based on individuals, groups, projects, and team spaces provides you with the highest level of control. The solution leverages the existing infrastructure such as LDAP or Active Directory for authentication and authorization.

A web-based rules engine enables business users to define the business and content rules appropriately without the help of programmers and IT staff. Alfresco supports a graphical tool to define the workflow and business process management for content flow in collaborative environments.

Users can discuss the content using discussion forums and discussion threads tied to the content. Users can subscribe to content and receive email notifications when content is added or updated. The solution supports both inbound and outbound RSS syndication to share content both inside and outside corporate firewalls.

The interfaces such as **Common Internet File System (CIFS)**, SMB, and WebDAV allow each team member or departmental system to map the folder on the server as a local network drive. This enables bulk transfer of files between your local system and the central server repository. Users can use their favorite editors to edit the content that is mapped in the local network drive.

Knowledge Management (KM) refers to a range of practices used by organizations to identify, create, represent, and distribute knowledge for reuse, awareness, and learning across the organization.

Key features include:

- Team spaces
- Full audit control
- Discussion forums
- Message boards
- RSS syndication
- Ad-hoc security
- A version controlled content repository
- Full-text search of various content items
- User-controlled routing

- Integration of enterprise systems
- High availability, fault tolerance, and scalability
- Business process-driven content management

Using Alfresco for Enterprise Content Search

Most ECM systems do not consider Search to be an important part of enterprise content management. Search helps to locate information quickly, generate business reports, and helps to make business decisions. The following features of Alfresco will provide you an enterprise search solution.

- Provides single-point access to enterprise content repository
- Provides full-text search of documents
- Helps to index the documents and provide metadata searching
- Helps you to build and share reports using saved searches
- Helps search for users and collaborative groups
- Searches archived content

Applications of Alfresco

Since the architecture is flexible and extensible, you can build various applications using Alfresco such as:

- Enterprise document repository
- Intranet
- Enterprise knowledge management portal
- Scalable content repository
- Corporate websites
- Marketing communications
- On demand publishing
- Compliance and records management
- Financial applications that involve security, forms handling, and approval process
- Research portals for collaboration and sharing of information

Alfresco's website (http://www.alfresco.com) has a list of customer case studies. Going through these case studies will help you understand the type of applications you could develop using Alfresco.

How does the Future Look with Alfresco?

The current release of Alfresco is 1.4. The Alfresco system will constantly evolve towards a broad-scoped Enterprise Content Management system.

More Feature Enhancements

It is planned to have Alfresco 2.0 release by the end of 2006 or early 2007. Full-featured web content management is the key focus area for this release. Along with versioning, the web content management will provide additional features such as content publishing, virtualization and in-context preview, workflow, dependency management, and content deployment.

Content federation and federated search is going to be supported in this release. The web client user interface will be redesigned using AJAX to significantly enhance the browsing, searching, and contribution process through the web client. Records management capabilities will be enhanced to get DoD5015.2 certification.

There has been so much interest from international organizations, governments, and multi-national corporations that translation seems a natural extension of the Alfresco model. More languages will be supported out of the box.

This release will provide publishing and multi-channel solutions against the Alfresco repository. In particular, managing XML with schemas such as DITA and Docbook has a high level of interest.

The lifecycle aspect will be an additional feature. The lifecycle aspect can be attached to any object to provide lifecycle control of that object. The lifecycle aspect will keep track of state and use the actions capability to provide alerts and manage workflows and location of the object.

Better Support Options

Alfresco comes with multiple support options. Firstly, it is supported by the company Alfresco, which gives users direct access to the Alfresco's engineering team and most recent bug fixes. This is currently the best way to get high-quality support for the Alfresco software. However, as more and more people adopt the software, the options for quality support beyond Alfresco, the company, will improve.

At any given point in time, the following three support alternatives exist for Alfresco open source software:

- In-house Development Support: As the source code is open source, you can train your developers in-house to support your application built using Alfresco.

- Community Support: Alfresco already has a big community world wide. With a growing community, you can always get help through Alfresco community forums, though the quality of support can vary.

- Alfresco Enterprise Network Support: As mentioned, Alfresco Inc. today provides the highest quality option for production and development support. This support is provided to the company's customers using the Enterprise product. It includes direct access to the engineers who write the Alfresco code, the up-to-date bug fixes, configuration assistance, and a range of other services.

Free Upgrades

For every new release, you will get free upgraded software. You might have to take care of your specific customization to upgrade to a later version of the software. It is important to follow best practices while implementing Alfresco, so that upgrades are easier and less expensive to handle.

Implementing an Example Solution Using Alfresco

Subsequent chapters of the book contain an extended example to help you implement your requirements using Alfresco. The example is an attempt to solve similar content management problems to those that you would encounter in a typical enterprise. The example is something you can relate to.

By providing an extended example in this book, my idea is to:

- Engage you, and keep the material feeling real-world.

- Help you apply the features of Alfresco to business decisions. You see in the fictional example that decisions are made for particular reasons, and can contrast those reasons (and thus the decisions) with your own situation.

- Give the book an overall theme—even a narrative engine to keep things moving and not feeling like technical documentation.

Where do You get More Information?

The best place to start looking for more information is Alfresco's corporate website (http://www.alfresco.com) itself. You can find the latest news and events, various training programs offered worldwide, presentations, demonstrations, and hosted trials.

Alfresco is 100% open source and all the downloads are available from the SourceForge.net website at `http://sourceforge.net/project/showfiles.php?group_id=143373`.

The Alfresco Wiki (`http://wiki.alfresco.com`) contains documentation such as a tutorial, user guide, developer guide, administrator guide, roadmap, etc.

Alfresco discussion forums (`http://forums.alfresco.com`) are the best place to share your thoughts, and to get tips and tricks about Alfresco implementation.

If you would like to file a bug or to know more details about the fixes in a specific release, then you must visit the bug tracking system at `http://issues.alfresco.org/`.

Summary

Alfresco is the leading open-source alternative for Enterprise Content Management. It couples the innovation of open source with the stability of a true enterprise-class platform. The open-source model allows Alfresco to use best-of-breed open-source technologies and contributions from the open-source community to get higher quality software produced more quickly at much lower cost.

Alfresco provides key features for a scalable, robust, and secure Content Management System to deliver trusted and relevant content to your customers, suppliers, and employees.

2
Installing and Getting Started with Alfresco

One of the remarkable features of Alfresco is the ease with which it can be installed and deployed. The simple out of the box installation is quite straightforward with preconfigured options that are aimed at having a complete, working content management system in no time. This chapter provides you with a basic understanding of Alfresco architecture, various installation options, and the key terminologies used. By the end of this chapter you will be well equipped with the information to make a choice on the suitable operating system, database, application server, and other software required for your installation. This chapter is essential reading for anyone not already familiar with Alfresco.

By the end of this chapter you will have learned how to:

- Determine what is the right installation option for you
- Install Alfresco and all the required software
- Log in to the Alfresco web client application
- Use the administration console and perform system administration tasks
- Use Alfresco for basic document management

Installing Alfresco

Before directly delving into installation, it is important for you to understand the architecture behind Alfresco and various installation options available to you. This will help you to make good decisions in selecting the suitable software for your business application.

Out-of-the-Box Installation Architecture

The out-of-the-box deployment of Alfresco is a typical web application architecture consisting of client, application server, and storage layers as shown in the next figure. While the client layer is implemented as a web browser on the user's machine, the application server hosts the Alfresco application providing the presentation and domain logic. The storage layer stores the data in a relational database and file system. The layered architecture of Alfresco provides the benefits of an easily manageable, flexible, and highly scalable content management solution.

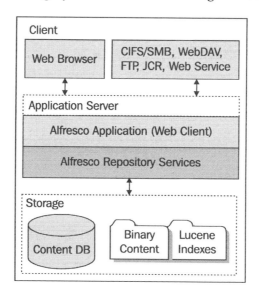

Where is Your Content Stored?

The content in Alfresco is stored in persistent back-end systems such as a database and file system. There is a reason for using both database and file system as content storage. Any content within Alfresco consists of two elements, the content itself and information about the content (metadata).

The actual content can be anything from simple documents (HTML, XML) to images, audios, and videos. The actual content and its related versions are stored as binary files in the file system. Storing content on a file system has its own advantages. It allows for very large content, random-access streaming, and options for different storage devices. It is important to note that the file system that Alfresco application works on is operating-system agnostic.

Alfresco uses Lucene—a popular open-source search engine, to provide metadata search and full text search capabilities of the content. Apart from the actual binary content, Lucene index files are also stored on the file system.

The content metadata, which is stored in the relational database, includes information like:

- The format of the content
- Date created
- Language
- Security settings

What are the Components of Alfresco Application Server?

The application server hosts the user interface and domain logic. It provides an abstraction and enables communication between the client and storage layers. In the case of Alfresco, the application server houses the Alfresco application (also known as the web client) and Alfresco repository.

The Alfresco repository provides a set of reusable cross-cutting content management services such as content storage, query, versioning, and transformation, which may be utilized by one or more applications.

An Alfresco application provides a complete solution tailored for a specific area of content management such as document management and records management. The user interface for all these applications is referred to as a web client, which is highly customizable and configurable according to the user-specific requirements. The out-of-box web client gives you lot of packaged functionality. With the web client management console, you can manage users, security, content, business rules, etc.

How Can You Access the Application?

There is no installation or configuration required for the Alfresco user interface. Any number of web browsers can connect to the application without prior client installation costs.

The out-of-box installation comes with a web client where you can connect to Alfresco repository through a web-based application.

Apart from the web client, the Alfresco out-of-the-box installation supports various client applications to access Alfresco content with Web Services or protocols such as FTP, WebDAV, and CIFS:

- **File Transfer Protocol (FTP)**: This is useful to transfer files from your local file system to the remote server.

- **WWW Distributed Authoring and Versioning (WebDAV)**: This is primarily designed for editing and managing files on remote web servers in a structured way. For example, an application like Adobe Photoshop can directly open and edit a file in the Alfresco content repository. This gives you the flexibility of using your own favorite editor to edit the content on the Alfresco server.
- **Common Internet File System (CIFS)**: This helps you to map Alfresco content as your local file system folder.

Web Services: Most of the ECM products that are on the market store content in a proprietary format, which is like a "black box". Alfresco content is stored as per the JCR (Java Content Repository-JSR 170) open standards. Any JCR-compliant client application can read the content that is stored in Alfresco repository. This is one of the key selling points of Alfresco. An API is provided out of the box so that you could connect to the Alfresco repository from your applications through web services or JCR integration.

Which Installation Option is Suitable for You?

Alfresco is 100% open-source software, which is developed using open standards. Hence it runs on various operating systems, relational databases, application servers, web browsers, and portals and supports various languages. Let us examine all the choices and determine which option is right for you.

Enterprise and Community Editions

Alfresco currently provides two types of product download options:

- Alfresco Community Network
- Alfresco Enterprise Network

Both the options have the same code base and features, and are 100% open source. For both options, you can use Alfresco documentation (wiki), community support (forums), and community contributed add-on products. Alfresco Community Network is free. Alfresco Enterprise Network includes a per CPU license fee.

If you are implementing Alfresco for a major corporation, financial, insurance, government or healthcare organization, I would recommend you to go for Alfresco Enterprise Network support. The primary benefit is that with the support of Alfresco and its certified partners you would get a stable, reliable, certified, and supported application with warranty and indemnity. Your Alfresco version will be certified on all available stacks such as Linux, Windows, MySQL, Oracle, etc. You will benefit from Alfresco support, which includes problem resolution, compatibility advice, migration advice, and upgrade support. For mission-critical applications you will get 24 x 7 support from Alfresco experts.

Operating Systems—Windows, Linux, UNIX, MacOS

Choosing an operating system to run Alfresco will be based on various factors. For some companies it depends on in-house expertise. For example, if you have administrators and IT staff who can easily manage business applications running on a Microsoft Windows platform, then your choice could be to go with a Windows operating system. For some companies it is based on the integration requirements with the existing systems.

If you do not have any preferences, I would recommend you to go with a Linux operating system for production use. Linux source code is freely distributed. Tens and thousands of programmers have reviewed the source code to improve performance, eliminate bugs, and strengthen security. No other operating system has ever undergone this level of review. The key advantages of Linux are listed below:

- The best technical support available
- No vendor lock-in
- Runs on a wide range of hardware
- Exceptionally stable
- Supports many tools and applications you need
- Interoperates with many other types of computer systems
- Low total cost of ownership

Databases—MySQL, Oracle, MS SQL Server

The Alfresco application internally uses an open-source software component called Hibernate. Hibernate abstracts the database layer and provides seamless integration between the Alfresco repository and any relational database.

If you have already chosen a Microsoft Windows operating system, then the natural choice for you could be MS SQL Server. If you already have an Oracle license, then Oracle database is the best choice for you.

If you do not have any preference, I recommend that you go with the MySQL database, which costs nothing if you go with open-source version. The MySQL database has become the world's most popular open-source database because of its consistent, fast performance, high reliability, and ease of use. It's used in more than 10 million installations ranging from large corporations to specialized embedded applications. MySQL runs on more than 20 platforms including Linux, Windows, OS/X, HP-UX, AIX, and Netware, giving you the kind of flexibility that puts you in control.

Application Servers—Tomcat, JBoss

Alfresco runs on any J2SE 5.0-compliant application server. Hence there are no application server-specific dependencies. However it is important to make a choice of application server before moving into production.

Alfresco uses **Spring** framework and not the Enterprise Java Beans (EJB) framework. So there is no dependency on JBoss or any other application server that provides an EJB container. If you are developing a standalone application then Tomcat might be a good option. Apache Tomcat powers numerous large-scale, and mission-critical web applications across a diverse range of industries and organizations. It is the most widely accepted web application server in the market.

On the other hand you must consider using JBoss application server, which has the highest market capture (> 35%) in J2EE-based application servers in the world. JBoss internally uses Tomcat and hence you get the benefits of the Tomcat servlet engine as well.

Alfresco utilizes JBoss cache's ability to distribute and maintain data caches, making it possible to build large-scale systems that outperform traditional enterprise content management systems. Alfresco also utilizes the clustering, failover, and load-balancing facilities of the JBoss application server to increase scalability. Alfresco's business process management features are powered by the JBoss jBPM tool.

If you have already invested in JBoss, then Alfresco provides complementary industry-leading enterprise content management technology to the JBoss enterprise middleware system suite.

Portals (Optional)—JBoss Portal, Liferay

It is optional for you to go with a portal of your choice; if you already have an enterprise portal you can integrate Alfresco with it. If you do not have a portal in place and you would like to leverage the portal framework, then you can consider using either JBoss portal or Liferay portal. Both of these are based on J2EE technology; both of them are open-source and open-standards-based and both of them have built-in Alfresco support.

JBoss Portal provides an open-source platform for hosting and serving a portal's web interface, publishing and managing its content, and customizing its experience. While most packaged portal frameworks help enterprises launch portals more quickly, only JBoss Portal delivers the benefits of a zero-cost, open-source license combined with a flexible and scalable underlying platform.

Liferay is the most downloaded and popular portal with 40,000 downloads per month. It runs on top of any J2EE servlet such as Tomcat, so a full installation of

JBoss is not required, but can run against most full application-servers out of the box including JBoss, JRun, BEA, WebLogic, and Orion. It has a full set of web service interfaces to the portal. Liferay supports 800+ portlets (products) and has wider adoption in the market.

Choose the Suitable Software for Your Installation

You need to make the best choice of software to install Alfresco. If you do not have any specific requirements, you might consider a complete open-source stack for production usage and go with Alfresco **Enterprise** Edition on a **Linux** operating system with a **MySQL** database running on a **JBoss** application server with **Liferay** portal.

The examples in this book were created and tested with the following choice of Alfresco installation:

- Alfresco Edition: Community
- Operating System: Windows
- Database: MySQL
- Application server: Tomcat
- Portal: None

Installing on Microsoft Windows

In our earlier section, you have noticed that repository application server is the default deployment option chosen. This means that the out-of-box Alfresco installation is a typical web application where the web application server becomes the host for an embedded repository and is accessible through the HTTP protocol. In this section, we discuss the requirements and procedures for simple installation of Alfresco using the installer on a Windows platform.

Requirements

The default installation of Alfresco software requires installing the Windows community version `alfresco-<version>-windows-community.exe` downloaded from the SourceForge project location (`http://sourceforge.net/projects/ alfresco`). At the time of writing this book the latest version was 1.4 and the installer file `alfresco-1.4Preview-windows-community.exe` is approximately 183 MB in size.

This installer will install:

- Java Development Kit (JDK), version 5.0
- MySQL database, version 4.1.16

- Apache Tomcat, version 5.5.12
- Portable Open Office, version 2.0.3
- Alfresco, version 1.4 which is packaged as a Web Archive (WAR) file and deployed on the Tomcat server

To install and run Alfresco, you need at least 500 MB disk space and at least 512 MB RAM on the desktop or server.

Installation of Community Edition with Tomcat and MySQL

The following steps are a simple way of installing community edition with Tomcat and MySQL:

1. Start the installation of Alfresco by double-clicking on the Alfresco installer. You will see this first screen:

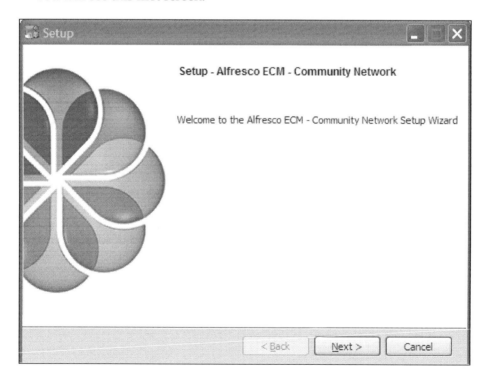

2. After you click **Next** at the bottom, you will see the license agreement screen. Accept the agreement and click **Next**

3. You will see the option to choose the installation folder. Let us install it in the default folder given by the installer, `C:\Program Files\alfresco-1.4`. Please note that you have the option to browse and select your chosen folder by clicking the ⬛ icon. Once you are done with the folder selection, click on **Next**.

4. In the next screen, you will be prompted to enter the passwords for the root and anonymous accounts of MySQL. This step involves installing MySQL database and setting the appropriate permissions for Alfresco application to connect to the database. You will need this password in case you want to access and perform manual Create, Read, Update, and Delete operations (CRUD) on the database. You can enter any password of your choice. Click on **Next** to proceed to the next screen.

5. You will be asked whether you want to install it as a service that Windows starts automatically when you log in as shown in the next screenshot, If you choose **Yes** here, it will install two services `alfrescomysql` and `Apache Tomcat alfrescoTomcat` on your Windows machine. For default installation, we recommend to use it as a service. The user need not worry about manually starting the database and the Tomcat server. Click on the **Next** button to go to the next screen:

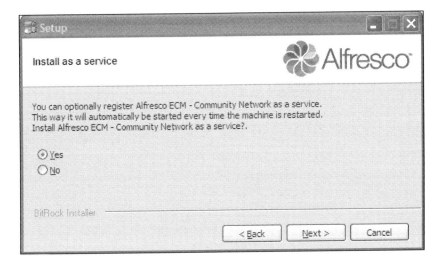

6. Start the installation procedure by clicking the **Next** button. The installation will take a while and you will see a progress bar.

7. Once you are done with the installation, the final installation screen will be as shown in the screenshot overleaf. Do not forget to read the contents of the `Readme` file, as it contains information about using CIFS and some troubleshooting tips. Clicking **Finish** will launch the application.

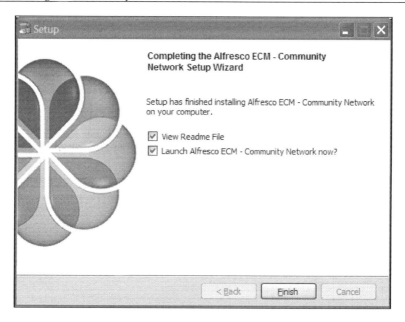

8. Once you see the default page, you are sure that the application is successfully deployed and started. Wait a few seconds to allow Tomcat to start and fire up your web browser and browse to `http://127.0.0.1:8080/ alfresco`. Since it is the first time you are using Alfresco, use admin as username and password.

Using HSQL or MySQL Database

Some windows installations of Alfresco are pre-configured to use the HSQL database, but can easily be configured to use other databases. HSQL is a light-weight database used for demonstrations or for building proof of concept applications. You can still use HSQL database and complete all the sample exercises given in this book. However, for production usage, you need to configure a database such as MySQL.

To use MySQL database, install MySQL 4.1 or higher. To create a database, navigate to `<alfresco_installation_folder>\extras\databases\mysql` folder, and run `db_setup.bat` file. This creates a MySQL database named `alfresco` with a user account and a password of `alfresco`. If `db_setup` fails, this may be because either the MySQL service is not running or the MySQL command cannot be found. Either correct this or setup the Alfresco database and user manually by loading the `db_setup.sql` file into MySQL, for example, `mysql -u root -p <db_setup.sql>`.

To convert the default installation to MySQL, you simply need to remove three files from the `tomcat/shared/classes/alfresco/extension` directory that are set to use HSQL. Those files are:

- `custom-db-and-data-context.xml`
- `custom-db-connection.properties`
- `custom-hibernate-dialect.properties`

Installation Folder Structure

Let's take a peek into the installation directory `C:\Program Files\alfresco-1.4` (from now on referred as `<install_folder>`) to look at the folders:

- `alfresco`: All the shortcuts to installing, uninstalling, starting, and stopping Alfresco as a Windows service, and restarting, stopping, and starting Alfresco as a normal console application, from the **Start** menu of Windows point to this folder.

- `alf_data`: All the Alfresco content and Lucene indexes are stored in this directory.

- `bin`: This directory contains the sub-installations of Alfresco. The main installation script in the `alfresco` directory calls the sub-scripts in this folder to start the sub Alfresco `Tomcat` component of the installation, creating and setting up the permissions for the Alfresco MySQL database. This folder is very useful for people going for a manual installation rather than using an installer.

- `extras`: Contains additional files such as a blank template for a records management file plan, which can be imported into the Alfresco repository.

- `java`: As is evident by the name, this contains the Java Development Kit. All the Alfresco development is done using Java as the core programming language.

- `licenses`: This directory contains the licenses for Alfresco, MySQL, Apache, and licenses for the other-third party applications used inside Alfresco.

- `mysql`: This directory holds the MySQL database installation.

- `tomcat`: Again, as evident from the name, this directory holds the Tomcat installation where the Alfresco application is deployed as a WAR file. You can see the `alfresco.war` file in "webapps" sub-folder of this directory.

- `PortableOpenOffice`: This directory contains the entire portable office suite installation that is used for word processing, spread sheet processing, etc.

- The `README` file gives information about using CIFS and some troubleshooting tips.

You can uninstall the program by clicking the `uninstall.exe` application.

Starting and Stopping the Alfresco Application as a Service

The options for Alfresco service can be viewed by clicking **Start | All Programs | Alfresco ECM - Community Network | Alfresco Service** as shown in the following screenshot:

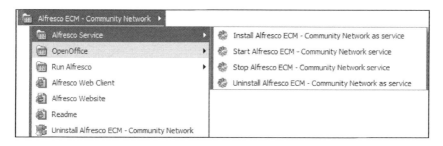

The various options in the above screenshot are discussed below:

Stop Alfresco ECM - Community Network service: This option is used to stop the Alfresco service. It stops the MySQL server and the Tomcat application server.

Start Alfresco ECM - Community Network as service: Use this option to start the service. This will start the MySQL server and the Tomcat server.

Install Alfresco ECM - Community Network as service: Choose this option if you want to install Alfresco as a service, if you have not chosen to do so during the original installation.

Unistall Alfresco ECM - Community Network as service: This option will uninstall Alfresco as a service. However, you can still run Alfresco using the normal console option.

Starting and Stopping Alfresco as a Console Application

The options for starting and stopping Alfresco as a console application can be viewed by clicking **Start | All Programs | Alfresco ECM - Community Network | Run Alfresco**. The options there are discussed below:

Stop Alfresco ECM - Community Network: This option is used to stop Alfresco. It stops the MySQL server and the Tomcat application server.

Start Alfresco ECM - Community Network: Use this option to start the Alfresco as a console application. This will start the MySQL server and the Tomcat server.

Restart Alfresco ECM - Community Network: Choose this option for stopping and restarting the Alfresco application.

Alternatively, you can always start, stop, and restart the Tomcat application server and the MySQL database server manually, by going to their respective directories. It gives more control to the user. However, the service option and console option give batch files to perform the start/stop procedures in a consolidated way, relieving the user of any unwanted errors.

Installing on Linux

Alfresco provides a nice package that includes all of the programs you need for using Alfresco on your Linux machine. Download it from the SourceForge location (`http://sourceforge.net/projects/alfresco`) by selecting the latest version of `alfresco-<version>-linux-community.bin` file.

This installer file contains MySQL, Java (JRE), Tomcat, Open Office, and Alfresco. Make sure you have permissions to execute the installer.

Use the following command to change the permissions on the installer so that it can be executed:

```
> chmod a+x ./alfresco-<version>-linux-community.bin
```

Become root (super) user to install by executing the following command (some platforms that have the super user account disabled by default might require "su –s").

```
> su
```

Now execute the installer directly on the command prompt as follows.

```
./alfresco-<version>-linux-community.bin
```

Follow the instructions presented by the installer:

1. You will be asked for a location to install the software. If you choose to skip the 'Become root' step above, your home folder is selected by default. If you intend for Alfresco to be run by other users, or start on startup, you should change this to a different location. Exit the installer and become root. If you are root, the default of **/opt/alfresco-<version>** will be selected. If you want to change it, **/usr/local/alfresco-<version>** will often be another good choice.

2. You will be asked to provide an initial password for the MySQL database.

3. You will be prompted for a MySQL port. If you already have a MySQL server on your machine you will need to change this. The quick installer cannot use a pre-existing MySQL installation. You can change the database once Alfresco has been installed.

4. You will be asked for the name of the local domain.

5. Press *y* and your computer will begin installing Alfresco.

6. Decide if you want to view the Readme.

7. Press y to start Alfresco.

Wait a few seconds to allow Tomcat to start and fire up your web browser and browse to `http://localhost:8080/alfresco`. Since it is the first time you have logged in use admin as username and password.

Introduction to the Web Client

Alfresco web client is the web-based application bundled and shipped along with the Alfresco repository. Using any web browser you can connect to the web client application. You will be able to manage users, security, content, business rules, and everything related to your enterprise content stored in Alfresco through the web client.

Log in to Alfresco as Administrator

To begin, if Alfresco was installed from the Tomcat bundle, access the web client from `http://localhost:8080/alfresco`. If Alfresco was installed from the JBoss bundle, you may use the same URL as for Tomcat, or access the web client in the portal from `http://localhost:8080/portal` and navigate to the web client from the page menu and then maximize the portlet.

If you have started Alfresco for the first time, then Alfresco creates the initial database content that is required to manage content. The first time you use Alfresco, your username will be **admin** and your password will be **admin**. You can change the admin password once you login. Depending on your installation, you may have a choice of languages in the language drop-down menu. This book assumes that your selected language is English.

Screen Layout

Once you log in, you will see the **My Alfresco Dashboard**. You can browse through the web client by clicking on the **Company Home** link provided at the top. A typical web client page is shown in the screenshot below. Let us examine various sections of the web client layout.

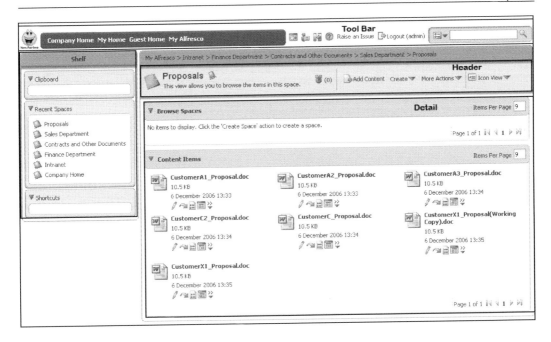

Tool bar

The **Tool Bar** on the top provides the following information:

- Logo
- Links to home spaces, **My Alfresco** dashboard
- *Administration Console* icon ▦ to perform system administration functions
- *User Options* icon ▦ to change your options and settings
- Icon ▦ to *hide or show the shelf*
- *Help* button ▦ to launch online help
- **Raise an Issue** link to submit bug reports to Alfresco
- Login and logout options
- Search box with basic and advanced search options

Shelf

The **Shelf** includes the clipboard, recent spaces, and shortcuts.

- The clipboard is useful to cut or copy content and to paste in multiple spaces. The clipboard also facilitates creating links to actual content item or space.

- Recent spaces provide the list of recently visited spaces and are thus useful to go back to a specific space with one click. The information in the recent spaces is refreshed every time you log in to Alfresco web client.

- Shortcuts are similar to favorites. You can create shortcuts to your frequently visited spaces.

Breadcrumbs

Breadcrumbs help you navigate through various spaces. Typically breadcrumbs provide the path to parent spaces.

Header

The header screen provides information about the current space, the number of business rules applied on the current space, options to create content, menu actions to manage content, and options to use various views to display the information in the current space.

Detail

The detail screen provides information about the sub-spaces and content that is part of the current space.

You can click on the icon or title of a space or content item in the detail screen to access the information.

Actions are listed as icons for each space or content. Additional action items will be listed if you click on the double-arrow icon ⏬ .

Administration Console

The administration console in the web client is useful to perform all the system-administration tasks. You can access the administration console by clicking on the administration console icon in the tool bar as shown in the following screenshot. This icon is visible and accessible only to users with admin previlages. Refer to the following screenshot to view the list of administration functions that can be performed by the system administrator.

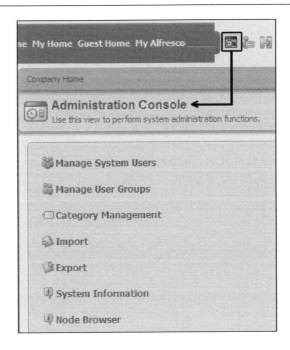

User and Group Management

You can add and delete users, and update user information using the **Manage System Users** functionality. When you first install Alfresco, there will be two users, namely *admin* and *guest*, created by the installer. You can create new users using this functionality.

The **Manage User Groups** functionality is useful to create groups of users and sub-groups within the groups. Groups are useful to provide authorization to the content.

Category Management

Categorization allows content information to be classified in a number of different ways. This aids searching of content. Categories can be editable only by the administrator. Categories can have sub-categories and content can be linked to one or more categories.

Data Management

Export and **Import** functionality is useful to bulk extract and load personal, department, or team information from one location to another location within the repository or to another repository. Export and Import functionality is covered in detail in Chapter 12.

System Information

System Information functionality is useful to view session information and the HTTP header information. The content in Alfresco is stored in an industry-standard Java Content Repository (JCR) where every folder and file is represented as a **Node**. The sub-folders are represented as branches of a node, which are nodes themselves. **Node Browser** functionality is useful to navigate through the entire repository through nodes and sub-nodes.

Getting Started with Content Creation

The remaining chapters of the book cover the content creation, management, and delivery aspects of Alfresco in detail. In this section you will be introduced to the key terminology and you will get a basic understanding of content creation in Alfresco.

Create Space

An Alfresco space is a folder with additional properties such as business rules and security. Similar to a folder, a space can hold sub-spaces and any type of content. To create a space within a space, click on the **Create** icon in the header and click on the **Create Space** link as shown in the following screenshot:

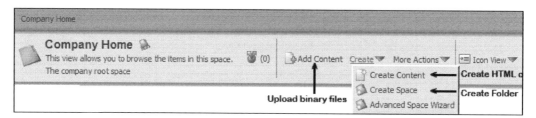

The **Create Space** wizard will be displayed as shown in the following screenshot. **Name** is a mandatory property (as you can tell from the small star next to the label), whereas **Title** and **Description** are optional properties. You can associate an icon with this space. Fill out the information and click on the **Create Space** button to create the space.

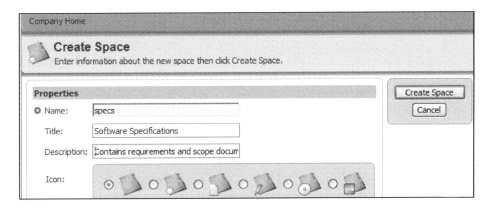

Each space supports various actions such as **Delete**, **Copy**, and **Paste All** as shown in the screenshot below. For each logged-in user, the actions for a specific space will be different, based on the security permissions. For example if you do not have permission to delete on a space, you will not see the **Delete** link or icon in the **More Actions** menu.

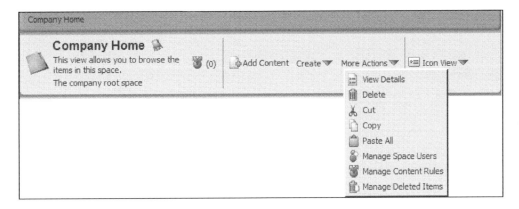

Create Content

In Alfresco content is any kind of document, such as a Microsoft Office file, Open Office file, PDF, HTML, XML, text, image, audio, or video file.

Each content item is made of two main elements, the content itself and the information about the content, called metadata or properties. By default each content item will have properties such as title, description, author, and audit trail information such as creator, creation date, modifier, and modification date. Additional properties can be added as needed.

To add a document in a space, click on the **Add Content** link in header as shown in the screenshot at the top of the page opposite. To create HTML or text content in a space, click on create icon and click on the **Create Content** menu link as shown in the same screenshot.

Every content item supports various actions such as **Delete**, **Update**, **Cut**, and **Copy** as shown in the following screenshot. For each logged-in user, the actions for a specific content item will be different, based on the security permissions.

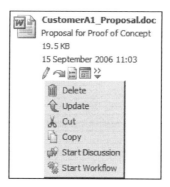

Create a Link to Content

A link (or shortcut) to content is a special type of file that serves as a reference to another file. This is similar to the symbolic links commonly used in Unix-like operating systems. A link only contains a symbolic path to content stored elsewhere in the Alfresco repository. Thus, when a user removes a link, the file to which it points, remains unaffected.

There might be situations where you need to have the same file in two spaces. For example, you might want to have a product data sheet in the engineering department space as well as in the marketing department space. Instead of creating two copies of the same file, you can keep one copy at one place and create links to the target file in other spaces.

Users should pay careful attention to the maintenance of links. If the target of a link is removed, the document vanishes and all links to it become orphans. Conversely, removing a symbolic link has no effect on its target.

Follow this process to create a link to content.

1. Identify the target document and click on the **Copy** action (as shown in the screenshot on the previous page).

2. The document will be placed in the clipboard as shown in the screenshot below.

3. Go to the space where you would like to create the link to the content.

4. Click on the **Paste Content as Link** icon ▣ in clipboard to create the link as shown in the screenshot below.

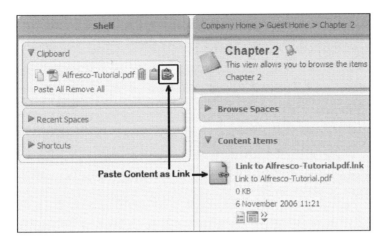

Summary

You have so many options to choose from while installing Alfresco. Alfresco installers on Windows and Linux operating systems make the installation process so simple that you can install all the installation software such as JDK, MySQL, Open Office, JBoss, and Alfresco within minutes. On the Windows platform you can run Alfresco as a service or as console application.

A web client, which is Alfresco's built-in web application, provides an intuitive user interface so that beginners can start using the system without any specialized user training.

In this chapter you have learned the key terminology in Alfresco such as web client, administrator console, space, content, category, aspects, actions and rules.

3
Planning

Planning is the most critical phase of any implementation project. During this phase, most of the decisions to customize specific features in a particular way are made. You define the security framework, custom-content types, folder structure, categories, workflow, reporting, business rules, and collaboration. During the planning phase, you will scope your implementation, prioritize the requirements, and finalize the project plan. This chapter provides you with information required for your planning exercise before implementing your system using Alfresco.

By the end of this chapter you will have learned how to:

- Follow best practices for implementing Alfresco
- Configure the relational database of your choice
- Configure the email and log files
- Configure the file-system interface to drag-and-drop content into repository
- Define multilanguage support
- Create a blueprint for your application

Follow Best Practices

Well, you must be wondering about the 'best practices' to be followed for implementing a project using open-source software. Is it so different than the best practices we follow for traditional commercial closed-source software development? The answer is YES.

Open-source strategy, development, packaging, deployment, documentation, training, support and maintenance, and other activities are very different form commercial closed-source software. The entire open-source development model is based on collaboration. You either develop your product on top of some open-source platform/framework or you share the development with people who are external to your organization. Hence it is very important to follow best practices such as:

- Common coding standards
- Upfront story boarding to satisfy all the business users
- Global identity management for your systems
- Version control
- Secure access

The open-source release process is also different as you will potentially have millions of testers around the world to test your software, and to provide you with feedback. Hence it is very important to have best practices for packaging, release, licensing, testing, and bug fixing.

This section covers some of the important practices you need to consider while implementing open-source software and specifically Alfresco.

Finalize Requirements and Scope of Implementation

The most difficult part of requirements gathering is not documenting what the users want but the effort of helping users figure out what they need that can be successfully provided within the cost and schedule parameters available.

Part of the requirements process is to prioritize requirements. This is important, because rarely is there enough time and money to provide everything that is wanted. It is also beneficial to focus on product benefits, not features. Benefits refer to the necessary requirements. Adding unnecessary features adds design constraints and increases costs.

To finalize the requirements, you need to go through the entire content acquisition, management, categorization, composition, and delivery processes.

- **Acquisition**: How is data captured? Where does it originate?
- **Management**: How is data approved, stored, managed, and tracked?
- **Categorization**: How is data organized and secured?
- **Composition**: How is data packaged?
- **Delivery**: How is data delivered?

Finalize the scope of your implementation by identifying the following design aspects:

- Membership (identity management)
- Content types with attributes
- Content associations

- Content functionality
- Content intelligence (reports)
- Business process management/workflow
- User interface
- Integration with external systems

Start with Documentation

The biggest complaint with most implementations is lack of documentation. For some projects, except source code, you can not locate a single line of documentation. Definitely you don't want to end up in that situation.

Start the project with documentation. Whether you are customizing an existing open-source project or integrating many open-source projects, documentation is very critical. Another good reason for you to focus on documentation is that some of your projects might involve external developers (out of your organization) on a contract/project basis.

The following documents are mandatory for any project whether it is small or large:

- Requirements document
- Project plan
- Criteria for user acceptance testing
- Design document
- System (hardware and software) configuration
- User manual
- Backup/recovery/maintenance documentation

You can include additional documentation based on the nature of the project, but make sure the above documents are part of your project deliverable. Plan for the time and budget for documentation.

Define Security for Groups and Not for Individuals

While designing your security system, consider using groups for defining the security instead of individuals.

Consider a scenario where you allowed Mr. Joe to be the contributor of space "X" and editor of spaces "Y" and "Z". If you delete Mr. Joe from the system, you need to manually remove him from spaces X, Y, and Z. Alfresco, at present does not provide any report to indicate all the spaces to which a particular user has access in the system. This becomes a security issue in the long run.

Consider another scenario, where two users, who belong to sales department, are added as contributors to the "Sales" space and "Finance" space and some more spaces as required. Let us say a new sales person joins the company, you need to add him or her to all these spaces and this is a big maintenance issue. Instead, if you provide access to the sales group on these spaces, the additions and deletions of individual members of the sales group will automatically take care of the security and collaboration requirements of the system.

Hence always group individual users. A user can belong to more than one group. Use groups to define security for various spaces.

Create Various Use Cases for Testing

A use case is a picture of actions a system performs, depicting the actors. Use cases and scenarios (descriptions of sequences of events) facilitate team communication. They provide a context for the requirements by expressing sequences of events and a common language for end users and the technical team.

Create use cases with the following details for testing your system:

- Who are all the users (actors) of the system?
- What are they allowed to do?
- How the process flow works
- Workflow and business process management
- Who approves? How?
- What is the escalation process?
- How to handle exceptions

Involve end users in testing to ensure the success of your implementation.

Identify Data to be Migrated

Most of the time, data migration happens after the application is built. You will save time and money if you can identify the data to be migrated before the implementation. For example, if you have hundreds of users who need to be migrated to the new system, then you might have thousands of documents and content (with metadata) to be migrated to the new system.

The nature of the data to be migrated will provide you with additional requirements. Hence it is a good practice to identify the data to be migrated in the earlier stages of the project.

Define Development, Staging, and Production Set up

Since Alfresco is the new technology, some of the enterprise customers are trying out proof of concept (POC) implementations. In the case of POC or smaller implementations, the development, testing, and production deployment happens on the same server.

Irrespective of the size of the implementation, consider having hardware for at least three different deployment setups for development, staging (or testing), and production.

This drives your hardware requirements and helps you set up a process for development, testing, and deployment.

Refer to the Alfresco Wiki, Forums, and Bug-Tracking Systems

Alfresco software is being enhanced in an incredibly short period of time. It is important to follow the release schedules and the upcoming features of Alfresco. For example, the current version (release 1.4) includes very important features such as business process management, records management, and document life cycle management. The Alfresco Wiki contains information related to current features and the roadmap.

It is quite possible that the feature you are trying to customize using Alfresco is already being developed by somebody in the community. Alfresco forge is a place where community developers collaborate to create additional features and add-on products.

Alfresco forums provide a platform to exchange ideas, tips, and best practices. Similarly the Alfresco bug-tracking system is open to everyone. You can see the list of bugs open and the fixes that are going to be released.

You can find the URLs related to the Alfresco Wiki, forums, forge, and bug-tracking systems in the Alfresco website `http://www.alfresco.com`

Contribute Back to the Community

Open source enables faster innovation. As the source code is open, there is more cooperation and input on the development of new capabilities. You can contribute the functionality that you have found useful and think others might as well. Of course, you would not contribute code that is sensitive to your organization or that has some intellectual property and licensing issues.

You will have many benefits if you contribute your code back to the community. Some of the benefits are listed below:

- You are giving some thing valuable to the community.
- Your code will be tested by thousands of testers worldwide. This helps you in saving time in testing.
- If your code becomes the part of the core product, then you don't have to personally maintain it for yourself or for your customers. It will be maintained and supported by Alfresco and the community as a part of product support.

Start with Basic Configuration

Now that you have planned your implementation, you can start configuring Alfresco as per your business needs. This section covers basic configuration settings such as the relational database, email server, etc. required before using the system.

Extend Alfresco Configuration

Alfresco configuration items are completely exposed as XML files, so you can override the default out-of-the-box Alfresco by customizing individual configuration items.

Default Configuration Files

The default configuration files for Alfresco are in the application WAR file. When the server starts, the files are expanded to `<configRoot>`, which is either:

JBoss: `<JBOSS_HOME>/server/default/tmp/deploy/`
`tmp*alfresco-exp.war/WEBINF/classes`

Tomcat: `<TOMCAT_HOME>/webapps/alfresco/WEB-INF/classes`

The default configuration files, maintained by Alfresco, are contained in `<configRoot>/alfresco` folder. The repository properties file (`repository.properties`) in this folder defines some of the core system properties including the following:

- **dir.root**: This is the folder (alf_data) where the binary content and Lucene indexes are stored. It is relative by default, but should be pointed to a permanent, backed-up location for permanent data storage.
- **db.***: These are the default database connection properties.

The web-client configuration files are located in the web-client *.xml files. Examine the other configuration files in the <configRoot>/alfresco folder.

Alfresco Extension Folder

You can override or extend the Alfresco configuration by placing the custom configuration files in the extension folder. If you have downloaded one of the bundles you will find the sample files in the following location:

JBoss: <alfresco>/jboss/server/default/conf/alfresco/extension

Tomcat: <alfresco>/tomcat/shared/classes/alfresco/extension

Configuration Approach

When Alfresco starts, it reads all the default configuration files, and then reads the customized configuration items (in the extension folder). So, depending upon the type of item, the customization either extends, or overrides the default configuration item.

The example given below extends the advanced search form. The first file contains the default configuration. This file can be found in the folder from the path given below: tomcat/webapps/alfresco/WEB-INF/classes/alfresco/web-client-config.xml:

```
<alfresco-config>
...
...
...
  <config evaluator="string-compare" condition="Advanced Search">
    <advanced-search>
      <custom-properties>
        <meta-data aspect="rma:filePlan"
                        property="rma:recordCategoryName" />
        <meta-data aspect="rma:filePlan"
                        property="rma:recordCategoryIdentifier" />
        <meta-data aspect="rma:record"
                        property="rma:recordIdentifier" />
        <meta-data aspect="rma:record"
                        property="rma:orginator" />
        <meta-data aspect="rma:record"
```

```
                        property="rma:orginatingOrganization" />
        <meta-data aspect="rma:record"
                                    property="rma:dateReceived" />
        <meta-data aspect="rma:record"
                        property="rma:supplementalMarkingList" />
      </custom-properties>
    </advanced-search>
  </config>
 ...
 ...
 ...
</alfresco-config>
```

The web-client configuration file in the extension folder (see the following path) adds an additional property called `cm:effectivity` to the advanced search form. `tomcat/common/classes/alfresco/extension/web-client-config-custom.xml:`

```
    <alfresco-config>
      <config evaluator="string-compare"
                                    condition="Advanced Search">
        <advanced-search>
          <custom-properties>
            <meta-data aspect= "cm:effectivity" property="cm:to" />
          </custom-properties>
        </advanced-search>
      </config>
</alfresco-config>
```

Web-client configuration files can contain configuration that either augments the standard configuration or replaces it.

Replacement is performed at the `config` level by adding a `replace="true"` attribute to the configuration element, for example:

```
    <config evaluator="xx" condition="yy" replace="true">
```

Any configuration found within a section marked this way will replace any configuration found in the Alfresco maintained files. For example, if you wanted to replace the list of languages shown on the log-in page you could add the following:

```
    <config evaluator="string-compare" condition="Languages"
                                                  replace="true">
      <languages>
        <language locale="fr_FR">French</language>
        <language locale="de_DE">German</language>
      </languages>
    </config>
```

On the other hand if you just wanted to add French to the list of languages, you would add the following:

```
<config evaluator="string-compare" condition="Languages">
    <languages>
        <language locale="fr_FR">French</language>
    </languages>
</config>
```

Whenever you make changes to these configuration files, you need to restart Alfresco to see the effect of the changes.

Packaging and Deploying Java Extensions

If your customization only consists of Alfresco configuration files or properties files i.e. `web-client-config-custom.xml` or `webclient.properties`, you can place the customization files in the `extension` folder.

However, if you are changing the Java source code the process is little different. Java classes are typically packaged within a `.jar` file; this then has to go in the web application's `WEB-INF/lib` directory. If you have Java code, you are more than likely going to have at least one other file type as part of your extension i.e. configuration files. These too can be contained within the `.jar` file, simply package them within the `.jar` file in the `alfresco/extension` folder.

Another alternative is to add your `.jar` file to the `alfresco.war` file. In JBoss, if you deploy a web application as a WAR file the application gets exploded to a temporary directory each time the application server starts. Thus there is nowhere to copy the `.jar` file to. One solution is to use an exploded deployment. Create a directory called `alfresco.war` under the deploy directory and extract the contents of `alfresco.war` (the file) into it. Then copy your `.jar` file to deploy/`alfresco.war/WEB-INF/lib` and restart JBoss.

Install the Enterprise License File

If you have installed the enterprise version of Alfresco, then you have to install the enterprise license file. Otherwise by default the Alfresco enterprise software expires in 30 days after installation.

Get the `.lic` file from Alfresco. Copy the `.lic` file to the `<config>/extension/license` directory (e.g. `tomcat/shared/classes/extension/license`). Once it is in place, restart the Alfresco server. Information about the license being set will be visible in the logs; also the license file is renamed with `.installed`. The Administration Console within Alfresco also gives details of the license status.

Change the Default Administrator Password

The administrator is the super user of the system. The administrator user ID is `admin` and password is `admin`. You can change the password by logging in to Alfresco web client as `admin` and changing the password.

Another way of overriding this password (during startup) is to update the web-client configuration file in the extensions folder with the following code:

```
<admin>
    <initial-password>admin</initial-password>
</admin>
```

Configure Relational Database

Refer to Chapter 2 for more details about installation. During installation, if you use either Windows installer or the Linux binary, then the installer automatically installs a local MySQL database, and configures it for you.

If you are installing the database and configuring it manually, then you need to follow the steps given in the section.

To configure the MySQL database:

1. Create a new `alfresco` user and *alfresco* database.
2. Grant all permissions to user `alfresco` on the *alfresco* database.
3. Override the database properties in the `<configRoot>/alfresco/repository.properties` file as follows:

   ```
   db.schema.update=true
   db.driver=org.gjt.mm.mysql.Driver
   db.name=alfresco
   db.url=jdbc:mysql:///${db.name}
   db.username=alfresco
   db.password=alfresco
   db.pool.initial=10
   db.pool.max=20
   db.pool.maxIdleTime=120
   ```

4. Restart Alfresco.

Alfresco supports MySQL or Oracle or MS SQL Server databases. Steps to configure a database remain the same for any of these databases.

Configure Email

You can configure the Alfresco repository to send emails from an SMTP server. Currently the repository does not support secure SMTP servers. Follow the steps given below to configure email:

1. Browse to the file: `<configRoot>/alfresco/repository.properties`.

2. Copy the following block of email properties:

   ```
   # Email configuration
   mail.host=
   mail.port=25
   mail.username=anonymous
   mail.password=
   ```

3. Create a new file in the **<extension>** directory.

4. Copy the email properties block into this file.

5. Modify any property to your required value as follows (you can delete any unmodified property, because it will retain the default value from `repository.properties`):

   ```
   mail.host=<the name of your SMTP host>
   mail.port=<the port that your SMTP service runs on
                                       (the default is 25)>
   mail.username=<the username of the account you want e-mail to
                                       be sent from >

   mail.password=<the password>
   ```

6. Save the file with a meaningful name that ends with `.properties`.

7. Ensure that your new file is pointed to, so that it can be found at server startup.

From Email Address

To change the 'from' email address used when users are invited to a space, add the following to the `web-client-config-custom.xml` file in the `extension` folder.

```
<config>
  <client>
    <from-email-address>someone@your-domain.com
                                  </from-email-address>
  </client>
</config>
```

Configure Log Files

Log files hold very important run-time system information. For a Tomcat installation, the log files are located at `<install_folder>` itself. Tomcat application server creates a log file per day. The current log file is named `alfresco.log` and at the end of the day, the log file will be backed up as alfresco.log.YYYY-MM-DD (for example, `alfresco.log.2006-09-18`).

You can configure the log file by updating the `<configRoot>/log4j.properties` file. You can set the level of logging as either `info` or `debug` or `error` based on the amount of information you need (For example, `log4j.logger.org.alfresco.web=info`). For example, the option *debug* will provide you very detailed information; however, it creates performance issues in high-traffic installations.

Configure CIFS Desktop Actions

CIFS helps you to map Alfresco space as your local file system folder, thus giving you flexibility in working with files in the repository as if they are in your local file system. You will be able to upload bulk files to server and edit them directly using your desktop applications.

For the drag-and-drop feature to work with CIFS, you need to make some configuration settings. The configuration file `<configRoot>\alfresco\file-servers.xml` contains information about the desktop actions. The custom version of the configuration file is available in Alfresco's extension folder. Open the `<extension>/file-servers-custom.xml` file, and make sure the following block is uncommented.

```xml
<!-- Desktop actions -->
<!-- Uses a client-side application to trigger a server-side
                                                action -->
<!-- Echo - displays a message echoed from the server -->
<!-- URL  - launches a URL via the Windows shell >
<!-- CmdLine - launches the Notepad application -->
<!-- CheckInOut - checks files in/out, drag and drop files onto the
                                                application -->
<desktopActions>
  <global>
    <path>alfresco/desktop/Alfresco.exe</path>
  </global>
  <action>
    <class>org.alfresco.filesys.smb.server.repo.desk.
                                        EchoDesktopAction</class>
      <name>Echo</name>
        <filename>__AlfrescoEcho.exe</filename>
```

```
    </action>
    <action>
      <class>org.alfresco.filesys.smb.server.repo.desk.
                                    URLDesktopAction</class>

        <name>URL</name>
          <filename>__AlfrescoURL.exe</filename>
    </action>
    <action>
      <class>org.alfresco.filesys.smb.server.repo.desk.
                                    CmdLineDesktopAction</class>

        <name>CmdLine</name>
          <filename>__AlfrescoCmd.exe</filename>
    </action>
    <action>
      <class>org.alfresco.filesys.smb.server.repo.desk.
                                    CheckInOutDesktopAction</class>

        <name>CheckInOut</name>
          <filename>__AlfrescoCheckInOut.exe</filename>
    </action>
  </desktopActions>
```

Restart Alfresco server after making changes.

Configure Default Logos

While using the Alfresco web client, you will have noticed Alfresco logos appear on the log-in page, in the web-client tool bar. You can configure the custom logos as per your branding requirements.

All the logos that appear in the web-client application are kept in the logos folder in the file system. In a Tomcat installation, the logo's folder is `<install_folder>\tomcat\webapps\alfresco\images\logo`.

Examine some of the logos in this folder:

- `AlfrescoLogo32.png` is the site logo. This logo is always displayed on the top left corner of the web client. This logo is 32 pixels wide and 30 pixels high.

- `AlfrescoLogo200.png` is the log-in page logo. This logo is displayed on the log-in page in the log-in window along with user name and password. This logo is 200 pixels wide and 60 pixels high.

- `AlfrescoFadedBG.png` is the log-in page background logo. This is the blurred logo displayed as background image on the log-in page. This logo is 428 pixels wide and 422 pixels high.

To customize these logos, first rename the existing logos to `AlfrescoLogo32_OLD.png`, `AlfrescoLogo200_OLD.png`, and `AlfrescoFadedBG_OLD.png` respectively, for backup purpose. Create three new logos with the original names with the same sizes. For example a custom site logo with the file name `AlfrescoLogo32.png` (32 x 30 pixels size).

Now your Alfresco application displays new custom logos, instead of the old default ones. In some browsers you might not be able to see the new logos due to the fact that the old logos are cached in the browser. Refresh the browser cache to view the new logos in the Alfresco web client.

Customize Look and Feel using CSS

Cascading Style Sheets (CSS) files define how to display HTML elements, in other words the look and feel of the Alfresco web client. The font size, font color, background color, font style, text alignment, table structure — everything is controlled by the CSS files.

The CSS files are located in the file system `<install_folder>\tomcat\webapps\alfresco\css` folder. You can customize the look and feel by changing the values in the `main.css` file. For example, you can customize the title look and feel by editing the following block in `main.css` file.

```
headbarTitle
  {
    color: #003366;
    font-size: 11px;
    font-weight: bold;
    margin-bottom: 5px;
  }
```

 It is a good practice to backup the `main.css` file before making any changes to it.

Configure Multilanguage Support

You can configure Alfresco to support various languages like:

- Chinese
- Dutch
- English

- French
- German
- Italian
- Japanese
- Russian
- Spanish

The support for other languages is being developed. The beauty of true open-source development is that most of these language packs are developed and donated by community users.

The following are the steps to configure support for a specific language for your Alfresco application:

1. Download Alfresco language packs from SourceForge website; `http://sourceforge.net/project/showfiles.php?group_id=143373`

2. Copy the required language packs to the `<configRoot>/alfresco/messages` folder in the file system.

3. Edit the `web-client-config-custom.xml` file in the extension folder and include the following XML code to configure the specific languages.

```
<!-- English is the default language.  Add additional languages to
                                 the list in the login page -->
  <config evaluator="string-compare" condition="Languages">
    <languages>
      <language locale="de_DE">German</language>
      <language locale="es_ES">Spanish</language>
      <language locale="fr_FR">French</language>
      <language locale="it_IT">Italian</language>
      <language locale="ja_JP">Japanese</language>
    </languages>
  </config>
```

4. Restart Alfresco.

The Alfresco web-client log-in screen displays all the configured languages in the drop-down list. The languages appear in the log-in option and will be in the same order as they are defined in the configuration file. Select the language of your choice as shown in the following screenshot:

Create a Blueprint for Your Application

Now that the configuration is done, the next step is to create the blueprint for your application. The blueprint is nothing but a skeleton application on Alfresco without the actual content. This includes the security framework, folder structure within the Alfresco repository, categories for taxonomy, workflow and business rules, and so on.

Enterprise Intranet as a Theme

We will build an intranet for your enterprise where each department has its own space, document management and security, and business rules. All departments collaborate to create an effective enterprise knowledge management portal.

This example solution is extended in all the chapters. Hence reading the chapters in the proper sequence would help you to understand the features of Alfresco in a systematic manner. While reading each chapter, you will get the concepts of Alfresco, and at the same time you will be developing the solution. Though the extended sample is related to an enterprise intranet, it is created in such a way that you will learn all the features of Alfresco.

Let us name your enterprise Have Fun Corporation, which has the following groups of people:

- **Administrator**: Manages membership, groups, categories, security, business rules, workflow, templates
- **Executive:** Has highest authority on the content and manages approvals
- **HR**: Manages corporate policy documents
- **Corporate Communications**: Manages external PR, internal news releases, syndication
- **Marketing**: Manages website, company brochures, marketing campaign projects, digital assets
- **Sales**: Manages presentations, contracts, documents and reports
- **Finance**: Manages account documents, scanned invoices and checks, notifications
- **Engineering**: Collaborates on engineering projects, workflow, XML documents, presentation templates

Features You are Going to Implement

These are the high-level features you are going to implement as a part of solution.

- **Security and Access Control**: Give de-centralized control to each department to manage its own content and yet share with others.
- **Document Management**: This includes version control, check-in and checkout, categorization, notifications, bulk upload, Advanced Search features etc. Every group will use these features.
- **Space templates for engineering projects and marketing projects**: Each engineering project will follow a standard structure, workflow, and security rules. Similarly each marketing project will follow specific workflow, transformation, and publishing rules.
- **Content transformations**: This is used for marketing and sales material.
- **Imaging Solution**: The Finance group will use this feature to handle scanned invoices and checks.
- **Presentation templates including dashboard views**: The Corporate Communications group will use these to display news and the latest PR files. The Finance group will use them to have thumbnail views of scanned checks, the Engineering group will use them to display XML documents.
- **Automated Business Rules**: Each group uses these in a specific manner. For example the HR group might send an email notification to a specific group when a document is updated. The Sales group will automatically convert a PPT to Flash; the Finance group will trigger an approval process whenever a scanned check gets into the system etc.

Summary

When Alfresco starts, it reads all the default configuration files, and then reads the customized configuration items in the extensions folder. So, depending on the type of item, the customization either extends, or overrides the default configuration item. You have flexibility in choosing the database and membership framework of your choice. You can configure email, multi-language support, and the look and feel of the application. Applications built on top of Alfresco are highly configurable, customizable, extensible, and scalable. If you plan it right by following the best practices, Alfresco provides you the highest return on your technology investments.

4
Implementing Membership and Security

In this chapter you will learn about the concepts and the underlying framework behind Alfresco's security model and membership system. The Alfresco security model is flexible and allows you to choose either built-in security or an external security model defined by your organization via systems such as LDAP and Active Directory. You will understand various security models and learn to choose the one most suited to your enterprise's requirements. Alfresco's membership system is highly scalable and can cater for hundreds and thousands of users and content managers.

By the end of this chapter you will have learned how to:

- Create, update, and delete users
- Group users based on the activities they perform
- Search for and locate users and groups
- Extend the security policy
- Secure spaces and individual content as per your organizational security requirements
- Choose a suitable security model
- Migrate existing users and groups to Alfresco

Alfresco Membership and Security Model

A content management system requires a membership system for its users to access content, to allow setting up user preferences, and to allow its users to receive notifications and alerts. Members of the system can collaborate with other members by selectively sharing documents, and sharing ideas via discussion forums. Members can control and follow the business process through a workflow.

Traditional membership models address basic authentication (who can access) and authorization (what they can do). Alfresco extends this model by providing capabilities to manage groups and subgroups of members, member attributes, and member workspace and provides a set of administrative tools to configure and control membership.

Users and Groups

Users are individual members, whereas groups are logical categorizations of users.

In Alfresco, a user is identified by a unique user ID, also known as a log-in ID. The administrator is like a super user of the system. Alfresco identifies registered users (users not logged in as guest). The name of such a logged-in user is shown on the top right-hand corner of the web-client screen.

Alfresco groups logically group a set of users in the system for security and collaboration purposes. A group can have any number of sub-groups. There is a default group called **EVERYONE**, which represents all users of the system.

A user can belong to more than one group and sub-group as shown in the following diagram in the next page. For example user *Mike ExecEngg* belongs to two groups: *Executive* and *Engineering.*

A group can have more than one user. For example the sales group in the following diagram contains two users *Amit Sales* and *Candace Sales.*

A user belonging to a sub-group will automatically belong to the parent group. For example, *Chi EnggDoc* belongs to the *Engineering Documentation* sub-group and thus automatically belongs to *Engineering* group.

This is how a typical organization hierarchy works. An employee belongs to a particular department or sometimes more than one department.

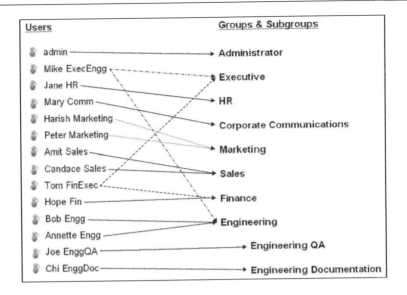

Permissions and Roles

Permissions define access rights on spaces and content. Out of the box, Alfresco supports extensive permission settings on spaces and content. More detailed description is provided in later sections of this chapter.

Permissions are identified by a string. A particular permission, for example `ReadChildren`, may be granted or denied to an authority: a user, group, administrator, owner, etc. The children of a node, sub-folders or files in a folder, will inherit permissions from their parents. So by default, the files in a folder will inherit their permissions from the folder. Permissions set on a node take precedence over permissions set on the parent nodes. Permissions inheritance may be turned off for any node.

A permission group is a convenient grouping of permissions such as `Read` made up of `ReadProperties` and `ReadChildren`. Each one of these permissions is applicable to node, space, space properties, sub-space, content, content properties, and business rules. The following are typical permissions groups:

- Read
- Edit
- Add
- Delete

Roles are collections of permissions assigned to a user. Each role comprises of a set of permissions. Alfresco provides out-of-the-box support for the following roles:

- **Consumer** can read content
- **Editor** can read and edit content
- **Contributor** can read and add content
- **Collaborator** can read, edit, and add content
- **Coordinator** can read, edit, add, and delete content (full access)

Alfresco roles and permissions may be extended to support your requirements.

Authentication

Alfresco imposes authentication using the user name and password pair. Authentication is performed at the following entry points to the Alfresco repository:

- Web client
- CIFS
- FTP
- WebDAV
- Web services
- Spring beans exposed as public services in Java

When a call is made to the repository through the public service API, the caller must first be authenticated. This can be done by logging in using a username and password to validate a user. Some applications and authentication mechanisms may support single sign-on. For example, a user can access the Alfresco repository through a web client program or another application can access the Alfresco repository through a web services protocol. No matter how a user or an external system connects to Alfresco, they all should go through the same authentication process to access data from the Alfresco repository.

How is Security Imposed in Alfresco?

Alfresco imposes authorization by assigning a role to a specific user or group for a specific space or content.

Spaces and content in Alfresco can be secured in a number of ways. By default, a space or content in Alfresco can be managed only by the owner who created it. For each space, you need to give specific roles (groups of permissions) to specific users (or groups of users) to set the permissions on that space. Sub-spaces may inherit parent space permissions. Security rules may be specified at the individual content level that may be different from security rules for its parent folder or space.

Refer to the previous figure, where users *Tom FinExec* and *Hope Fin* both belong to the *Finance* group. Let us say you have a space called *Finance Department* and you would like to give *full access control* to only people who belong to the *Finance* group and give *Read* access to the people who belong to the *Sales* and *Executive* groups.

As an administrator to *Finance Department* space, you can invite the *Finance* group as **Coordinator** (full access) and the *Sales* and *Executive* groups as **Consumer** (read access). Refer to the table given below, which shows examples of space structure and roles assigned to specific groups and individual users on a space:

Space Title	Group	Assigned Role
Finance Department	Finance	Coordinator — Full Access
	Sales	Consumer — Only Read Access
	Executive	Consumer — Only Read Access
Company Policies	HR	Coordinator — Full Access
	EVERYONE	Consumer — Only Read Access

Manage System Users

You have to log in to Alfresco web client as an administrator (*admin*) to create accounts for each Alfresco user. Only an admin user can manage user accounts.

To add users, you need to know the user ID, password, and other details as listed in the *Create New Users* section below.

In Alfresco, each user can have his or her individual space. The location and name for a space can be specified while creating a user account. The user for which a space is created becomes the owner of that space. As an owner, the user can have full access to his or her space.

Create a Space for All Users

It is good practice to create a single space to contain spaces for all individual users. First, you create a space for all users and then you add users.

To create a new space for users, follow the steps below:

1. Click on the **Company Home** menu link in the tool bar (top left).
2. In the header click on **Create | Create Space**.
3. The create space dialog is displayed as shown in the following screenshot.
4. In the **Name** text box, type **Users Home**.

5. In the **Description** text box, type **Contains spaces for all users**.

6. Click on the **Create Space** button to create the space.

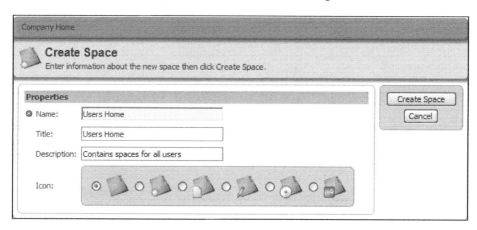

You are returned to the **Company Home** space with the **Users Home** space added as shown in the screenshot below:

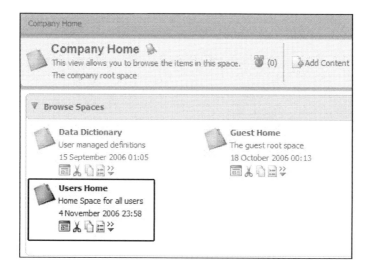

Create New Users

Before adding users, you will need to know the following details for each user:

*   First Name
*   Last Name
*   Email ID (valid corporate email address)

- Company ID (for customer extranet, this could be customer's company name)
- User name (log-in ID)
- Password
- Home space name (usually user name)

Refer to the first figure in this chapter for the list of users to be created for your intranet. Follow the steps below to create a user:

1. In any space, click on the administration console button provided in the top tool bar as shown in the screenshot below:

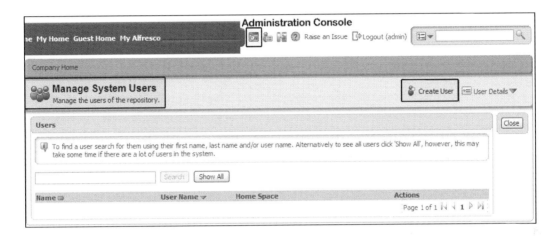

2. The administration console pane appears. Click on the **Manage System Users link**. The **Manage System Users** pane appears as shown in the above screenshot.

3. In the header, click the **Create User** link (highlighted in the above screenshot).

4. The first pane of the **New User Wizard** appears as shown in the screenshot overleaf. This is the **Person Properties** pane, as you can see from the list of steps at the left of the pane.

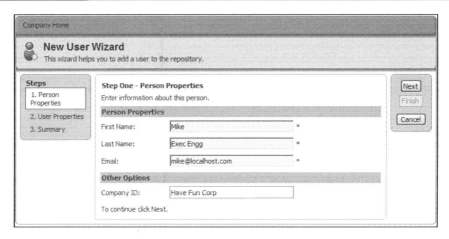

5. For the user **Mike ExecEngg,** provide **Mike** as the **First Name**, **Exec Engg** as the **Last Name**, `mike@localhost.com` as the **Email** and **Have Fun Corp** as the **Company ID**. In fact, you may also provide the employee ID in the **Company ID** field.

6. Click on the **Next** button to the right of the pane. The second pane of the **New User Wizard** appears as shown in the screenshot below. This is the **User Properties** pane, as you can see from the list of steps at the left side of the pane.

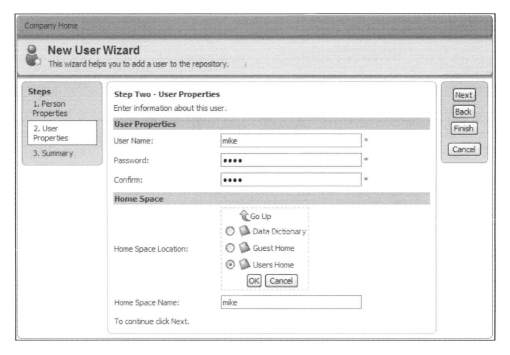

7. Choose **mike** (all lower case) for **User Name** and **Password**. Choose **Users Home** as the parent space and **mike** as the **Home Space Name**. Note that the username and password must be between 3 and 32 characters in length.

8. Click on the **Next** button to the right of the pane. The third pane, which is the **Summary** pane for the **New User Wizard**, appears.

9. Verify all the information and click on the **Finish** button to confirm.

> For every wizard in Alfresco, you need to click on the **Finish** button to confirm; otherwise, the information you provided earlier will be lost.

Similarly, create all the users listed in the first figure (except *admin*, which is already created out of the box).

> Do not proceed to the subsequent sections without first creating the users. The remaining sample solutions are based on these users and the groups they belong to.

Search for Existing Users

Alfresco provides a user-search tool to find a user by using their first name, last name, and/or user name. Follow the steps below to search for existing users:

1. In any space, click the administration console icon. The administration console pane appears.

2. Click the **Manage System Users link**. The **Manage System Users** pane appears.

3. In the search box, provide the user's first name or last name to search for. Alternatively, to see all users click the **Show all** button without providing any information in the search box.

The search results will be displayed as shown in the screenshot overleaf. If there are many users in the system then the search will return multiple pages with pagination numbers.

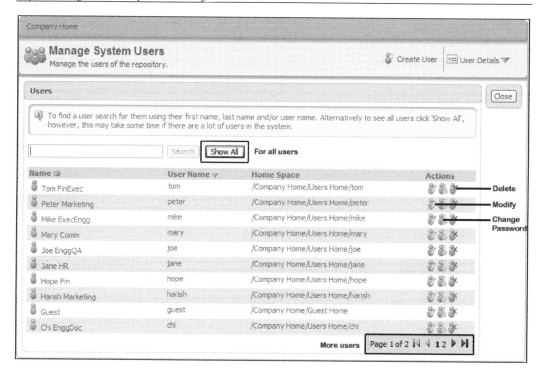

Modify User Details

Search for a system user as explained in the *Search for Existing Users* section above. To edit user detail information, click on the **Modify** icon belonging to that user, as shown in the above screenshot.

The first pane of the **Edit User Wizard** appears. You can edit and make corrections as required and then click the **Finish** button to confirm.

Deleting a User

Search for a system user as explained in the *Search for Existing Users* section above. To delete user detail information, click on the **Delete** icon belonging to that user, as shown in the above screenshot. You need to be very careful while deleting a user from the system as the user will no longer be able to access the system.

Even if the user is deleted from the system, his or her home space will not be deleted from the system. Hence you need to remove the user space manually if you want the deleted user's content removed from the system.

Alfresco provides a content recovery tool to recover the deleted content. However there is no way to recover the deleted user. Hence, you need to be careful while deleting a user from the system.

Individual User Access

Once a user account is created by the administrator, the user can log in to the system. The administrator can set up an automated script to send an email to the user with user id and password information. You will learn more about such email notification template scripts in later chapters.

New User Log in and My Home Page

Log in to Alfresco, by entering the following URL in your browser:
`http://server_name:8080/alfresco`.

If you are already logged in as an administrator, logout by clicking on the **Logout** button given in the top tool bar.

The log-in page appears as shown in the screenshot on the previous page. In the **User Name** text box enter your user name as **mike** and in the **Password** text box enter your password as **mike**. Note, that the user **Mike ExecEngg** was created as a new user account in the earlier section.

Depending on your installation, you may have a choice of languages in the **Language** drop-down menu. This example assumes that your selected language is **English**. Click on the **Login** link and enter your credentials. Your home space appears as shown in the screenshot below:

Update Personal Details and Password

You can update your profile information and password by clicking on the user options icon given on the top tool bar as shown in the screenshot below.

Click on the edit personal profile icon to update your name and user ID. Click on the **Change Password** link to update the password.

Under the general preferences block, select the **Start Location** as the landing page once you log in to Alfresco web client.

Manage User Groups

Alfresco comes with one default user group called **EVERYONE**. The **EVERYONE** group logically includes all the system users irrespective of the groups they belong to. This is useful to give 'read' access to **EVERYONE** on certain common spaces, e.g. HR Policies etc. You can create and manage your own groups. In order to create groups, log in to Alfresco web client as an administrator.

Create Groups and Sub-Groups

Before adding a group or sub-group (hierarchical groups), you will need to finalize group names. The group name (identifier) should be unique and cannot be changed once set.

Refer to the first figure in this chapter for the list of groups to be created for your Intranet. Follow the steps given below to create a group:

1. In any space, click on the administration console icon. The **Administration Console** pane appears.

2. Click the **Manage User Groups** link. The **Groups Management** pane appears.

3. In the header, click **Create | Create Group**. The **Create Group Wizard** appears as shown in the screenshot below. Specify **Executive** as **Group Identifier**, which is the group used for all company executives. Click on the **Create Group** button to confirm.

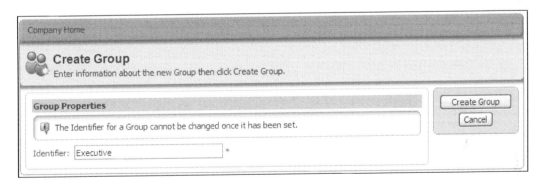

Similarly, create all the groups listed in the first figure except 'Administrator' (which is already created out-of-the-box).

Do not proceed to the subsequent sections without creating the groups. The remaining sample solutions rely on the existence of these groups for security and collaboration.

Click on the **Engineering** group and create two sub-groups called **QA** and **Documentation**.

Now you can see the groups at root level as shown in the following screenshot. You will notice that **QA** and **Documentation** are not part of the root level groups, as they are sub-groups under the **Engineering** group.

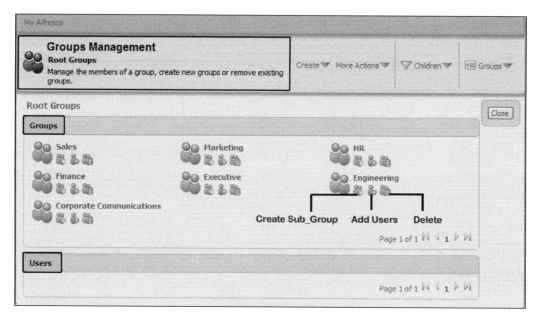

Add Users to a Group

To add users to a group, click on the add users icon as shown in the above screenshot. The **Add User** dialog will pop up. You can search for the system users and add them to a group as shown in the next screenshot. Click on the **Finish** button to confirm the operation.

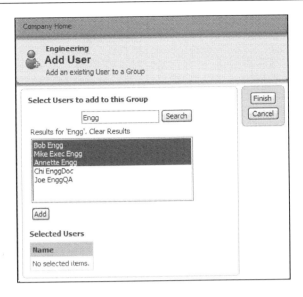

Add users to the newly created groups as explained in the first figure. For example, add user Jane HR to the HR group. Add user Mary Comm to the Corporate Communications group. Similarly, add user Joe EnggQA to the QA sub-group of the Engineering group, and so on.

Remove Users from a Group

Users can be removed from a group by clicking on the remove user icon as shown in the screenshot on the next page.

A user may belong to one or more groups. If a user is deleted from the system users list, then that user will be automatically removed from all the groups.

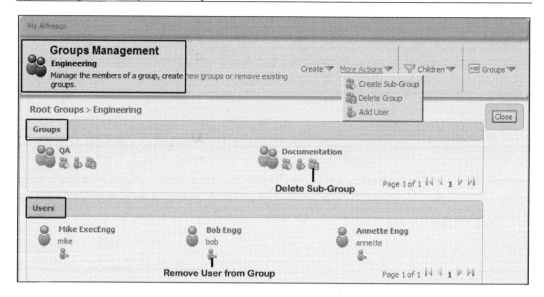

Extend Security Permissions and Roles

Out of the box, Alfresco supports an extensive set of permissions to provide security controls. Alfresco supports a set of roles by grouping these permissions. The security permissions and roles can be extended. However, before extending the permissions and roles, you need to evaluate and understand the existing permissions and roles and justify the decision to extend them.

Default Permissions

Alfresco supports a number of permissions to access the spaces, content, properties, etc. The following are some of the permissions for spaces:

- ReadProperties — Read space properties
- ReadChildren — Read the content within a space
- WriteProperties — Update properties such as title their description
- DeleteNode — Delete space
- DeleteChildren — Delete content and sub-spaces within a space
- CreateChildren — Create content within a space

The following are some of the permissions for content items:

- ReadContent — Read file
- WriteContent — Update file

- ReadProperties — Read file properties
- WriteProperties — Update file properties such as title, description, etc.
- DeleteNode — Delete file
- ExecuteContent — Execute file
- SetOwner — Set ownership on a content item

A complete list of default permissions and roles is provided in the Alfresco configuration file `<config>\model\permissionDefinitions.xml`.

Default Roles

Roles are collections of permissions assigned to users in a specific space. Sub-spaces may inherit permissions from their parent space. Roles may also be applied to individual content items. The following table lists the default roles supported out of the box by Alfresco:

Role	Permission
Consumer	Read spaces and content
Editor	Consumer + edit existing content
Contributor	Consumer + add new content
Collaborator	Editor + Contributor
Coordinator	Full Control

Create a Custom Role

You can add a new custom role as per your security requirements. You will have to include details of the custom role in `permissionDefinitions.xml`, which is the permission definitions file located at `<config>\model\`. For a Tomcat installation, you can find this file at `tomcat\webapps\alfresco\WEB-INF\classes\alfresco\ model\ permissionDefinitions.xml`

You need to define your own permissions group (say "TestRole") and assign permissions as shown below:

```
<permissionGroup name="TestRole" allowFullControl="false"
                                            expose="true" >
  <includePermissionGroup permissionGroup="Read" type="sys:base" />
  <includePermissionGroup permissionGroup="AddChildren"
                                            type="sys:base"/>
  <includePermissionGroup type="cm:lockable"
                                    permissionGroup="CheckOut"/>

</permissionGroup>
```

Once you make the changes to the XML file, you need to restart Alfresco to see the new role added to the system.

Secure Your Spaces

A space can be secured by assigning a role to a specific user (or group) on that space.

User Roles on a Space

Alfresco uses roles to determine what a user can and cannot do in a space. These roles are associated with permissions. The following table lists the allowed permissions for each role on a given space. A user (or group) with the *Consumer* role on a space can read all the content within that space. Similarly, a user (or group) with the *Contributor* role on a space can create content within the space.

Permission	Consumer	Contributor	Editor	Collaborator	Coordinator
Read Content within space	X	X	X	X	X
Read Space Properties	X	X	X	X	X
Read Sub-spaces	X	X	X	X	X
Read Forums, Topics, Posts	X	X	X	X	X
Copy	X	X	X	X	X
Preview in Template	X	X	X	X	X
Create Content within space		X		X	X
Create Sub-Spaces		X		X	X
Create Forums, Topics, Posts		X		X	X
Reply to Posts		X		X	X
Start Discussion		X		X	X
Edit Space's Properties			X	X	X
Add/Edit Space users			X	X	X
Delete Space users					X
Add/Edit Space rules			X	X	X
Delete Space rules					X

Permission	Consumer	Contributor	Editor	Collaborator	Coordinator
Cut Content/ Sub-Spaces					X
Delete Content/Sub-Spaces					X
Check-out Content			X	X	X
Update Content			X	X	X
Take Ownership					X

Invite Users to Your Space

You can grant permission the users (or groups) to do specific tasks in your space. You do this by inviting users to join your space. Each role applies only to the space in which it is assigned. For example, you could invite a user (or group) to one of your spaces as an editor. You could invite the same user (or group) to a different space as a collaborator. That same user (or group) could be invited to someone else's space as a coordinator.

Follow the steps given below to invite a group of users to your space:

1. Click on the **Company Home** menu link in the tool bar (top left).

2. In the header click the **Create | Create Space** link.

3. Create a new space called **Intranet**.

4. Within the **Intranet** space create a sub-space called **Finance Department**. Ensure that you are in the **Finance Department** space.

5. In the space header, click **More Actions | Manage Space Users**. The **Manage Space Users** pane appears as shown in the following screenshot:

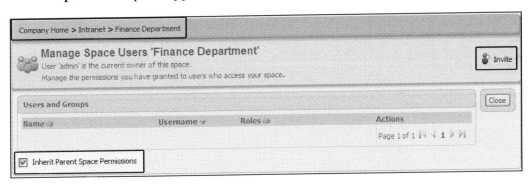

6. Leave the **Inherit Parent Space Permissions** option as checked (selected). When it is not selected, uninvited users cannot see the content item. Only invited users can see the content item, and can access it according to their assigned role.

7. In the header, click the **Invite** link. The **Invite User Wizard** pane appears as shown in the following screenshot:

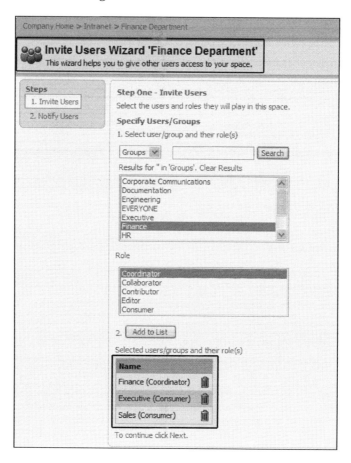

8. Before continuing with your invitation, you can experiment with the Search feature. Select the **Groups** from the drop-down box and click on the **Search** button.

9. From the search results, select the **Finance** group, give it the **Coordinator** role and click on the **Add to list** button.

10. The finance group is added to the list of invitees.

11. As an administrator of the *Finance Department* space, you can invite the *Finance* group as coordinator (full access) and the *Sales* and *Executive* groups as consumer (read access).

12. Click on the **Next** button to go to the second pane, where you can notify the selected users.

13. Do not select this option as you do not have to notify these selected users in this sample. Click on the **Finish** button to confirm.

Notice the permissions given to the groups on this space as shown in the screenshot below:

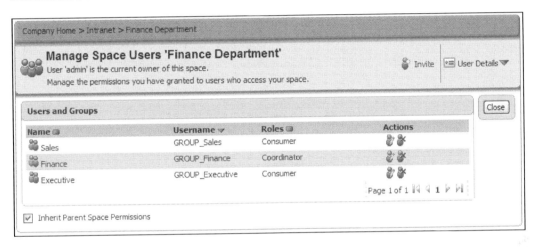

Define and Secure Your Spaces

In the example above, you created a space called Finance Department and you gave the Coordinator role (full control) to the Finance group and gave the Consumer role (read access) to the Sales and Executive groups.

Next, go to your **Company Home | Intranet** space and create spaces as given in the first column of the table overleaf. Invite groups and assign roles as indicated in the second column of the table:

Space Name	Group (Assigned Role)	Individual (Assigned Role)
Executive and Board	Executive (Coordinator)	
Company Policies	HR (Coordinator) EVERYONE (Consumer)	
Press and Media	Corporate Communications (Coordinator) EVERYONE (Consumer)	
Marketing Communications	Marketing (Coordinator) EVERYONE (Consumer)	
Sales Department	Sales (Coordinator) Executive (Consumer)	Mr. CEO (Coordinator)
Finance Department	Finance (Coordinator) Sales (Consumer) Executive (Consumer)	
Engineering Department	Engineering (Coordinator) EVERYONE (Consumer)	Mrs. Presales (Coordinator)

Secure Your Content

Content can be secured by assigning a role to a specific user (or group) on that content.

User Roles for Content

Alfresco uses roles to determine what a user can and cannot do with the content. These roles are associated with permissions. The table below shows each role and the permissions for that role for content:

Permissions	Consumer	Contributor	Editor	Collaborator	Coordinator
Read Content	X	X	X	X	X
Read Content Properties	X	X	X	X	X
Copy	X	X	X	X	X
Preview in Template	X	X	X	X	X
Start Discussion		X		X	X

Permissions	Consumer	Contributor	Editor	Collaborator	Coordinator
Edit Content			X	X	X
Edit Properties			X	X	X
Apply Versioning			X	X	X
Apply Categorization			X	X	X
Check-out			X	X	X
Update			X	X	X
Take ownership					X
Cut					X
Delete					X

Invite Users to Your Content

Typically security and access control rules are defined at the space level. It is not advised to secure individual content items as it may become unmanageable with large numbers of files. It is the best practice to secure the parent space rather than securing the content itself. However, you can still control the access to a specific content item.

Follow the steps below to invite users to your content item:

1. Go to a space and add a file by clicking on the **Add Content** link.
2. Click on the **View Details** icon for the file to see the detailed view of the content.
3. From the right-hand side **Actions** menu, click on the **Manage Content Users** link, to assign users to this content item for collaboration.
4. Search and select a user and assign a **Collaborator** role to the user.

Now the user can collaborate on the file.

Choosing the Right Security Model for You

It is very important to choose a suitable security model at the beginning of Alfresco implementation. The authentication mechanism, user profile data storage, security settings, business rules, etc. are all based on the security model you choose.

Alfresco imposes authentication through user log-in ID and password. This is where you choose a security model such as Alfresco's built-in membership system, NTLM (Windows NT LAN Manager) or LDAP (Lightweight Directory Access Protocol). These security models are explained in detail in the subsequent sections of this chapter.

Alfresco imposes authorization by assigning a role to a specific user (or group) for a specific space (or content). This will be the same irrespective of which model you choose.

The security model you choose will be based on the requirements of your enterprise. Let us consider the following sample scenarios:

Scenario 1: I would like to build an extranet as a stand-alone application to share documents with my customers. I have over 500 customers who will access the site, and I would like to control and manage the security. I need a flexible and highly scalable membership system.

In this scenario, the out-of-the-box Alfresco membership system would be able to solve the problem.

Scenario 2: I work in the IT department of a large university. Over the years, the various departments have developed their own sites with local authentication and authorization. Our university has a directory-based central authentication system. How can I consolidate all the sites and provide a central point of authentication and authorization for all our sub-sites?

In this scenario, it would make sense configure Alfresco with LDAP for centralized identity management.

Scenario 3: In my enterprise we have various systems such as customer support, ERP, proprietary content management systems, and the open-source ECM Alfresco. Our employees have different accounts on all these different systems and it is becoming unmanageable for us. We are looking at a single sign-on solution to access all our systems with one log-in ID and password. In this scenario Alfresco can be configured to use NTML to provide single sign-on.

Use Alfresco Out-of-the-Box Membership System

Alfresco out of the box security includes the following functionality:

- User management
- Provision of user personal information

- User authentication
- Group management
- Ownership of nodes within the repository
- An extendable permission model
- Access control, to restrict calls to public services to authenticated users

Examples in this book are based on the out-of-the-box Alfresco security model.

Configuring LDAP for Centralized Identity Management

LDAP evolved from X.500 OSI Directory Access Protocol. LDAP directory is the central authentication engine for the enterprise, and serves as yellow pages for access to users, and their profile information. The biggest advantage of LDAP is that your enterprise can access the LDAP directory from almost any computing platform, using any one of the increasing numbers of readily available LDAP-aware applications. In fact, LDAP is finding much wider industrial acceptance because of its status as an Internet standard.

You can use LDAP with any directory server, such as iPlanet, Novell's eDirectory, Microsoft's Active Directory, or OpenLDAP. If you are planning to implement an LDAP directory in your organization, you may consider *OpenLDAP*, which is a stable and widely accepted open-source directory server.

Active Directory supports LDAP-based authentication. It can also support authentication using JAAS+Kerberos and NTLM authentication. Only NTLM will give you a single-sign-on solution. It is possible to use any of these authentication methods against an Active Directory server and extract user and group information via LDAP.

There are three parts to Alfresco LDAP configuration:

- Authentication
- Scheduled jobs for loading people and groups
- The authentication context (which configures LDAP authentication and how people and groups are extracted from LDAP).

 A template configuration is provided in `alfresco/extensions/ldap-authentication-context.xml.sample`.

Configuring NTLM for Single Sign-on

NTLM is an authentication protocol used in various Microsoft network protocol implementations, and is also used throughout Microsoft's systems as an integrated single-sign-on mechanism.

NTLM authentication can be used to provide single sign-on to Alfresco. Using this protocol, the password that is sent over the network is more secure than when using basic authentication. NTLM pass-through authentication can also be used to replace the standard Alfresco user database and instead use a Windows server/domain controller, or list of servers, to authenticate users accessing Alfresco. This eliminates the task of creating user accounts within Alfresco.

By using NTLM authentication, the web browser can automatically log on when accessing Alfresco and Alfresco WebDAV sites. When NTLM is configured, Internet Explorer will use your Windows log on credentials when requested by the web server. Firefox and Mozilla also support the use of NTLM; for these you will be prompted for the username/password details, which can then optionally be stored using the password manager. Opera web browser does not support NTLM authentication. If an Opera browser is detected, you will be sent to the usual Alfresco log on page.

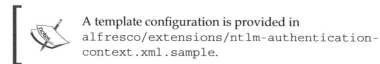

A template configuration is provided in `alfresco/extensions/ntlm-authentication-context.xml.sample`.

To enable NTLM authentication you need to edit the `web.xml` file (the location of the file depends on the application server used) and uncomment `<filter>` elements for NTLM.

To enable NTLM pass-through you need to replace the file `<config>/authentication-services-context.xml` with the `<config>/authentication-services-context.ntlm` file.

Migrate Existing Users to Alfresco

If you are planning to migrate an existing application to Alfresco, then you might want to migrate its existing users to Alfresco as well. If you use LDAP or NTLM-based security model, then you don't have to migrate the existing users to Alfresco. Instead, you can directly connect to those user sources from Alfresco. This model is always preferred as you can manage users and groups at one centralized location and access the user information in many applications.

What follows is applicable if you are using Alfresco's out-of-the box security model.

Using Command-Line Scripts to Bulk Upload Users

You can bulk upload users to Alfresco using **command-line scripts**. In order to bulk upload users, you need to create a user data XML file. A sample file is shown below for your reference:

person.xml

```
<?xml version="1.0" encoding="UTF-8"?>
  <view:view xmlns:d="http://www.alfresco.org/model/dictionary/1.0"
             xmlns:cm="http://www.alfresco.org/model/content/1.0"
           xmlns:view="http://www.alfresco.org/view/repository/1.0">
    <cm:person view:childName="cm:person">
      <cm:userName>fredb</cm:userName>
      <cm:firstName>Fred</cm:firstName>
      <cm:lastName>Bloggs</cm:lastName>
      <cm:email>fredb@alfresco.org</cm:email>
    </cm:person>
    <cm:person view:childName="cm:person">
      <cm:userName>sues</cm:userName>
      <cm:firstName>Sue</cm:firstName>
      <cm:lastName>Sanderson</cm:lastName>
      <cm:email>sues@alfresco.org</cm:email>
    </cm:person>
  </view:view>
```

Once the XML file is created with the user details, the next step is to run a command-line script to upload the users given in the `person.xml` file.

The syntax to call the script may change based on the operating-system platform. Here is a sample script that reads user data from `person.xml` file and uploads to Alfresco.

```
java -classpath classes;
lib\repository.jar;lib\core.jar;lib\spring.jar;
lib\jibx-run.jar;lib\xpp3.jar;lib\commons-logging.jar;
lib\ehcache-1.1.jar;lib\dom4j-1.6.1.jar;lib\acegi-security-0.8.2.jar;
lib\hibernate3.jar;lib\quartz.jar;lib\pdfbox-0.7.2.jar;
lib\poi-2.5.1.jar;lib\jooconverter.jar;lib\jid3lib-0.5.jar;
lib\freemarker.jar;lib\log4j-1.2.8.jar;lib\cryptix-jce-provider.jar;
lib\commons-codec-1.2.jar;lib\
            commons-dbcp-1.2.1.jar;lib\commons-pool.jar;lib\jta.jar;
```

```
lib\mail.jar;lib\activation.jar;lib\jug.jar;lib\
                                commons-collections-3.0.jar;
lib\cglib-nodep-2.1.jar;lib\antlr-2.7.5H3.jar;
lib\tm-extractors-0.4_patched.jar;lib\ridl.jar;
lib\juh.jar;lib\jurt.jar;lib\sandbox.jar;lib\jut.jar;
lib\lucene-1.4.3.jar;..\..\..\common\lib\
                                mysql-connector-java-3.1.12-bin.jar;
lib\saxpath.jar;lib\jaxen-1.1-beta-8.jar org.alfresco.tools.
    Import -user admin -pwd admin -store workspace://SpacesStore -path
                                sys:system\sys:people person.xml
```

Bootstrapping the Alfresco Repository with Pre-Defined User Data

The Alfresco repository supports a bootstrap process, which is initiated whenever the repository is first started. The process populates the repository with information that is required upon first log in, such as system users, data dictionary definitions, and important root folders.

Detailed information about bootstrapping Alfresco repository is provided in Chapter 12 *Maintaining the System*.

Using the Web Services API to Create Users

You may also use the web services API to programmatically create users in Alfresco. This is useful if you already have another software application to manage users and you would like to create users in Alfresco from that application as needed.

Summary

The Alfresco membership framework is very secure, flexible, scalable, and customizable. Roles are collections of permissions assigned to users (Consumer, Contributor, Editor, Collaborator, and Coordinator). You can manage system users and groups through the administration console. Security is imposed by assigning a role to a specific user or group for a specific space or content. Authentication is possible using Alfresco's built-in membership system, NTLM, and LDAP. You can bulk upload users to Alfresco using command-line utilities and the web services API.

5
Implementing Document Management

This chapter introduces you to the basic features of creating and managing content in Alfresco. Using Alfresco, you can manage any type of documents such as HTML, text, XML, Microsoft Office documents, Adobe PDF, Flash, scanned images, media, and video files. You will also learn about the concepts of creating and using categories and smart spaces. This chapter also focuses on the most important aspect of adopting a new enterprise content management system, which is migrating the existing data and using it effectively.

By the end of this chapter you will have learned how to:

- Create spaces and fill them with documents
- Automatically control the document versioning
- Lock, check-in, and check-out the documents
- Categorize content to facilitate searching
- Recover deleted content
- Create and use space templates
- Access documents in the Alfresco repository from your web browser, or a networked drive, FTP, or WebDAV
- Migrate existing documents to Alfresco

Managing Spaces

A space in Alfresco is nothing but a folder, which contains content as well as sub-spaces. Space users are the users invited to a space to perform specific actions such as editing content, adding content, discussing a particular document, etc. You need to have the administrator, contributor, collaborator, or coordinator role, on a space to create sub-spaces. Similarly you need to have the administrator, editor, collaborator, coordinator role, to edit space properties. For more information about user roles on a space, refer to Chapter 4.

Space is a Smart Folder

Space is a folder with additional features such as security, business rules, workflow, notifications, local search, and special views. These additional features that make a space a smart folder are explained below:

- Space Security: You can define security at the space level. You can specify a user or a group of users who may perform certain actions on content in a space. For example, on the *Marketing Communications* space in *Intranet*, you can specify that only users of the marketing group can add the content and others can only see the content.

- Space Business Rules: Business rules such as transforming content from Microsoft Word to Adobe PDF and sending notifications when content gets into a space can be defined at space level.

- Space Workflow: You can define and manage content workflow on a space. Typically, you will create a space for the content to be reviewed, and a space for approved content. You will create various spaces for dealing with the different stages the work flows through, and Alfresco will manage the movement of the content between those spaces.

- Space Events: Alfresco triggers events when content gets into a space, or when content goes out of a space, or when content is modified within a space. You can capture such events at space level and trigger certain actions such as sending email notifications to certain users.

- Space Aspects: Aspects are additional properties and behavior, which could be added to the content, based on the space in which it resides. For example, you can define a business rule to add customer details to all the customer contract documents in your Intranet's *Sales* space.

- Space Search: Alfresco Search can be limited to a space. For example, if you create a space called *Marketing*, you can limit the search for documents within *Marketing* space, instead of searching the entire site.

- Space Syndication: Space content can be syndicated by applying RSS feed scripts on a space. You can apply RSS feeds on your *News* space, so that other applications and websites can subscribe for news updates.

- Space Content: Content in a space can be versioned, locked, checked-in and checked-out, and managed. You can specify certain documents in a space to be versioned and others not.

- Space Network folder: A space can be mapped to a network drive on your local machine enabling you to work with the content locally. For example, using the CIFS interface a space can be mapped to the Windows network folder.

- Space Dashboard View: Content in a space can be aggregated and presented using special dashboard views. For example, the Company Policies space can list all the latest policy documents that have been updated during the past one month or so. You can create different views for the Sales, Marketing, and Finance departmental spaces.

Why Space Hierarchy is Important

Like regular folders, a space can have spaces (called sub-spaces) and sub-spaces can further have sub-spaces of their own. There is no limitation on the number of hierarchical levels. However, the space hierarchy is very important for all the reasons specified above in the previous section. Any business rule and security defined at a space is applicable to all the content and sub-spaces underlying that space.

In the previous chapter, you created system users, groups, and spaces for various departments as per the example. Your space hierarchy should look like the one given below:

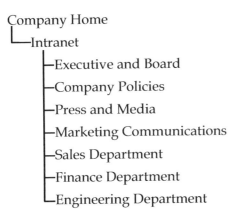

Space hierarchy enables you to define various business rules, dashboard views, properties, workflow, and security for the content belonging to each department. You can decentralize the content management by giving access to departments at individual space levels.

The Intranet space in our example should contain sub-spaces as shown in the screenshot on the next page. If you have not already created spaces as per the example given in the previous chapter, you must do it now by logging in as the administrator. The examples used in the remaining chapters of this book refer to these spaces. Also, it is very important to set security (by inviting groups of users to these spaces) as explained in the previous chapter.

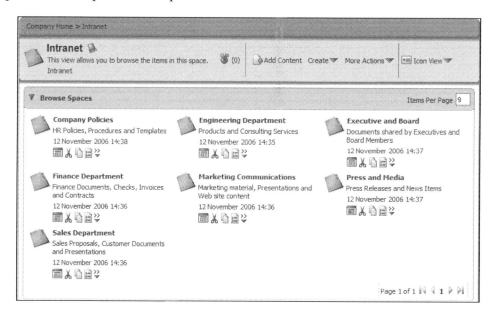

Edit Space

Using the web client, you can edit the spaces you have added previously. Note that you need to have edit permissions on the spaces to edit them as explained in the previous chapter.

Edit Space Properties

Every space listed will have clickable actions as shown in the following screenshot:

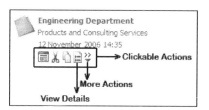

These clickable actions will be dynamically generated for each space based on the current user's permissions on that space. If you have copy permission on a space you will notice the copy icon as a clickable action for that space. On clicking the **View Details** action icon the detailed view of a space will be displayed as shown in the next screenshot:

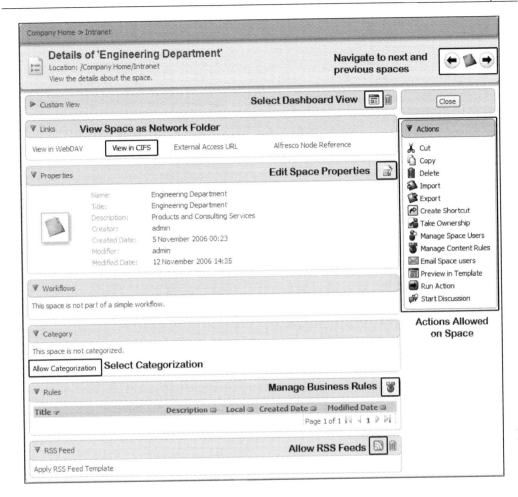

The detailed view page of a space allows you to select a dashboard view, to view and edit existing space properties, to categorize the space, to set business rules, and to run various actions as shown in the above screenshot.

To edit space properties, click on the edit properties icon shown in the above screenshot. You can change the name of the space and other properties as needed.

Delete a Space and Its Contents

From the list of space actions, you can click on the **Delete** action to delete the space. You need to be very careful while deleting a space as all the business rules, sub-spaces, and the entire content within the space will also be deleted.

Move or Copy a Space Using the Clipboard

From the list of space actions, you can click on the **Cut** action to move a space to the clipboard. Now you can navigate to any space hierarchy, given that you have the permission, and paste this particular space as required.

Similarly, you can use the **Copy** action to copy the space to some other space hierarchy. This is useful if you have an existing space structure (such as a marketing project or engineering project) and you would like to replicate it along with the data.

The copied or moved space will be identical in all aspects to the original (source) space. When you copy a space its properties, categorization, business rules, space users, entire content within the space, and all sub-spaces along with their content will also be copied.

Create a Shortcut to a Space for Quick Access

If you need to frequently access a space, you can create a shortcut (similar to a browser favorite) to that space to reach the space in one click. From the list of space actions, you can click on the **Create Shortcut** action to create a shortcut to the existing space. Shortcuts are listed in the left-hand side **shelf**.

Choose a Default View for Your Space

Out of the box, four different views (as shown in the screenshot on the next page) are supported to display the space information.

Details View provides listings of sub-spaces and content in horizontal rows.

Icon View provides title, description, timestamp, and action menus for each sub-space and content item present in the current space.

Similarly, **Browse View** provides title, description, and a list of sub-spaces for each space.

The **Custom View** is disabled and appears in grey. This is because you have not enabled a dashboard view for this space. In order to enable a dashboard view for a space, you need to select a dashboard view (refer to the icon in the earlier screenshot).

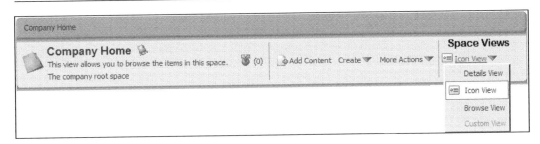

Sample Marketing-Project Space Structure

Let us say you are launching a new marketing project called 'Switch to open source ECM'. You can create your own space structure within the marketing project space to manage content. For example, you can have a space called *Drafts* to keep all the draft marketing documents and so on. Go to the **Company Home | Intranet | Marketing Communications** space and create a new space called *Switch to open source ECM* and create various sub-spaces under that as shown in the screenshot below.

The new marketing project space and the sub-spaces created are used in the remaining examples listed in this chapter to manage content.

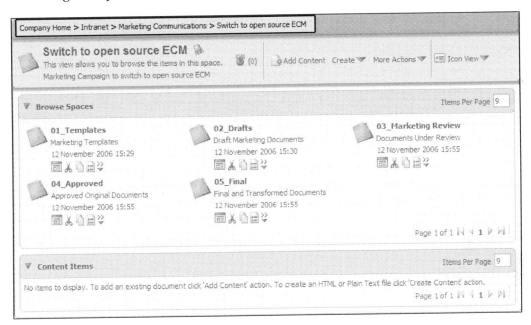

Managing Content

Content could be of any type as mentioned at the start of this chapter. Using the Alfresco web client application, you can add and modify content and its properties. You can categorize content, lock content for safe editing, and you can maintain several versions of the content. You can delete content and you can recover the deleted content as well.

This section uses the space you have already created as a part of your *Intranet* sample application. As a part of sample application, you will manage content in the **Intranet | Marketing Communications** space. As you have secured this space earlier, only the administrator (*admin*) and users belonging to the Marketing group (*Peter Marketing* and *Harish Marketing*) can add content in this space. You can log in as *Peter Marketing* to manage content in this space.

Create Content

The web client provides two different interfaces for adding content: one to create inline editable content such as HTML, Text, and XML and the other to add binary content such Microsoft office files and scanned images.

You need to have the Administrator, Contributor, Collaborator, Coordinator role on a space to create content within that space. For more information about user roles on a space, refer to Chapter 4.

Creating Text Documents—HTML, Text, and XML

To create an HTML file in a space, follow the steps given below:

1. Ensure that you are in the **Intranet | Marketing Communications | Switch to open source ECM | 02_Drafts** space.

2. On the header, click **Create | Create Content**. The first pane of the **Create Content** wizard appears as shown in the screenshot on the next page. In this wizard, and in any Alfresco wizard, you can track your progress through the wizard from the list of steps at the left of the pane.

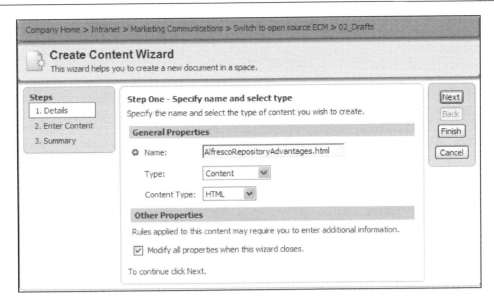

3. Provide the name of the HTML file, select HTML as **Content Type**, and click the **Next** button. The **Enter Content** pane of the wizard appears as shown in the next screenshot. Note that **Enter Content** is now highlighted in the list of steps at the left of the pane.

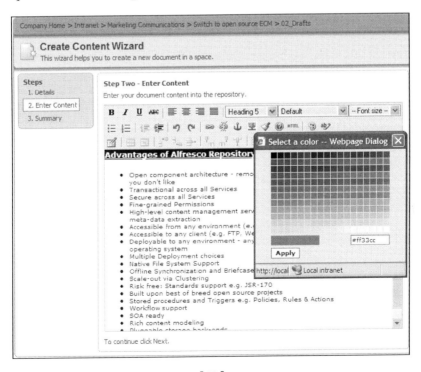

4. You can see that there is a comprehensive set of tools to help you format your HTML document. Enter some text, using some of the formatting features.

5. If you know HTML, you can also use an HTML editor by clicking on the HTML icon given. The HTML source editor is displayed. Once you have updated the HTML content, click on the update button to return to the **Enter Content** pane in the wizard, with the contents updated.

6. After the content is entered and edited in the **Enter Content** pane, click **Finish**. You will see the **Modify Content Properties** screen to update metadata associated with the content as shown in the screenshot below:

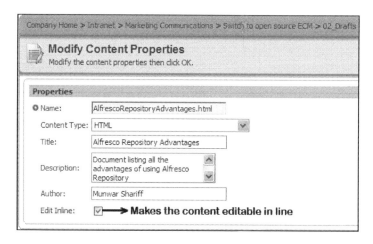

7. If you are satisfied with the properties, click the **OK** button to return to the **02_Drafts** space, with your newly created file inserted.

You can launch the newly created HTML file by clicking on it. Your browser launches most of the common files such as HTML, text, and PDF. If the browser could not recognize the file, you will be prompted with the Windows dialog box containing the list of applications, from which you must choose an application. This is the normal behavior if you try to launch a file on any Internet page.

Uploading Binary Files—Word, PDF, Flash, Image, and Media

Using the web client, you can upload content from your hard drive. Choose a file from your hard disk that is not an HTML or text file. I chose *Alfresco_CIGNEX.doc* from my hard disk for the sample application. Ensure that you are in the **Intranet | Marketing Communications | Switch to open source ECM | 02_Drafts** space.

To upload a binary file in a space, follow the steps given below:

1. In the space header, click the **Add Content** link.

2. The **Add Content** dialog appears.

3. To specify the file that you want to upload, click **Browse**. In the **File Upload** dialog box, browse to the file that you want to upload. Click **Open**. Alfresco inserts the full path name of the selected file in the **Location** text box.

4. Click the **Upload** button to upload the file from your hard disk to the Alfresco repository. A message informs you that your upload was successful as shown in the following screenshot.

5. Click **OK** to confirm.

6. The **Modify Content Properties** dialog appears. Verify the pre-populated properties and add information in the text boxes. Click **OK** to save and return to the **02_Drafts** space.

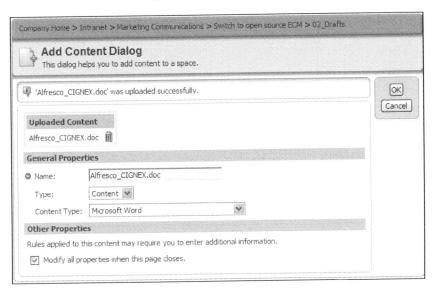

The file that you uploaded appears in the **Content Items** pane. Alfresco extracts the file size from the properties of the disk file, and includes the value in the size row. Now that you have two files, you can edit them as you like.

Edit Content

Using the web client you can edit the files that you have added previously. Note that you need to have edit permissions on the content to edit them as explained in the previous chapter.

Inline Editing of HTML, Text, and XML

HTML files and plain text files can be created and edited inline. Each file type is edited in its own WYSIWYG editor. If you have edit access to a file, you will notice a small pencil (edit) icon as shown in the screenshot below. Clicking on the pencil icon will open the file in its editor.

Upload an Updated Binary File

If you have edit access to a binary file, you will notice the **Update** action icon in the more actions link as shown in the screenshot below. On clicking on the update icon, the update pane opens. Click on the **Browse** button to upload the updated version of the document from your hard disk.

Content Actions

Content will have clickable actions as shown in the screenshot on the next page. These clickable actions (icons) will be dynamically generated for a content based on the current user's permissions for that content. For example, if you have copy permission for the content, you will notice a copy icon as a clickable action for that content.

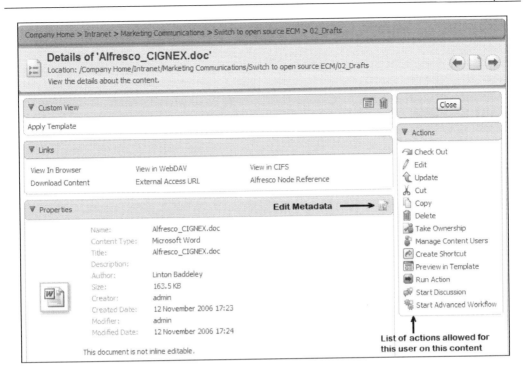

Delete Content

Click on the **Delete** action, from the list of content actions, to delete the content.

Move or Copy Content Using the Clipboard

From the list of content actions as shown in the previous screenshot, you can click on the **Cut** action to move the content to the clipboard. Now you can navigate to any space hierarchy and paste this particular content as required.

Similarly, you can use the **Copy** action to copy the content to another space.

Create a Shortcut to Content for Quick Access

If you have to access particular content very frequently, you can create a shortcut (similar to a browser favorite) to that content to reach the content in one click. From the list of content actions as shown in the **View Details** page, you can click on the **Create Shortcut** action to create a short cut to the existing content. Shortcuts are listed in the left-hand side **Shelf**.

Managing Content Properties

Every content item in Alfresco will have properties associated with it. Refer to the screenshot on the tenth page to see the list of properties such as **Title**, **Description**, **Author, Size**, and **Creation Date**. These properties are associated with the actual content file `Alfresco_CIGNEX.doc`.

The content properties are stored in the relational database and are searchable using advanced search options.

What is Content Metadata?

Content properties are also known as *Content Metadata*. Metadata is structured data, which describes the characteristics of content. It shares many similar characteristics with the cataloguing that takes place in libraries. The term Meta derives from the Greek word denoting a nature of a higher order or more fundamental kind. A metadata record consists of a number of pre-defined elements representing specific attributes of content, and each element can have one or more values.

Metadata is a systematic method for describing resources, and thereby improving access to them. If access to the content will be required, then it should be described using metadata, so as to maximize the ability to locate it. Metadata provides the essential link between the information creator and the information user.

While the primary aim of metadata is to improve resource discovery, metadata sets are also being developed for other reasons, including:

- Administrative control
- Security
- Management information
- Content rating
- Rights management

Metadata Extractors

Typically, in most content management systems, once you upload the content file, you need to add the metadata (properties) such as title, description, and keywords to the content manually. Most of the content such as Microsoft Office documents, media files, and PDF documents contain properties within the file itself. Hence, it is a duplicated effort having to enter those values again in the content management system along with the document.

Alfresco provides built-in metadata extractors for popular document types to extract the standard metadata values from a document and populate the values automatically.

This is very useful if you are uploading the documents through FTP, CIFS, or WebDAV interface, where you do not have to enter the properties manually, as Alfresco will transfer the document properties automatically.

Editing Metadata

To edit metadata, you need to click the edit metadata icon ▨ in the content details view. Refer to the edit metadata icon shown in the screenshot that shows the detailed view of the file `Alfresco_CIGNEX.doc`. You can update the metadata values such as **Name** and **Description** for your content items. However, certain metadata values such as **Creator**, **Created Date**, **Modifier** and **Modified Date** are read-only and you cannot change them. Certain properties such as **Modifier** and **Modified Date** will be updated by Alfresco automatically, whenever the content is updated.

Adding Additional Properties

Additional properties can be added to the content in two ways. One way is to extend the data model and define more properties in a content type. More information is provided in the chapter titled *Extending the Alfresco Content Model*.

The other way is to dynamically attach the properties and behavior through **Aspects**. Using aspects, you can add additional properties such as *Effectivity*, *Dublin Core Metadata*, and *Thumbnailable* to the content. More information is provided in the chapter titled *Implementing Business Rules*.

Library Services

The library services are the common document management functions for controlling users with permissions to create multiple instances of a document (versioning) and users with access a document to make changes (checking in/out).

Versioning

So far you have learned about creating spaces, adding files, and editing them. You might have more than one person who can edit a document. What if somebody edits a document, and removes a useful piece of information? Well, you can use versioning features to avoid such issues.

Versioning allows the history of previous versions of a content item to be kept. A content item needs to be *versionable* for versions to be kept. You can enable versioning in four different ways.

- Individually: To enable versioning for an individual content item, go to the **View Details** page and click on the **Allow Versioning** link. The screenshot on the next page illustrates the way to enable versioning on an individual content item.

- Using Smart Spaces: A business rule can be set for a space to allow versioning of all the content or selective content within that space. More information about this is provided in the chapter titled *Implementing Business Rules*.

- By Type: By default, versioning is disabled for all content types in the Alfresco content model. Versioning can be enabled for a specific content type in the Alfresco content model, irrespective of the location of the content. More information about this is provided in the chapter titled *Extending the Alfresco Content Model*.

- Globally: Alfresco can be configured globally to enable versioning for all the content throughout the site. More information about this is provided in the chapter titled *Extending the Alfresco Content Model*.

Enable versioning for the sample file you have already uploaded to the system. Go to the **Intranet | Marketing Communications | Switch to open source ECM | 02_Drafts** space and view details of `Alfresco_CIGNEX.doc`. Click on the **Allow Versioning** link to enable versioning as shown in the screenshot below, and you will immediately notice that a version with 1.0 is created.

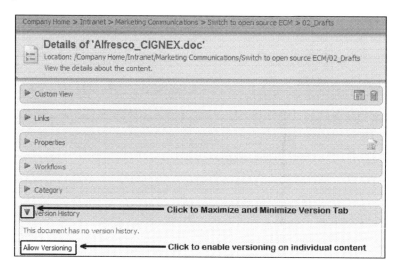

At the time of writing this book (Alfresco version 1.4), reverting back to an older version of the content is not supported. There is plan to support this feature in the future releases of Alfresco. The work-around is to download the older version and upload it again as the current version.

For a checked-out content item, the version is updated when the content is checked in. The version number is incremented from the content version number that was checked out.

Auto Versioning

Auto versioning can be enabled by editing the content properties and selecting the **Auto Version** checkbox.

If auto versioning is enabled, each **Save** of the content results in an incremented version number when it is edited directly from the repository. Each **Update** (upload) of the content also results in an incremented version number.

If auto versioning is not enabled, the version number is incremented only when content is checked in.

Check-in and Check-out

Using the versioning feature, you can ensure that all the changes made to a document are saved. You might have more than one person who can edit a document. What if two people edit a document at once, and you get into a mess with two new versions. To resolve this issue, you'll need the library services.

The library services provide the ability to check out a document, reserving it for one user to edit while others can only access the document in a read-only mode. Once the necessary changes are made to the document, the user checks in the document and can either replace the original or create a version of the original.

Check-out locks the item and creates a working copy, which can be edited (content and details). Check-in replaces the original item with the working copy and releases the lock.

Checking out Documents

Ensure that you are in the **Intranet | Marketing Communications | Switch to open source ECM | 02_Drafts** space. Click on the check-out action of Alfresco_CIGNEX. doc as shown in the screenshot below:

The **Check Out** pane is displayed as shown in the screenshot below. You can either check out the file in the current space or to any other pre-defined space. Typically, in a production environment the file resides in the **Published** space and you can check it out to a drafts space to make modifications to the file.

For the current example, choose the file check-out in the current space option and click on the **Check Out** button. You will return to the **02_Drafts** space.

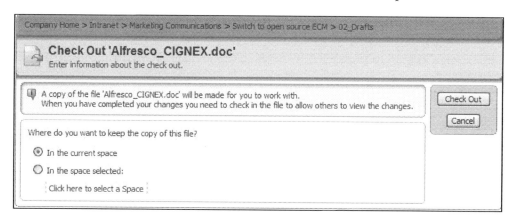

You will see two copies of the same document as shown the following screenshot. The original version of the file has a lock. This indicates that no one else can check out this file until you have checked it in again. The original version of the file cannot be edited (no pencil icon) or checked out (no check-out icon). The desired effect of all these features is that you cannot edit a checked-out file deliberately or accidentally.

You can only update the working copy. The checked-out file has **Working Copy** inserted in the file name. The working copy can be edited and checked in.

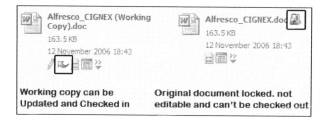

Checking in the Working Copy

Update the working copy **Alfresco_CIGNEX (Working Copy).doc** file. Updating the document is explained earlier in this chapter in the *Upload the Updated Binary File* section. After you update the working copy, you can check it in by clicking the check-in button as shown in the above screenshot. Once you click on the check-in action, you will see the **Check In** dialog window as shown in the following screenshot:

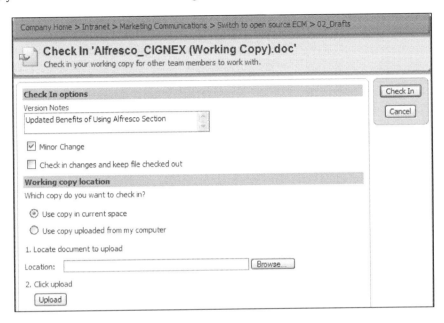

If you have only made minor changes to the file, you will check the **Minor Change** checkbox. By selecting the *Minor Change* checkbox, you will be able to increment only the number after the decimal (from 1.0 to 1.1); else you will increment the number before the decimal (from 1.0 to 2.0).

For this example, select the **Minor Change** option and provide some meaningful version notes. Version notes are very important documentation to help understand the differences between various versions of the same document.

The option **Check in changes and keep file checked out** is an useful option if you intend to keep the file locked for several days. You can continually mirror your changes from the working copy to the locked copy. This means that if another user wants to look at the file, they will see a more up-to-date copy than if they had to wait until you checked in the file.

You now have two options to check in the file:

- **Use copy in current space**: You would use this option if you had previously used **Update** on the working copy.

- **Use copy uploaded from my computer**: If you use this option, you do not need to have previously used the **Update** option.

There will be situations where either of these options is preferable. For this example, select the **Use copy in current space** option and click on the **Check In** button. You are returned to the *02_Drafts* space.

There will no longer be a working copy of the document. Notice the latest modification timestamp of the original document. If you click on the **View Details** action and scroll down to **Version History**, you will see that the history has been updated as shown in the following screenshot:

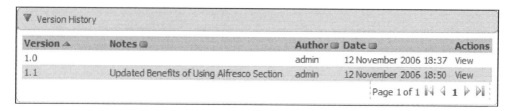

Undo Check-Out to Unlock a Document

Now that you can use library services, you might still have questions such as; How long does a file remain checked out? Can we see who checked it out and when? And who can cancel the lock?

A document remains in the checked-out state (locked) forever till the working copy is checked in or till somebody cancels the checked-out status from the working copy. To cancel check-out, locate the working copy of the document, click on the **More Actions** icon and select the **Undo Check Out** option as shown in the following screenshot. **Undo Check Out** will delete the working copy and release the lock, as if the check-out had not happened.

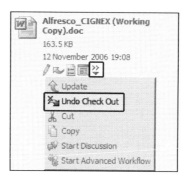

You can enable auditing on the Alfresco repository, and find out audit trail information such as who locked the content and when. More information about the auditing is covered in Chapter 7.

The owner of the document, or a coordinator, or an administrator can unlock the document by executing the **Undo Check Out** action on the working copy. Other users, who have read access to the space, can still see the working copy of the document but they can never edit or check in the document. The possible actions on a working copy by other users are shown in the following screenshot:

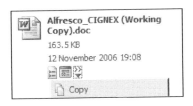

Categorizing Content

Categorization helps to classify information in a number of ways. Various technologies use various terminologies such as hierarchies, taxonomies, and ontology for the same concept.

In Alfresco, all content can be linked to one or more categories. Categories are defined and managed by administrators only. Categories can have sub-categories and there is no limitation on the number of categories or the depth of the hierarchy.

Categorization aids in searching and the advanced search form in Alfresco allows you to search the content filtered by various categories.

Managing Categories

Follow the steps below to create two new categories called Technology and Products for your example application.

1. In any space, click on the **Administration Console** icon in the top tool bar. The **Administration Console** pane appears.

2. Click on the **Category Management** link. The **Category Management** pane appears as shown in the following screenshot. Notice the existing categories such as **Software Document Classification**, **Regions**, and **Languages**.

3. In the header, click the **Create | Add Category** link to create a new category.

4. As an example, create a new category called *Open Source Products*. Under that new category, create few sub-categories such as *Alfresco* and *Plone*.

You can add additional categories and sub-categories and you can edit the existing categories.

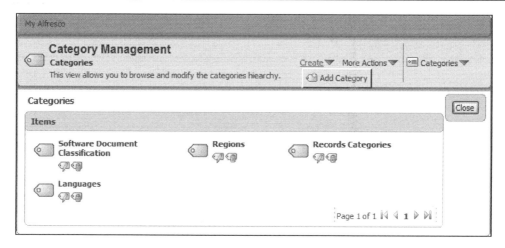

Adding Categories to Content

In order to categorize content, you need to have an Administrator, Editor, Collaborator, Coordinator role on that content.

To enable categorization for an individual content item (say `Alfresco_CIGNEX.doc`), go to the **View Details** page, and click on the **Allow Categorization** link. Click on the **Change Category** icon as shown in the following screenshot overleaf to apply categorization to the content.

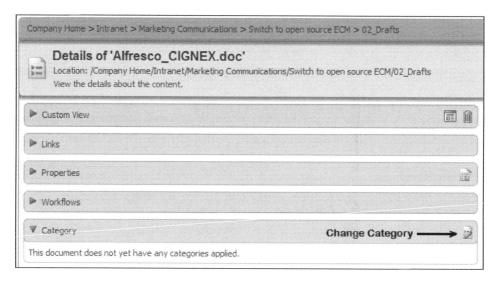

You will see the **Modify categories** dialog as shown in the screenshot below page. Apply two different categories to the content. Click on the **OK** button to confirm.

You will notice these two categories associated with your document in the **View Details** page.

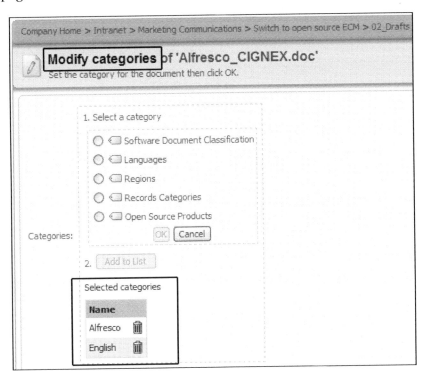

Search Content by Category

Categorization helps to narrow down a search or filter the search results. From the earlier example, we will search for the marketing documents, with a text called *Content* and categorized under **Open Source Products | Alfresco**.

Click on the **Advanced Search** link from the drop-down list of the search menu. From the form options, click on the **Show me results in the categories** pane. Click on the **Click here to select a category** link. Select **Open Source Products | Alfresco** as an option and provide text in the **Look For** text box and then click on the **Search** button.

Recovering Deleted Content

When you delete an item (content or space) in Alfresco, the item will not be deleted from the server; it will be moved to a temporary store called the **Archive Space Store**. This gives you a chance to recover items that were deleted earlier.

A deleted item will be in the temporary store forever, or till you decide to either recover or purge the deleted item. This feature is available to administrators through the **Manage Deleted Item** action.

To test these features, log in as an administrator, create a couple of dummy files in Alfresco and delete them. In any space, click **More Actions | Manage Deleted Items**. The **Manage Deleted Items** pane appears as shown in the following screenshot:

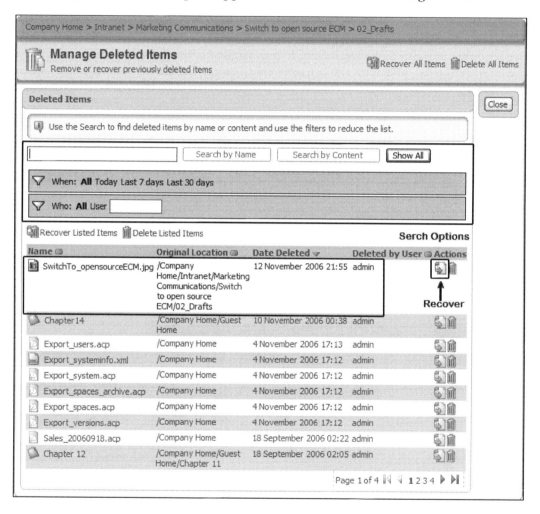

You can list all the deleted content by clicking on the **Show All** button as highlighted in the above screenshot. You can also search the deleted items by name, content, date, or the person who deleted them using the search options provided. Select the item that you deleted earlier and click on the **Recover Listed Items** icon as shown in the screenshot above. You will notice that the item has been recovered to the original space.

When an item is recovered, it will be removed from the archive space store and moved to the original space from where it was deleted.

Purged items are deleted forever and can not be recovered. Since the deleted items will be in the temporary store forever, it is best practice to purge them periodically. It is also recommended to take regular backups of your data. More information about maintenance and backup is provided in the *Maintaining System* chapter of this book.

Use Network Drives to Manage Content

The out-of-the-box installation comes with a web client, where you can connect to the Alfresco repository through a web-based application. Apart from the web client, the Alfresco out-of-the-box installation supports various client applications to access Alfresco content using protocols such as FTP, WebDAV, and CIFS.

CIFS

CIFS, an enhanced version of **Microsoft Server Message Block (SMB)**, is the standard way for the computer users to share files across intranets and the Internet. CIFS enables collaboration on the Internet by defining a remote file-access protocol that is compatible with the way applications already share data on local disks and network file servers.

CIFS supports the usual set of file operations like open, close, read, write, and seek. CIFS also supports file and record lock and unlocking. CIFS allows multiple clients to access and update the same file while preventing conflicts by providing file sharing and file locking. CIFS servers support both anonymous transfers and secure, authenticated access to named files.

CIFS helps you to map an Alfresco space as a folder in your local file system thus giving you flexibility in working with files in the repository as if they are in your local file system. You will be able to bulk upload files to the server and edit them directly using your desktop applications.

Mapping the Drive

As an example, you will now map one of your spaces, say **Intranet | Marketing Communications**, as a local folder.

To map a space in Windows Explorer as a network drive, follow the steps given below:

1. In Windows Explorer, click the **Tools | Map Network Drive** link. The **Map Network Drive** dialog appears as shown in the above screenshot.

2. Select an unused drive letter (say **M** for Marketing Communications space).

3. In the **Folder** text box, type **\\AlfrescoServerName_a\Alfresco\Intranet\ Marketing Communications**. The syntax is:

   `\\YourMachineName_a\alfresco\YourSpaceName`

4. Check the **Reconnect at logon** checkbox.

5. Click **Finish**. As the space is secured the system will prompt for your authentication.

6. Type your Alfresco user name and password when prompted.

Another easy way of mapping your space as a network folder in your local file system were using the web client. Go to the space and click on the **Open Network Folder** icon as shown in the following screenshot:

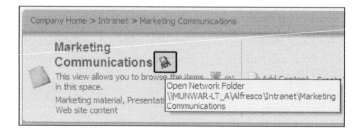

Once a space is mapped as a network folder, you can browse the space as if it were your local folder. The above screenshot illustrates that you could browse your Alfresco content on your local file system and the server name is *YourMachineName_A*.

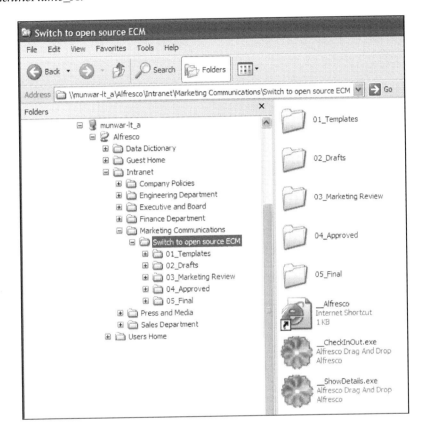

Drag-and-Drop Documents in Alfresco through CIFS

Once a space is mapped as a network drive, you can drag-and-drop files from your local hard disk to the Alfresco server. Similarly you can copy files from the Alfresco server to your local hard disk.

As an example, drag-and-drop an image file from your hard disk into your **Intranet | Marketing Communications | Switch to open source ECM | 02_Drafts** space.

People belonging to a department can map their department-specific space and transfer files from their local file system.

As an administrator, you can map the root space (Intranet) to your local drive and bulk transfer documents between the server and the local machine.

Check out and Check in Documents in CIFS

For the check-out and check-in feature to work with CIFS, you need to make some configuration settings. These settings are already explained in the *Configure CIFS Desktop Actions* section of Chapter 3. For more information, refer the custom configuration file `file-servers-custom.xml` in `<extension>` folder and view the configuration settings for the following XML block:

```
<desktopActions>
... xml configuration settings for desktop actions ...
</desktopActions>
```

Note that any configuration changes to XML files require restarting of server, otherwise the changes will not be effective.

Follow the following steps to try check-out and check-in of a document in CIFS:

1. In Windows Explorer locate the **02_Drafts** folder, drag-and-drop the `Alfresco_CIGNEX.doc` file (or any other file) onto `__CheckInOut.exe` to check out the file.

2. Observe that a working copy of the document is made and the original document is locked as shown in the following screenshot.

3. Make changes to the working copy by directly editing it using your favorite editor on your hard disk.

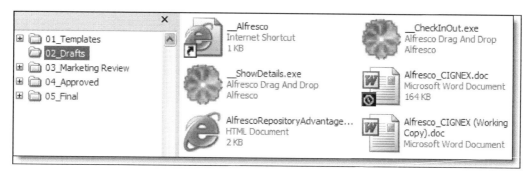

4. Click the `__`**Alfresco** icon (shown in the above screenshot) given in CIFS to open the web client interface directly from your CIFS folder. You can verify that the file has been checked out in web client interface as well. You will notice that the changes made to the Alfresco repository through the CIFS interface are visible in the web client user interface as well.

5. Again drag-and-drop the working copy onto __CheckInOut.exe to check in the file. You will see that the working copy file is checked in and deleted. The original file is updated and unlocked.

If auto versioning is enabled on the document, you will also notice that the changes made to the document are versioned as shown in the following screenshot. This is a great advantage to the content authors as they can edit the documents in their local file system using their choice of editors, and maintain various versions in the Alfresco repository automatically.

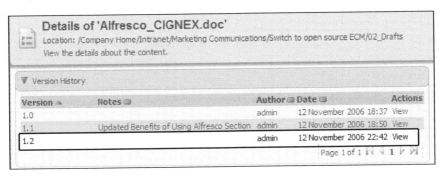

The sample works fine with Windows Internet Explorer and other browsers that already contain the CIFS plug-in. If you are using an older version of Firefox or any web browser that does not contain a CIFS plug-in, you need to install the plug-in to take advantage of this feature.

For Firefox (or Mozilla) browser, a plug-in is available on the sourceforge.net site. To install the Firefox extension, follow these steps:

1. Browse to the URL: http://sourceforge.net/projects/alfresco.
2. Click on the green box, **Download Alfresco Content Management**.
3. Scroll down to **Firefox extension**, and click on the **Download** link.
4. Click on the link **alfrescoext-0.9.xpi**.
5. In the list of download sites, click **Download** for the site nearest to you.
6. Allow permission to install the extension.

FTP

FTP is useful to transfer files from your local file system to the remote server. Using any FTP client, you can connect to Alfresco server as if it were a FTP site and upload and retrieve files.

If you are connecting to a space all of the rules are applied and all of the permissions are enforced. If versioning is enabled, then content will be versioned regardless of how it is updated.

Follow the steps below to use FTP on the Windows DOS prompt to upload a file from the local hard disk to your **Intranet | Marketing Communications | Switch to open source ECM | 02_Drafts** space.

```
> ftp localhost
Login as: admin/admin
> ls
> cd Alfresco
> ls
> cd Intranet
> ls
> cd Marketing*
> cd Switch*
> cd 02_Drafts
> put c:\press2A.txt
> ls
```

Verify that the text file is now in the Alfresco repository. Similarly, you can use any FTP client application to connect to the Alfresco repository and access files.

WebDAV

WebDAV is primarily designed for editing and managing files on remote web servers, in a structured way. For example, an application like Adobe Photoshop can directly open a file in the Alfresco content repository and edit it. This gives you the flexibility of using your own favorite editor to edit the content on the Alfresco server.

If you are connecting to a space all of the rules are applied and all of the permissions are enforced. If versioning is enabled, then content will be versioned regardless of how it is updated.

If you have a WebDAV client, then you can access the Alfresco server using the URL:

```
http://localhost:8080/alfresco/webdav/
```

To open a space in WebDAV, log in to the web client, go to the space, and click on the **Detailed View** link of the space and then click on the **View in WebDAV** link under the links section as shown in the next screenshot:

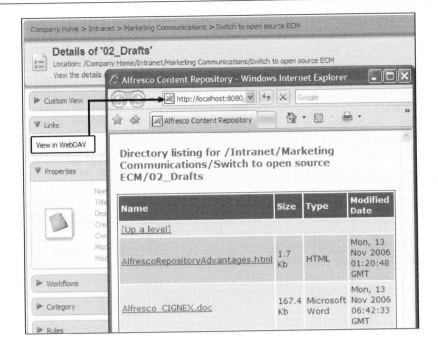

Data Dictionary and Space Templates

The **Company Home** space is the root space that contains the sub-spaces such as **Data Dictionary**, **Guest Home**, and **Users Home** spaces.

Data Dictionary Space

The **Data Dictionary** space contains all the user-managed definitions as shown in the screenshot on the next page:

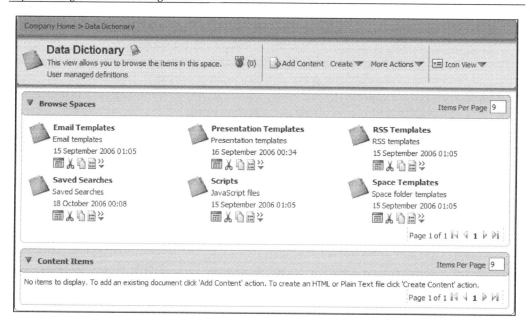

The **Data Dictionary** space contains the following sub-spaces. The scripts and the templates contained in these spaces are covered in detail in the further chapters of this book. For the time being, note that **Data Dictionary** is a shared resource. All the scripts and templates provided in the data dictionary can be defined by the administrators and used by the users.

- Email Templates: Contains email templates for notifying users of an invitation to a space or document and for sending notifications to users from a rule or an action. Email templates are written in the *FreeMarker* template language and have the .ftl extension.

- Presentation Templates: Contains presentation templates, which are useful to consolidate and view content in different ways. Presentation templates are written in the FreeMarker template language and have the .ftl extension.

- RSS Templates: Contains RSS templates, which are useful to provide RSS feeds on spaces. More information about RSS templates is provided in Chapter 10.

- Saved Searches: Contains pre-built queries, which are saved by a user from the search results page. Each user will have their private saved searches. This space will also contain all the saved searches that are publicly shared by the users.

- Scripts: Contains JavaScript files, which are used to perform certain operations on content.

- Space Templates: Space templates contain space structures that can be used as templates to create new spaces. Any space can be saved as a space template for future reuse of the space structure and data. More about space templates is covered in the following section.

Space Templates for Reusable Space Structure

In the earlier sections, you have created a marketing project in the **Company Home | Intranet | Marketing Communications | Switch to open source ECM** space. Let us assume that you are going to launch many such marketing campaign projects in your marketing department. Each marketing project space will have a similar structure to hold project information. For example, your marketing project space has marketing templates, draft documentation, and approved marketing collateral. Also, each project will have a hierarchy of spaces, security settings, business rules, notifications, and workflows.

Instead of having to repeatedly create the same structure for each project, you can maintain a *Marketing Project template* and keep on replicating it for every new project. Thus, all the work you do manually could be done in a few seconds simply by using such a template.

To give you an idea, **Company Home | Data Dictionary | Space Templates** contains a built-in space template called **Software Engineering Project** as shown in the next screenshot:

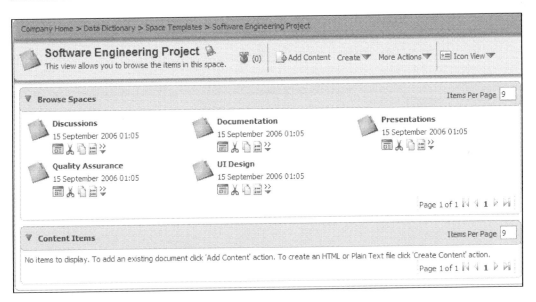

This represents a typical engineering project space structure with sub-spaces for documentation, discussions, quality assurance, user-interface design, and project presentations. You can use this *Sowftware Engineering Project template* and keep on replicating it for every new engineering project. If the template does not match your needs exactly, you can add or delete some spaces in the template itself.

Note that the **Software Engineering Project** does not contain rules. This is because rules will vary from one company to another. For example, workflow processes will vary. For your own company projects, adding rules and standard content will increase the value of the space template.

Create a New Space Template for Reuse

Follow the steps given to create your own space template for your **Marketing Projects** using the existing space structure.

1. Log in as the admin and go to the **Company Home | Data Dictionary | Space Templates** space.

2. Click on the **Create | Advanced Space Wizard** link. The **Create Space Wizard** pane appears.

3. Click on the **Based on an existing space** radio button option and then on the **Next** button to go to the second pane titled **Space Options**.

4. Browse and select the **Company Home | Intranet | Marketing Communications | Switch to open source ECM** space as shown in the screenshot below. Click on the **Next** button to go to the **Space Details** pane.

5. In the **Space Details** pane, give an appropriate title (such as *Marketing Project*) to your space template and click on the **Finish** button to confirm.

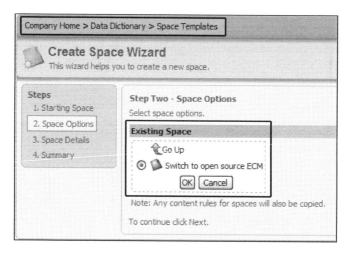

- You will notice a new space template called **Marketing Project** in the **Company Home | Data Dictionary | Space Templates** space. Examine the space structure.

Use an Existing Space Template to Create a New Space

You can reuse the *Marketing Project* space template to create new marketing projects. To create a new *Marketing Project*, ensure that you are in the **Company Home | Intranet | Marketing Communications** space and follow the steps given below.

1. In the space header, click **Create | Advanced Space Wizard**.

2. The first pane of the **Create Space Wizard** pane appears. Click on the **Using a template** radio button option and click on the **Next** button.

3. The **Space Options** pane of the wizard appears as shown in the following screenshot:

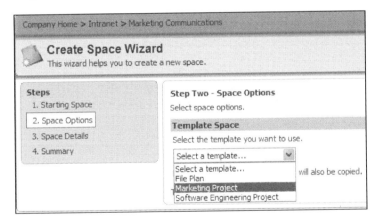

4. Choose the **Marketing Project** template and click the **Next** button.

5. The **Space Details** pane of the wizard appears as shown in the next screenshot.

6. Specify your new project name and click on the **Finish** button to confirm.

7. You can now browse around your new space and compare it with the *Marketing Project* space template. You will notice that the space contents are identical.

Migrating Existing Content into Alfresco

If you want your Enterprise Content Management initiative to be successful, you need to make sure that you can move the existing content into the new system. Most enterprises will have content in the form of files (in local or shared hard disks), email attachments, faxes (invoices) and scanned images. It is very important to move the content to a centralized and highly scalable content repository such as Alfresco.

Alfresco, being a powerful content management system for the enterprise, supports various ways to migrate existing content in the enterprise.

Drag-and-Drop Content to a Network Drive

You can drag-and-drop (bulk upload) content from your local hard disks to the Alfresco server using options such as CIFS, FTP, or WebDAV. Refer the *Use Network Drives to Manage Content* section in this chapter to know how to move content from your hard disk to the Alfresco server.

The only issue with this approach is that you will have to manually update the metadata (properties) of the content.

Using the Web Services API to Migrate Content

Alfresco provides a very rich web services API, using which you can transfer your files as well as metadata to the Alfresco server.

ACP Generator Bulk Upload Utility

The ACP Generator project provides a tool for bulk uploading of content into any Alfresco repository. It reads custom content models and a comma-separated variable (CSV) list of required property and category values for each content item and creates an ACP file.

The syntax is as follows:

```
acpGeneratr arg1 arg2 arg3 arg4 arg5
Where:
Arg1: The path and filename of the custom model to be used.
Arg2: The path to the directory where the content to be imported is
                                                located
Arg3: The destination path
Arg4: The content type we're dealing with
Arg5: The csv file of property values
```

Example:

```
acpGeneratr "D:\PIER\ACPGeneratr\sampleModel.xml"

            \ACPGeneratr\content   ..\ACPGeneratr\testDestDir dm:gqa

                            "D:\PIER\ACPGeneratr\faqlist.csv"
```

This will create the defined destination directory, and within it a directory with all the content and the required .xml file. All you need to do is zip it up into a .acp file and import to Alfresco. More details about this tool are provided in Alfresco Forge at http://forge.alfresco.com/projects/acpgeneratr/.

Summary

You can customize Alfresco features such as smart spaces, library services, and security to implement your enterprise document management requirements. Various interfaces such as web client, CIFS, FTP, and WebDAV can be used to manage content in the Alfresco repository. The content can be edited on your local desktop using your choice of favorite content editors. You can also use tools to migrate your existing content and to do bulk upload and retrieval of content.

6

Implementing Business Rules

So far, you have learned how to create system users, create user groups, create spaces, add content, check in and check out documents, use version control with documents, and use network folders to bulk upload content. In this chapter, you will learn about defining and using business rules as per your business requirements.

By the end of this chapter you will have learned how to:

- Automatically organize documents into specific spaces when you do a bulk upload of documents
- Define the sequence of business rules on a space
- Run time-consuming business rules in the background
- Automatically control document versions on specific documents in specific spaces
- Automatically categorize documents based on names
- Send notifications based on a specific event on a document
- Transform documents from one format to another
- Dynamically add custom properties to documents based on the location
- Configure business rules as scheduled actions to run periodically
- Extend business rules using customized JavaScript files

Using Business Rules on Spaces

You can leverage Alfresco's rules engine to define business rules based on your requirements. You do not require any programming expertise to define and deploy a business rule. You can choose to use a business rule from an extensive list of built-in rules or you can create your own business rules. Business rules can be applied to the entire content or a specific content item within a space, based on the conditions you set.

This section will provide you with various real-life examples of business rules and the steps to set and use business rules on spaces.

Organize Documents Automatically

In the previous chapter, you have learned that you can upload many documents (bulk upload) from your local folder to an Alfresco repository. However, each time you might end up manually moving them to specific spaces to organize them inside the repository.

Let us consider an example scenario. Let us say your finance department receives thousands of documents every day in electronic format from your customers, vendors, and internal departments. Your finance department receives checks from customers in the form of scanned images, invoices from vendors in the form of PDF documents, and contracts and other documents from various departments in the form of Microsoft Word documents. The department would like to upload them to the Alfresco repository and automatically organize them into various spaces, which are shown in the following figure.

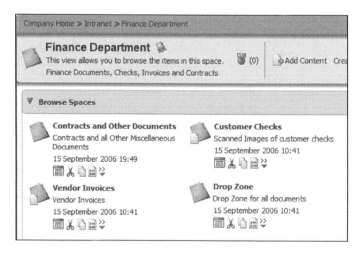

You can consider getting all these documents as a bulk upload in to a **Drop Zone** (a space which is mapped as a network folder). If the document name includes Check (say Client1Check_7003.jpg), then you would like to move it to the **Customer Checks** space. If the document name includes Invoice (say Vendor2Invoice_20060815.pdf), then you would like to move it to the **Vendor Invoices** space. You would like to move all other documents (say Project3Contract.doc) to the **Contracts and Other Documents** space. You will define a business rule that is triggered as soon as a document gets into the **Drop Zone**; it examines the file name and moves it to an appropriate space automatically.

This example uses the space called **Finance Department**, which you have already created as a part of your Intranet sample application. As you have secured this space earlier, only the administrator (*admin*) and users belonging to the *Finance* group (*Tom FinExec* and *Hope Fin*) can add content in this space. You can log in to Alfresco Web Client as **Tom FinExec** to manage content in this space. Go to **Company Home | Intranet | Finance Department** space and create the following four sub-spaces as shown in the previous figure.

- Drop Zone
- Customer Checks
- Vendor Invoices
- Contracts and Other Documents

Make sure that you are in the **Company Home | Intranet | Finance Department | Drop Zone** space. Follow the steps given below to define business rules on **Drop Zone**.

In the **Drop Zone** space, click on **More Actions | Manage Content Rules**. You will see the **Content Rules** pane as shown in the following figure:

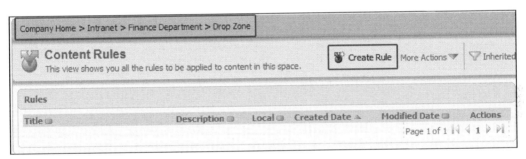

Clicking on the **Create Rule** link (as shown in the figure) opens the **Create Rule Wizard** window. As you may notice, **Create Rule Wizard** has four steps as shown in the following figure overleaf. The first step is to define the condition for selecting the documents, the second step is to define the desired action that will take place, the third step is to define the trigger type, and the fourth step is to confirm and commit the business rule.

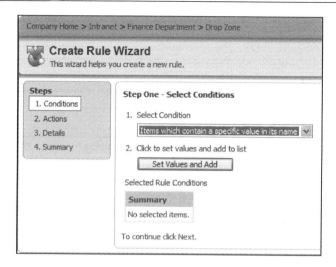

In the **Step One** window, you will notice that the **Select Condition** drop-down list displays all the built-in conditions that could be readily used for your business rules. We will examine all these conditions in later sections of this chapter. From the **Select Condition** drop-down list, select **Items which contain a specific value in its name** condition.

Click on the **Set Values and Add** button to set the condition values. You will notice a new window has popped up as shown in the following figure.

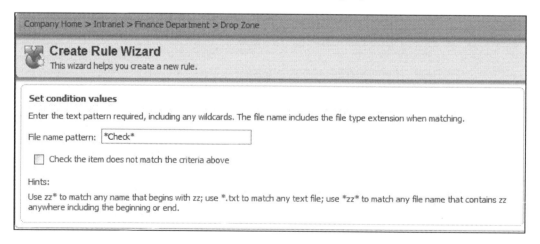

Refer to the figure in order to set the condition values. In **File name pattern**, you can Use **zz*** to match any name that begins with zz, use ***.txt** to match any text file, use ***zz*** to match any file name that contains zz anywhere including the beginning or end.

Select ***Check*** as the file name pattern. This means that this rule will be applied on any document that has `Check` anywhere in its name. For example this rule will be applied to documents that have names such as `Client1Check_7003.jpg` or `Check7003.jpg` or `20060815Client1Check.jpg`.

In the previous figure, you can see the checkbox that says **Check the item does not match the criteria above**, to define criteria that do not match this file pattern. This is how you can define the opposite criteria i.e., when check is not found within the filename string. For this example, do not select this checkbox. Click on the **OK** button to confirm the condition.

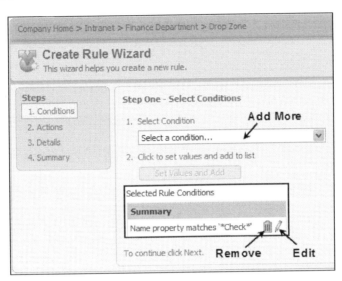

You may notice the selected rule conditions in the **Summary** section as shown in the figure above. You can edit the rule condition by clicking on the **Edit** (pencil) icon and you can delete the selected rule condition by clicking on the **Remove** icon.

You can define as many conditions as you like by selecting the condition and by clicking on the **Set Values and Add** button. Clicking on the **Next** button will take you to the **Step Two Actions** window as shown in the following figure overleaf:

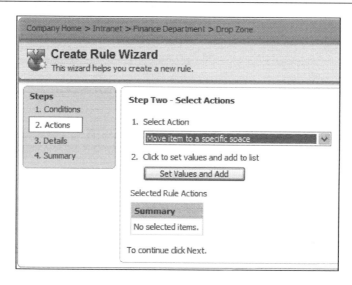

In the **Step Two** window, you will notice that the **Select Action** drop-down list displays all the built-in actions that could be readily used for your business rules. We will examine all these actions in the later sections of this chapter. From the **Select Action** drop-down list, select **Move item to a specific space** action.

Click on the **Set Values and Add** button to set the action values. In the **Set action values** window, click on the **click here to select the destination** link to select the destination space. You will notice a new window has popped up as shown in the following figure.

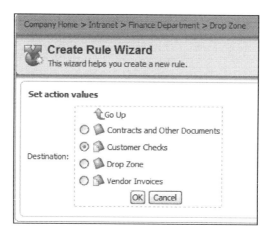

Select the **Customer Checks** space as the destination for the selected documents. Click on the **OK** button to confirm the action value.

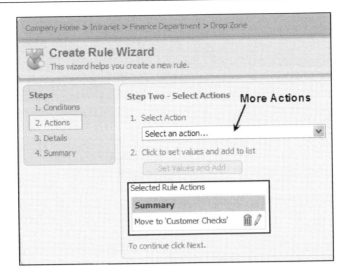

You will find the **Selected Rule Actions** in the **Summary** section as shown in the figure above. You can define as many actions as you like by selecting the action and by clicking on the **Set Values and Add** button. Clicking on the **Next** button will take you to the **Step Three** window as shown in the following figure.

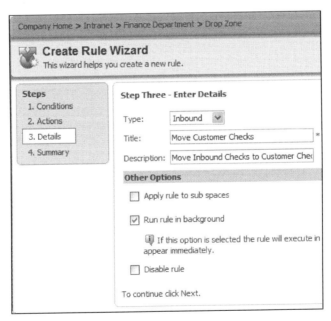

In the **Step Three** window, notice the business rule triggering options in the **Type** drop-down list.

- Inbound means this rule is triggered when a document is created (in the Web Client) or copied or moved (from some other space) or added (using the Web Services API) or dropped (using the drag-and-drop feature of CIFS, WebDAV, or FTP) in to the *Drop Zone* space.

- Outbound means this rule is triggered when a document is deleted or cut (to move it to another space) from the *Drop Zone* space.

- Update means this rule is triggered when a document in *Drop Zone* is updated. Again the update can happen by various means such as manual updating in the Web Client, updating through network drives (CIFS, FTP, or WebDAV), and updating through the Web Services API.

Select the **Inbound** type and give a meaningful **Title** and **Description** to your rule. You will notice three checkboxes in **Other options**. The option **Apply rule to sub spaces** will apply this rule to *Drop Zone* as well as all sub-spaces of *Drop Zone*. The option **Run rule in background** will execute this rule in the background as a separate process. The option **Disable rule** will allow you to define the rule but not activate it yet. You will learn more about **Other options** in the later sections of this chapter.

Select the **Run rule in background** checkbox leaving the other checkboxes unselected as shown in the figure on the previous page. Clicking on the **Next** button will take you to the **Step Four** window, which displays a summary of the rule.

Click on the **OK** button in the **Summary** window to confirm the rule. You will notice the rule listed for the *Drop Zone* space as shown in the following figure. You can make changes to an existing business rule by clicking on the **Edit Rule** icon as shown in the figure.

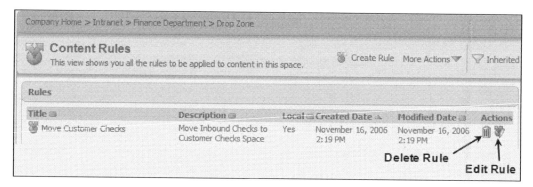

Now follow the steps and similarly create another new rule in the *Drop Zone* space to move all the documents that have Invoice (***Invoice***) in their name to the *Vendor Invoices* space.

Define a third business rule in the *Drop Zone* space that moves all the documents other than Checks and Invoices to the *Contracts and Other Documents* space. While selecting the condition, you have to select two conditions as indicated in the following figure to eliminate the previous two conditions and select all other documents. All the remaining steps are similar to those of the previous rules.

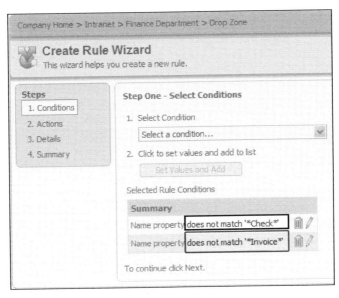

Once you are done with defining the rules, the **Content Rules** window for *Drop Zone* should display all the three rules as shown in the following figure. This is an example of setting the rules based on the name property of the document. You can think of other useful scenarios that might be applicable to your business.

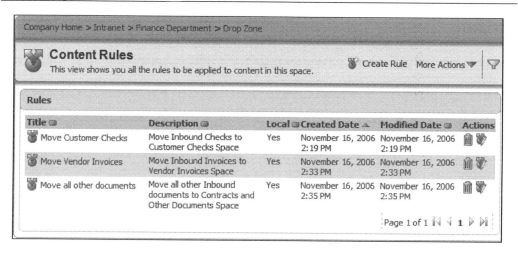

Now test the business rules you have set, by adding documents to the **Intranet | Finance Department | Drop Zone** space. On your personal computer, create files to test your business rules and choose the file names to match your business rules. For example create three files `Client1Check_7003.jpg` (Scanned Check), `Vendor2Invoice_20060815.pdf` (Vendor Invoice), and `Project3Contract.doc` (Contract Document). Drag and drop them to *Drop Zone* as shown in the following figure.

You will notice that the file containing `Check` has moved to the *Customer Checks* space, the file containing `Invoice` has moved to the *Vendor Invoices* space, and the third file has moved to the *Contracts and Other Documents* space automatically.

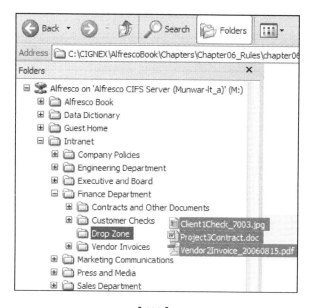

Run Rules in the Background to Improve Performance

Typically, business rules run in real time. Consider having a business rule that transforms 25 megabytes of Microsoft Word document to a PDF. Consider that rule being applied to hundreds of such files. If you upload a big Word document in the web client, then you might have to wait for a while till the business rule is completely executed. Similarly, think about having a business rule that sends email notifications to thousands of people. All these rules take significant amounts of time and resources to execute.

To improve the performance of the system, the best practise is to execute such business rules in the background. Refer to the earlier figure (under the section describing **Step Three**) where the rule has been selected to run in the background. If this option is selected the rule will execute in the background, so the results may not appear immediately.

Dynamically Add Properties to a Document

In the previous chapter, you have edited properties for each document. Those properties are default properties on every document. There might be situations where you need additional properties for all documents in a particular space. You can change the Alfresco content model to include additional properties of a document. But the issue with this approach is that all the documents in the repository will inherit these properties, causing unnecessary overhead on the storage.

You can define a business rule on a space to assign additional properties dynamically to all or a certain set of documents. Consider the example provided in the previous section, where *Finance Department* has various sub-spaces. Let us say you need to track the effective date and expiration date for all the documents in these sub-spaces. There is a built-in aspect called *Effectivity* that adds two properties to a document, namely, *effective date* and *expiration date*.

Follow the steps provided below to add the *Effectivity* aspect to all the documents in the *Finance Department* space.

1. Make sure that you are in the **Company Home | Intranet | Finance Department** space.

2. In the **Finance Department** space click on **More Actions | Manage Content Rules**.

3. Click on the **Create Rule** link and you will see the **Create Rules Wizard**.

4. In the **Step One** window, **Select Condition** drop-down list, select **All Items**, and click on the **Add to List** button. Then click on the **Next** button.

5. In the **Step Two** window, **Select Actions** drop-down list, select **Add aspect to item**, and click on the **Set Values and Add** button. Select the **Effectivity** aspect and click **OK**. Then click on the **Next** button.

6. In the **Step Three** window, select **Inbound Type** and provide appropriate **Title** and **Description** for this rule. Select the **Apply rule to sub-spaces** checkbox to apply this rule to all the documents within the sub-spaces as well. Now this rule will be applicable to all sub-spaces including *Customer Checks*, *Vendor Invoices*, and *Contracts and Other Documents*.

8. **Finish** the Rule.

Test this business rule by adding a document to the *Contracts and Other Documents* sub-space of the *Finance Department* space. You will notice two additional properties dynamically added to the document as shown in the following figure:

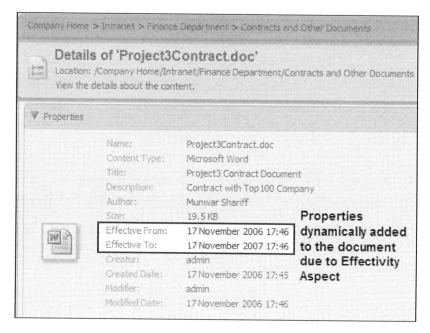

Automatic Versioning of Documents

In Alfresco, version control is disabled by default. In the previous chapter you enabled versioning for each individual document. It is a tedious job to enable versioning for each document if you have thousands of documents.

You can customize the Alfresco content model to enable versioning for every document. But this approach might be inefficient if you do not want to enable versioning for all the documents. Consider the example provided in the previous section, where *Finance Department* has four spaces, namely *Drop Zone*, *Customer Checks*, *Vendor Invoices*, and *Contracts and Other Documents*. *Drop Zone* is a temporary space; hence document versioning is not required. The *Customer Checks* space contains the scanned images of checks and versioning does not make sense as you need to have only one version of the scanned checks. This is the same with the *Vendor Invoices* space as well. The documents in the *Contracts and Other Documents* space require versioning support. Hence it makes sense to enable versioning only for the documents in the *Contracts and Other Documents* space.

Follow the steps provided below to enable versioning for all the documents in the *Contracts and Other Documents* space.

1. Make sure that you are in the **Company Home | Intranet | Finance Department | Contracts and Other documents** space.

2. In the **Contracts and Other documents** space click on **More Actions | Manage Content Rules**.

3. Click on the **Create Rule** link and you will see the **Create Rules Wizard**.

4. In **Step One**, **Select Condition** drop-down list, select **All Items** and click on the **Add to List** button. Then, click on the **Next** button.

5. In **Step Two**, **Select Actions** drop-down list, select **Add aspect to item** and click on the **Set Values and Add** button. Select **Versionable** aspect and click **OK**. Then click on the **Next** button.

6. In **Step Three**, select **Inbound Type** and provide appropriate **Title** and **Description** for this rule. Select the **Apply rule to sub-spaces** checkbox to enable versioning for all the documents within sub-spaces as well.

7. Finish the Rule.

Now versioning is enabled automatically for all the documents in this space. Test this business rule by adding a document to this space.

Send Notifications to Specified People

Email notification is a powerful feature where specified people can be notified immediately on certain events in the content management system. You can notify people when documents are added to some specific spaces such as public spaces. You can notify people when changes are made to certain important documents such as contract documents.

Let us say that in your organization the *Sales Group* is responsible for following up on contracts with customers. Follow the steps below to send email notifications to all the people in the *Sales Group* when a document in the *Contracts and Other Documents* space is updated.

1. Make sure that you are in the **Company Home | Intranet | Finance Department | Contracts and Other documents** space.

2. In the **Contracts and Other Documents** space click on **More Actions | Manage Content Rules**.

3. Click on the **Create Rule** link and you will see the **Create Rules Wizard**.

4. In the **Step One** window, from the **Select Condition** drop-down list select **All Items** and click on the **Add to List** button. Then click on the **Next** button.

5. In the **Step Two** window, from the **Select Actions** drop-down list select **Send an email to specified users** and click on the **Set Values and Add** button.

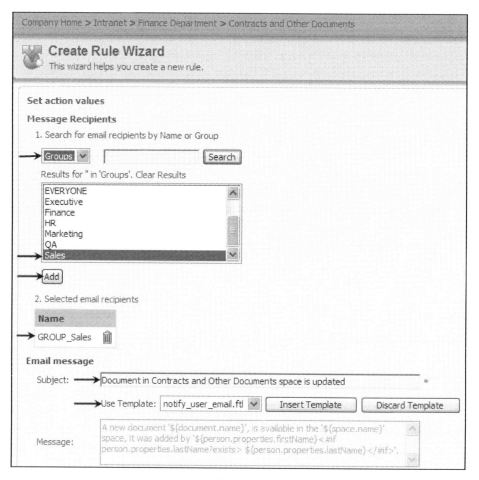

You will notice a **Set action values** window as shown in the figure. Select the **Sales Group** as email recipients. Use the built-in template called **notify_user_email.ftl** and click on the **Insert Template** button. Give an appropriate subject for the email.

- In the **Step Three** window, select the **Update Type**, to send notification on every document update.
- Finish the Rule.

Test this business rule by updating an existing document in this space. If your email server is configured right, then your sales people will receive email notifications with information about the document that is updated. Setting up your email server is detailed in Chapter 3 of this book.

Chaining All the Business Rules

You can have as many business rules as required on a specific space. In a space, all the rules defined locally in that space as well as all the rules inherited from the parent spaces will be applied. For example the *Contracts and Other Documents* space contains two local rules and one inherited rule (from its parent *Financial Department* space) as shown in the following figure:

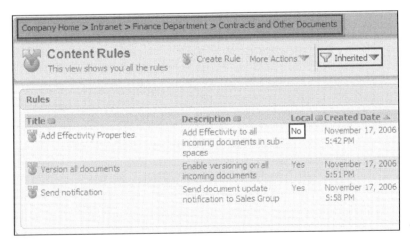

When a document is added to the *Contracts and Other Documents* space, it is automatically versioned due to the **Version all documents** local rule and two additional properties are added to the document due to the **Effectivity to all incoming documents** rule (from its parent space). When the document is updated then the **Send notifications to Sales Group** local rule will be executed.

Hence you can define business rules on spaces and sub-spaces and chain them together in a sequence to solve your business problem. For example, consider the following sequence of operations when a document titled ProjectXYZ_Contract.doc is dropped in **Company Home | Intranet | Finance Department | Drop Zone**.

- Due to the business rules defined in *Drop Zone*, the document ProjectXYZ_Contract.doc is automatically moved to **Finance Department | Contracts and Other Documents space**

- Due to **Effectivity** rule defined in the parent *Finance Department* space, two properties (**Effective From** and **Effective To**) are added to the ProjectXYZ_Contract.doc document.

- Due to the **Versioning** aspect rule defined in the space, the document ProjectXYZ_Contract.doc is automatically versioned.

However, there are certain things you need to remember while applying multiple rules on a space.

The **Inbound** rule will not be applicable to the documents that are already present in that space prior to creating the rule. The **Inbound** rule will be applicable only to the documents that are added after the rule is created.

- If a space has more than one rule, all the rules will be executed in a sequence.

- The rules defined in the parent spaces (with the **Apply rule to sub-spaces** option selected) will also be executed in the current space.

A document can be uploaded to a space in different ways, using the Web Client or FTP or WebDAV or CIFS. The **Inbound** rule in a space will be triggered when a document is uploaded to the space no matter how it is uploaded.

Built-In Business Rules

You can leverage the built-in business rules by applying them on appropriate spaces. You have already used some of them in the previous sections. This section will provide you with complete information about the built-in business rules and the Alfresco rules wizard.

How these Business Rules Work

Alfresco's underlying framework supports the latest technology, called **Aspect-Oriented Programming**, which is useful to change the behavior of the server dynamically without making changes to the code. Business rules leverage this technology so that you can define them at any space in Alfresco and change the behavior of the system.

Apart from the aspects available as built-in business rules, you can also define your own aspects as per your business requirements. More details about changing the data model and defining custom aspects are covered in Chapter 7.

Alfresco server follows a process to execute business rules:

- Whenever a document is added to a space (Inbound) or removed from a space (Outbound) or updated within a space (Update), Alfresco server checks whether that space or the parent spaces have any business rule to execute based on the triggering event type (Inbound, Outbound, or Update). The server checks if the business rule condition is satisfied. For example the business rule can be applied to documents that have certain pattern in their names.
- Then the server executes the action defined in the business rule.

The Alfresco Business *Rule Wizard* contains a sequence of screens (as steps) to capture the following:

1. The condition to apply the rule
2. The action to be performed as a result
3. The type of Event which triggers the action
4. The summary of the business rule to commit

The screens and the built-in features are described in this section.

How the Conditions are Checked

The first step in the *Rule Wizard* is to select the content items to apply the rule. The following can be checked against the content item.

- Does it have a particular name pattern?
- Is it in a particular category?
- Is it of a specific type or format?
- Does a property have a specific value?

You can define any number of conditions to select the content items. A content item must meet all the conditions to be selected.

What Actions are Executed

The second step in the *Rule Wizard* is to define the list of actions to be executed as a result. The following is the list of built-in actions to select from.

- Add aspect to item: Add additional properties and behavior to document
- Add simple workflow: Add approve and reject workflow
- Check in content: Check in the document
- Check out content: Check out the document to a space
- Copy item to a specific space: Copy the document to a space
- Execute a script: Execute a JavaScript as an action
- Extract common metadata fields from content: Extract document metadata
- Import Alfresco content package: Import as content package
- Link item to category: Link document to a specific existing category
- Move item to a specific space: Cut document from the current space and move to specified space
- Remove an aspect from an item: Remove property or set of properties from the document
- Send an email to specific users: Send email notifications to specific users or groups of users
- Specialize the type of an item: Define content type for the document
- Transform and copy content to a specific space: Transform content say from DOC to PDF and move the resultant file to the specified space
- Transform and copy image to a specific space: Transform and resize image say from JPG to PNG format and move the resultant image to the specified space

When you select the **Add aspect to item** action, you will have a list of built-in aspects to choose from as shown in the following figure:

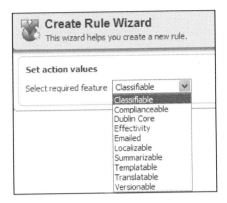

Each aspect has a different meaning as follows:

- Classifiable: Enable Categorization so that categories can be linked to the document.

- Complianceable: Add a compliance property called *Remove after* to the document.

- Dublin Core: Add Dublin core metadata to the document. Dublin core metadata includes properties such as *Publisher*, *Contributor*, *Subject*, and *Rights*.

- Effectivity: Add effectivity properties called *Effective From* and *Effective To* to the document.

- Emailed: Add a set of properties called *Email Data* to the document. This is useful to capture the email information if the document is an attachment to email.

- Localizable: Add a property called *Locale* to the document.

- Summarizable: Add a property called *Summary* to the document.

- Templatable: Enable template view.

- Translatable: Add a property called *Translations* to the document.

- Versionable: Enable versioning.

You can select one or more aspects to be applied as actions on the same document. For example a document can have the **Versionable** aspect as the well as **Effectivity** aspect.

When are these Rules Triggered?

The third step in the *Rule Wizard* is to define the triggering event types. The rules are triggered by something happening and specified by the **Type** field as follows.

- Inbound: content arriving into a space either new, copied, or moved
- Outbound: content leaving a space either deleted or moved
- Update: content updated either uploaded or saved

Applying Business Rules to Individual Content

In any business there will always be exceptions and there will be situations where you need to apply certain business rules to a specific document only. You can execute a business rule on a specific document directly without applying it on the space. This helps you if you want to apply certain business rules on an ad hoc basis to a specific document.

The business rules for content are invoked from **View Details** page of content item by clicking on the **Run Action** link in the **Actions** box. You are allowed to choose from the range of actions. You can also aggregate actions into a sequence that is applied in one go.

Removing an Aspect from Content

You have applied the **Versionable** aspect to all the incoming documents in the **Finance Department | Contracts and Other Documents** space. Consider a scenario where you would not want a specific document to be versioned but want all other documents to be versioned. The following are the steps for you to remove the **Versionable** aspect from a specific document.

Select a document in the **Finance Department | Contracts and Other Documents** space and go to the **View Details** page.

- From the **Actions** box, click on the **Run Action** link as shown in the following figure:

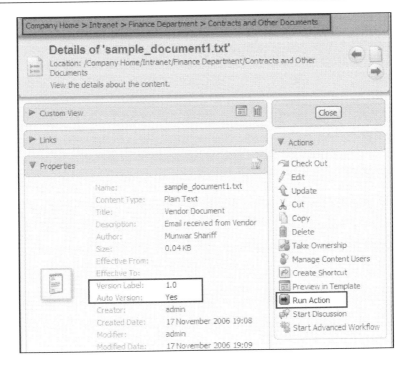

- The **Run Action Wizard** window will appear. From the **Select Action** drop-down list, choose the **Remove an aspect from an item** action.

- Click on the **Set Values and Add** button.

- From the **Set action values** window choose the **Versionable** aspect and click **OK**.

- Once you complete executing the rule you will notice that the properties related to versioning have been removed and the document no longer maintains versions.

Similarly you can use **Run Action** to execute business rules on a specific document such as sending email notifications, adding aspects, and executing scripts.

Handling Content Transformations

Content Transformation simplifies and accelerates the web-publishing process by transforming documents to web content. For example, you can leverage the built-in transformations engine to convert Word documents into HTML and PDF formats as directed by the user. Similarly you can resize and transform images as required. The underlying technology supports a cross-platform environment, including Windows, Linux, and Solaris. You can benefit from the increased consistency across multiple channels including print, Web, wireless, and other content-centric applications.

Transforming a Word Document to a PDF

Consider the following scenario as a staff member of the Marketing Department. You want to keep the source document in Microsoft Word format for editing. But you would like to send a PDF version of the document for publishing it on the website. Also, you would like to ensure that whenever you update the source document (in Microsoft Word format), the target document also gets updated (a PDF new PDF is generated).

This section uses the space you have already created as a part of your Intranet sample application in Chapter 5. As a part of sample application, you will manage content in **Intranet | Marketing Communications** space. As you have secured this space earlier, only the administrator (*admin*) and users belonging to the *Marketing* group (*Peter Marketing* and *Harish Marketing*) can add content in this space. You can log in as *Peter Marketing* to manage content in this space.

The following are the steps for you to transform and copy a Word document from the *Approved* space to a PDF document in the *Final* space.

1. Go to the **Company Home | Intranet | Marketing Communications | Switch to open source ECM | 04_Approved** space.

2. Click on **More Actions | Manage Content Rules**.

3. Click on the **Create Rule** link and you will see the **Create Rules Wizard**.

4. In the **Step One** window, **Select Condition** drop-down list, select **Items with the specified mime type**, and click on the **Set Values and Add** button.

5. From the **Set condition values** window (shown in the following figure), choose **Microsoft Word** as the required source format and click **OK**. Then click on the **Next** button.

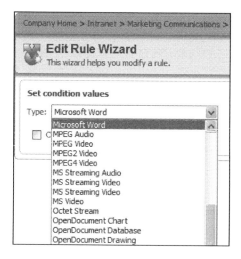

- In the **Step Two** window, **Select Actions** drop-down list, select **Transform and copy content to a specific space**, and click on the **Set Values and Add** button.

- From the **Set action values** window (shown in the following figure), choose **Adobe PDF Document** as the required format and choose the **05_Final** space as the destination space to which to copy the transformed PDF document.

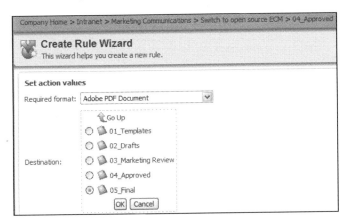

- In the **Step Three** window, select **Inbound Type** and provide appropriate **Title** and **Description** for this rule. You can also select **Update Type**, if you would like to create the destination PDF document whenever you update the source Word document.

- Select the **Run rule in background** checkbox.

- Finish the Rule.

Now transformation is enabled automatically for all the Microsoft Word documents in this space. Whenever a Word document is uploaded or moved to the *04_Approved* space, a PDF version of the document will be created in the *05_Final* space.

Test this business rule by adding a Word document to this space and testing the PDF document in the *05_Final* space.

Resizing and Transforming Images

Consider a scenario where you would like to keep the source image in PNG format and publish a fixed-size (say 200 x 200 pixels), JPEG version of the image on the website.

PNG is an extensible file format for the lossless, portable, well-compressed storage of raster images. Indexed-color, grayscale, and true-color images are supported, plus an optional alpha channel for transparency.

Joint Photographic Experts Group (JPEG) is a compression method standardized by ISO. The JPEG compression format was standardized by ISO and JPEG images are widely used on the Web. The amount of compression can be adjusted to achieve the desired trade-off between file size and visual quality. Progressive JPEG is a means of reordering the information so that, after only a small part has been downloaded, a hazy view of the entire image is presented rather than a crisp view of just a small part. It is part of the original JPEG specification, but was not implemented in Web browsers until rather later on, around 1996. It is now fairly widely supported.

The following are the steps for you to transform and resize the image from PNG format to JPEG format.

1. Go to the **Company Home | Intranet | Marketing Communications > Switch to open source ECM | 04_Approved** space.

2. Click on **More Actions | Manage Content Rules**.

3. Click on the **Create Rule** link and you will see the **Create Rules Wizard**.

4. In the **Step One** window, **Select Condition** drop-down list, select **Items with the specified mime type**, and click on the **Set Values and Add** button.

5. From the **Set condition values** window, choose **PNG Image** as the required source format and click **OK**. Then click on the **Next** button.

6. In the **Step Two** window, **Select Actions** drop-down list, select **Transform and copy image to a specific space**, and click on the **Set Values and Add** button.

7. From the **Set action values** window (shown in the following figure), choose **JPEG Image** as the required format. In the **Options** box, provide the resize options as **-resize 200x200**. Choose the **05_Final** space as the destination space to the copy the transformed image.

8. In the **Step Three** window, select the **Inbound Type** and provide appropriate **Title** and **Description** for this rule.

9. Select the **Run rule in background** checkbox.

10. **Finish** the Rule.

Test this business rule by adding a PNG image to the *04_Approved* space and testing the resized JPEG image in the *05_Final* space.

OpenDocument Format

OpenDocument Format (ODF) is an Open XML-based file format suitable for office applications. ODF is an open format for saving and exchanging office documents such as memos, reports, books, spreadsheets, databases, charts, and presentations.

The goal of ODF is to deliver an application-independent format that is vendor-neutral. This helps you to view, use, and update documents in the future when you no longer have software bought many years ago. You will have an advantage if your content is being shared across Governments, and citizens or multiple departments and organizations.

Alfresco's ODF Virtual File System offers a simple shared drive interface to any office application. Microsoft Office and Open Office users alike can save or drag content into intelligent drop-zones, where rules and actions transparently convert incoming content into the ODF vendor-neutral format.

The ability to share documents across organizations without being tied to the technology, strategy, pricing, and decisions of a single supplier is critical for businesses and government agencies today. The ability to access content without having a format and technology imposed on all users is equally important. Alfresco's ODF Virtual File System addresses these key issues.

Converting Microsoft Office Documents to ODF

The example in this section uses the **Intranet > Marketing Communications** space to create and test the ODF Virtual File System. The following are the steps for you to convert a Microsoft Word document to an ODF office document.

1. Go to the **Company Home | Intranet | Marketing Communications** space.

2. Create a space called **Marketing Documents** and create two sub-spaces under that space called **Inbox** and **ODF Virtual File System**.

3. Go to the **Company Home | Intranet | Marketing Communications | Marketing Documents | Inbox** space.

4. Click on **More Actions | Manage Content Rules**.

5. Click on the **Create Rule** link and you will see the **Create Rules Wizard**.

6. In the **Step One** window, **Select Condition** drop-down list, select **Items with the specified mime type** and click on the **Set Values and Add** button.

- From the **Set condition values** window choose **Microsoft Word** as the required source format and click **OK**. Then, click on the **Next** button.

- In the **Step Two** window, **Select Actions** drop-down list, select **Transform and copy content to a specific space** and click on the **Set Values and Add** button.

- From the **Set action values** window (shown in the following figure), choose **OpenDocument Text (OpenOffice 2.0)** as the required format and choose the **ODF Virtual File System** space as the destination space to the copy the converted document.

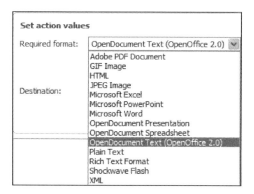

- In the **Step Three** window, select **Inbound Type** and provide appropriate **Title** and **Description** for this rule.
- Select the **Run rule in background** checkbox
- Finish the Rule.

Whenever a Microsoft Word document is uploaded or moved to the *Inbox* space, an ODF version of the document will be created in the *ODF Virtual File System* space.

Add a second business rule on the *Inbox* space, which converts incoming Microsoft Excel documents to OpenDocument Spreadsheet format and copies them to *ODF* the *Virtual File System* space.

Add a third business rule on the *Inbox* space, which converts incoming Microsoft PowerPoint documents to OpenDocument Presentation format and copies them to the *ODF Virtual File System* space.

The business rules on the *Inbox* space should be as shown in the following figure:

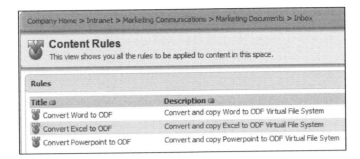

Test the business rules by copying Microsoft Word, Microsoft Excel, and Microsoft PowerPoint documents into the *Inbox* space. You should see the converted documents in the **ODF Virtual File System** space as shown in the following figure:

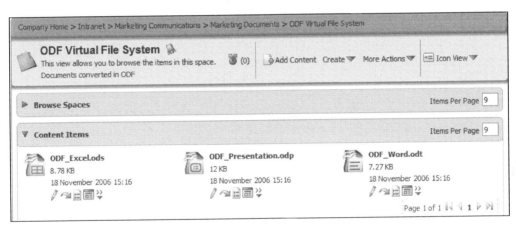

Built-In Transformations

You can apply the built-in content transformations in a variety of ways. For example, your marketing department might want to keep the source presentation in Microsoft PowerPoint format and publish the Flash version of the presentation on the website.

Try out the following transformations:

- Microsoft PowerPoint to Flash
- HTML to PDF
- HTML to JPEG image
- PDF to Text Document

Try out the various document and image transformations available out of the box.

Executing JavaScript as Business Rules

The built-in rules might not be sufficient to address all your business requirements. You can execute a JavaScript file as an action in your business rule. If you need even more flexibility, you can write business rules in custom JavaScript files and execute them as actions.

Use Built-In JavaScript Files as Actions

You can execute a JavaScript file by selecting **Execute a script** as an action in the **Rules Wizard**. The **Rules Wizard** displays the list of built-in JavaScript files such as:

- **backup.js**
- **append copyright.js**
- **backup and log.js**

For example the `backup.js` script creates backup of a file by copying it to a *backup* space. This might be required in some business situations. For a document in your space, try out `backup.js` as an action and observe the results.

Extend Business Rules with Custom JavaScript

The **Rules Wizard** lists all the JavaScript files that are available in the **Company Home | Data Dictionary | Scripts** space. You can extend your business rules by writing your own JavaScript files and placing them in this space so that they are visible to the **Rules Wizard**.

This is a very powerful feature. Consider the following scenario. Let us say your *Finance Department* has received a contract with $ amount as one of the properties. You can trigger a JavaScript that updates an external financial system with the information extracted from the document.

Let us consider another example. Let us say your *Marketing* group owns your internet website and manages the website content such as web pages, images, and documents. Upon approval, the website content is published in a *Staging* area, which has restricted access and is password protected. The content author schedules the website content to *move* from the *Staging* area and be published on the public site.

The example in this section uses the *Marketing Communications* space to execute a JavaScript file as a business rule. The JavaScript verifies the *Effective From* property of all the content items in the *Staging* space and moves the effective content to the *Production* space.

Set up Website Space

Set up a website space to implement the example mentioned on the previous page. Go to the **Company Home | Intranet | Marketing Communications** space. Create a space called *Website Documents* and create three sub-spaces under that space called *Staging*, *Production*, and *Archived*.

- The *Staging* space stages the transformed and approved content
- The *Production* space contains the effective content
- The *Archived* space contains the expired content

Go to the **Company Home | Intranet | Marketing Communications | Website Documents** space and create a business rule to add the *Effectivity* aspect to all the incoming documents in the sub-spaces. Refer to the section titled *Dynamically Add Properties to a Document* in this chapter to set up the business rule for the *Effectivity* aspect.

Now go to the **Company Home | Intranet | Marketing Communications | Website Documents | Staging** space and add a few sample documents. For each document in the *Staging* space, you will notice that two additional properties namely *Effective From* and *Effective To*, are present. Update the *Effective From* and *Effective To* properties of documents in the *Staging* space, making sure that some documents are effective as of today, so that they are ready to be moved to the *Production* space. Refer to the following figure for more details:

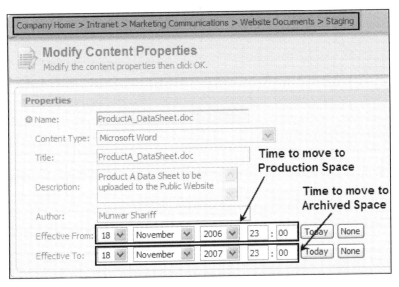

Create Custom JavaScript

Create a JavaScript file called `chapter6_publish_effective_content.js` in your personal computer with the following code. The script verifies the content in the **Intranet | Marketing Communications | Website Documents | Staging** space and moves the effective content (for which the *Effective From* property value is less than or equal to today's date) to the *Production* space.

```
// -----------------------------------------------------------------
// Name: chapter6_publish_effective_content.js
// Description: Moves effective content to Production site
// -----------------------------------------------------------------
var stagingFolder    = companyhome.childByNamePath("Intranet/Marketing
Communications/Website Documents/Staging");
var productionFolder = companyhome.childByNamePath("Intranet/Marketing
Communications/Website Documents/Production");

if(stagingFolder != null)
{
   var i=0;
   var today = new Date();

   stagingChildren  = stagingFolder.children;
   stagingTotal     = stagingChildren.length;

   for(i=0; i<stagingTotal;i++)
   {
      child = stagingChildren[i];
      if(child.properties["cm:from"] <= today)
      {
         child.move(productionFolder);
      }
   }
}
```

Go to the **Company Home | Data Dictionary | Scripts** space and click on the **Add Content** link and upload the `chapter6_publish_effective_content.js` file that you have created.

Execute Custom JavaScript as a Business Rule

You can apply a business rule on a space in two different ways. One way is to create a business rule on the space. Another way is to execute the business rule manually as a **Run Action** command on the space. For this example, let us follow the latter approach.

1. Go to the **Company Home | Intranet | Marketing Communications | Website Documents | Staging** space.

2. Go to the **View Details** page of the *Staging* space by clicking on the **More Actions | View Details** menu.

3. From the **Actions** box, click on the **Run Action** link.

4. The **Run Action Wizard** window will appear. From the **Select Action** drop-down list, choose the **Execute a script** action.

5. Click on the **Set Values and Add** button.

6. From the **Set action values** window choose the **chapter6_publish_effective_ content.js** script and click **OK**.

7. Once you complete executing the rule you will notice that all the effective documents in the *Staging* space have been moved to the *Production* space.

Try creating another custom JavaScript script that moves the expired content (the *Effective To* property value should be less than today's date) from the *Production* space to the *Archived* space. Test the custom script by applying it on the *Production* space content.

JavaScript API

The Alfresco JavaScript API allows script writers to develop JavaScript-compatible files that access, modify, and create Alfresco repository Node objects. Using the API script writers can find nodes (via XPath), walk node hierarchies, perform searches (including Lucene full-text searches), examine and modify the value of node properties, and modify the aspects applied to a node. In addition, scripts can create new files and folder objects and copy/move/delete nodes. All the usual Alfresco security and ACL permissions apply.

As JavaScript is a standard language there are many web resources, online tutorials and books to help developers in writing JavaScript files. It is suggested that potential script writers read up on JavaScript resources before starting to script the Alfresco repository.

Scripts can currently be executed in two different ways. The first is to create a **Content Rule** and select **Execute a script** from the list of available actions for the rule. The second way is to use direct URL addressing for a REST-style of execution. The Alfresco web client features a generic 'command' servlet that allows the execution of scripts directly via URLs. This feature allows direct access to scripts and the result of the script is returned as the HTML response stream. More information on this servlet is provided in the Alfresco Wiki (`http://wiki.alfresco.com`) website.

The default data model provides a set of scriptable *Node* objects that wrap the Alfresco repository Node concept and provide access to common services through a rich object orientated API suitable for scripting usage. The following objects are available to scripts by default in the root scope:

Named object	Description
companyhome	The Company Home node
userhome	Current user's Home Space node
person	Node representing the current user's Person object
space	The current space node (if any); note that for a script executing from a rule, the space object will be the space that the rule resides in
document	The current document
script	The node representing the script itself
search	A host object providing access to Lucene and Saved Search results
people	A host object providing access to people and groups in Alfresco
session	Session-related information (`session.ticket` for the authentication ticket)
classification	Read access to classifications and root categories

The `example test script.js` JavaScript file in the **Company Home | Data Dictionary | Scripts** space lists examples of various Alfresco API Calls.

```
var id = companyhome.id;
var name = companyhome.name;
var type = companyhome.type;
var noderef = companyhome.nodeRef;
var childList = companyhome.children;
var properties = companyhome.properties;
var assocs = companyhome.assocs;

// test various access mechanisms to get the same value
var childname1 = childList[0].name;            // special helper
                                    //for common 'name' property
var childname2 = childList[0].properties.name;
var childname3 = childList[0].properties["name"];
var childname4 = childList[0].properties["cm:name"];

// test accessing current document properties and modifying them
var docname = document.name.substring(0,
                 document.name.lastIndexOf('.'));
document.properties.name = "12345 " + document.properties.name;
document.save();
```

```
// modify the parent space name
space.name = space.name + " 1";
space.save();

// test accessing document content
var content = document.content;

// update the content by appending a string
document.content = content + "\r\nHere is another line added
                    from a script!";

// create a new file in the same space
var fileNode = space.createFile(docname + " - added by script.txt");
fileNode.content = "I am some content added by a script";

// create a new folder in the same space
var folderNode = space.createFolder(docname + " - added by script");

// copy the doc into the newly created folder node
var copy = document.copy(folderNode);

// move the folder node to companyhome
folderNode.move(companyhome);

// how to add a blank aspect to a node
copy.addAspect("cm:translatable");

// this is how to add an aspect with "mandatory" properties supplied
var props = new Array(1);
props["cm:template"] = fileNode.nodeRef;
document.addAspect("cm:templatable", props);

// and how to add one and set the properties individually later
copy.addAspect("cm:templatable", null);
copy.properties["cm:template"] = fileNode.nodeRef;
copy.save();

// example of hasAspect() and hasPermission() API functions
if (copy.hasAspect("cm:templatable") && copy.hasPermission("Write"))
{
    copy.name = "templatable " + copy.name;
    copy.save();
}

function result()
{
    return (childname1 == childname2 && childname2 == childname3
```

```
                    && childname3 == childname4);
}
result();
```

> A detailed description
> about Alfresco's JavaScript API is provided at:
> http://wiki.alfresco.com/wiki/JavaScript_API

Scheduled Actions

You know how to define and execute business rules. You also know how to trigger a business rule based on a condition such as when a document gets into a space or when a document is updated.

What if you want to execute a business rule at a specific time? What if you want to execute a business rule every day to check certain document status? What if you want to execute a business rule to send periodic reports? You can leverage the *Scheduled actions* feature of Alfresco to implement the solutions.

A scheduled action is made up of three parts:

- A cron expression
- A query template
- An action template

At the times specified by the cron expression, the query template is used to generate a query, and the query is run to select a set of nodes (Spaces and Documents). For each of these nodes, the action template is converted into an action, and then the action is applied to the node (Space or Document).

The query may be similar to

- A document has aspect
- It was created in the last month
- It is due in the next month
- It is in a category

You need to configure the scheduled action in an XML file and an sample file is located at `config\alfresco\extension\scheduled-action-services-context.xml.sample`

Example to Publish Effective Content to Production

Refer the sample custom JavaScript file (`chapter6_publish_effective_content.js`) you created earlier, which verifies the *Effective From* property of all the content items in the *Staging* space and moves the effective content to the *Production* space.

We have considered a scenario where the marketing group owns your internet website content. Upon approval, the website content is published in the *Staging* area, which has restricted access and is password protected. The content author schedules the website content to move from the *Staging* area and be published on the public site.

In the earlier example, you manually ran the script. In this section, you are going to create a scheduled action, which executes the custom JavaScript automatically every 15 minutes.

You need to create a schedule action XML configuration file in your extensions folder to specify the scheduled time and the custom JavaScript file. You will find the scheduled action sample file `scheduled-action-services-context.xml.sample` in the location below.

JBoss: `<alfresco>/jboss/server/default/conf/alfresco/extension`

Tomcat: `<alfresco>/tomcat/shared/classes/alfresco/extension`

Copy the scheduled action sample file as `scheduled-action-services-context.xml` in the same folder and edit the file as follows:

```
<?xml version='1.0' encoding='UTF-8'?>
<!DOCTYPE beans PUBLIC '-//SPRING//DTD BEAN//EN'
    'http://www.springframework.org/dtd/spring-beans.dtd'>

<beans>

    <!--
    Define the model factory used to generate object models
    suitable for use with freemarker templates.
    -->
    <bean id="templateActionModelFactory" class=
"org.alfresco.repo.action.scheduled.
FreeMarkerWithLuceneExtensionsModelFactory">
        <property name="serviceRegistry">
            <ref bean="ServiceRegistry"/>
        </property>
    </bean>
    <!--
```

```
     Example Chapter 6 : Action Definition
     Action is to execute the "Company Home > Data Dictionary >
      Scripts > chapter6_publish_effective_content.js" script
     -->

     <bean id="chapter6_runScriptAction" class=
"org.alfresco.repo.action.scheduled.SimpleTemplateActionDefinition">
         <property name="actionName">
             <value>script</value>
         </property>
         <property name="parameterTemplates">
             <map>
                 <entry>
                     <key>
                         <value>script-ref</value>
                     </key>
             <value>${selectSingleNode('workspace://SpacesStore',
'lucene', 'PATH:"/app:company_home/app:dictionary/app:scripts/cm:
chapter6_publish_effective_content.js"' )}</value>
                 </entry>
             </map>
         </property>
         <property name="templateActionModelFactory">
             <ref bean="templateActionModelFactory"/>
         </property>
         <property name="dictionaryService">
             <ref bean="DictionaryService"/>
         </property>
         <property name="actionService">
             <ref bean="ActionService"/>
         </property>
         <property name="templateService">
             <ref bean="TemplateService"/>
         </property>
     </bean>


     <!--
     Example Chapter 6 : The query and scheduler definition
     Query     - No specific query is used
     Scheduler - Run the script for every 15 minutes
     Action    - Call chapter6_runScriptAction defined above
     -->

     <bean id="chapter6_runScript" class=
```

```
"org.alfresco.repo.action.scheduled.
CronScheduledQueryBasedTemplateActionDefinition">
        <property name="transactionMode">
            <value>UNTIL_FIRST_FAILURE</value>
        </property>
        <property name="compensatingActionMode">
            <value>IGNORE</value>
        </property>
        <property name="searchService">
            <ref bean="SearchService"/>
        </property>
        <property name="templateService">
            <ref bean="TemplateService"/>
        </property>
        <property name="queryLanguage">
            <value>lucene</value>
        </property>
        <property name="stores">
            <list>
                <value>workspace://SpacesStore</value>
            </list>
        </property>
        <property name="queryTemplate">
            <value>PATH:"/app:company_home"</value>
        </property>
        <property name="cronExpression">
            <value>0 0/15 * * * ?</value>
        </property>
        <property name="jobName">
            <value>jobD</value>
        </property>
        <property name="jobGroup">
            <value>jobGroup</value>
        </property>
        <property name="triggerName">
            <value>triggerD</value>
        </property>
        <property name="triggerGroup">
            <value>triggerGroup</value>
        </property>
        <property name="scheduler">
            <ref bean="schedulerFactory"/>
        </property>
        <property name="actionService">
            <ref bean="ActionService"/>
```

```
        </property>
        <property name="templateActionModelFactory">
            <ref bean="templateActionModelFactory"/>
        </property>
        <property name="templateActionDefinition">
          <ref bean="chapter6_runScriptAction"/>
          <!-- This is name of the action (bean) that gets run -->
        </property>
        <property name="transactionService">
            <ref bean="TransactionService"/>
        </property>
        <property name="runAsUser">
            <value>System</value>
        </property>
    </bean>

</beans>
```

Restart the Alfresco server to ensure that the configuration changes are effective. Now go to the **Company Home | Intranet | Marketing Communications | Website Documents | Staging** space and add few sample documents. For each document in the *Staging* space, update the *Effective From* date property in such a way that these documents will be moved to the *Production* space at a specified time. Note that the custom JavaScript executes every 15 minutes to move the effective documents to the *Production* space.

XML Configuration File for Scheduled Actions

Note that `scheduled-action-services-context.xml` file has two blocks of XML configuration.

The first block, which starts with `<bean id="chapter6_runScriptAction"`, defines the action. This is where you specified the custom JavaScript to be executed. The important things to consider are as follows:

- `actionName`: The name of the action (the bean name for the implementation).
- `parameterTemplates`: A map of names and value templates. These are action specific.

The second block, which starts with `<bean id="chapter6_runScript"`, contains the query and scheduler definitions. This is where you specified the time interval to execute the custom JavaScript every 15 minutes. The important things to consider are as follows:

- transactionMode
    - ISOLATED_TRANSACTIONS: For each node the action is run in an isolated transaction. Failures are logged.
    - UNTIL_FIRST_FAILURE: For each node the action is run as an isolated transaction. The first failure stops this.
    - ONE_TRANSACTION: The actions for all nodes are run in one transaction. One failure will roll back all.

- queryLanguage: The query language to be used.
- stores: A list of stores to query (currently only one store is supported).
- queryTemplate: The template string to build the query.
- cronExpression: The cron expression to define when the query runs.
- jobName: The name of the scheduled job.
- jobGroup: The group for the scheduled job.
- triggerName: The name for the trigger.
- triggerGroup: The group for the trigger.
- runAsUser: The user with whose identity the action will run.
- templateActionDefinition: The bean that defines the action.

The cron Expression

A cron expression is six or seven text fields that are separated by whitespace.

Field Name	Position	Mandatory	Allowed Values	Special Characters
Seconds	1	Yes	0-59	, - * /
Minutes	2	Yes	0-59	, - * /
Hours	3	Yes	1-23	, - * /
Day of Month	4	Yes	1-31	, - * ? / L W
Month	5	Yes	1-12 or JAN-DEC	, - * /
Day of Week	6	Yes	1-7 or SUN-SAT	, - * ? / L #
Year	7	No	empty, 1970-2099	, - * /

An explanation of the special characters is provided in the following table:

*	All values.
?	No specific value.
-	This is used to specify a range. 1-5 in day of the week field would mean "on days 1, 2, 3, 4 and 5". 0-11 in the hours field would mean "each hour in the morning".
,	A list of values. In the minutes field 0,15,30,45 would mean "when the minute is 0, 15, 30, or 45". In the day field, MON,TUES would mean "on Mondays and Tuesdays".
/	After a value specifies increments. In the minutes field, 0/15 is equivalent to 0,15,30,45; */15 is equivalent to */15; and 10/15 is equivalent to 10,25,40,55. In the day of the month field 3/7 means "every seven days starting on the third of the month"; 3,10,17,24, ...
L	Last.
W	The nearest week day.
LW	The last week day of the month.
#	The nth day of the week.

Summary

Rules make a space smart. Rules are very powerful and you can use rules very creatively to address your business requirements. You can leverage the **Rules Wizard** to use the built-in rules as well as custom rules. Rules can be extended. You can have rules as scheduled actions and you can extend them using custom JavaScript files. The best practice is to document the business rules as they could affect the entire site globally.

7

Extending the Alfresco Content Model

In the previous chapters you were able to create content that had standard properties such as name, description, author, creation date, and timestamp. You were able to add aspects such as effectivity or the Dublin core metadata to the content using business rules. What if you need to have custom properties that are very specific to your business? What if you need to have custom content that handles the data and business rules in a way to suit your business needs? The Alfresco content model is highly configurable and easily extendable as per your business requirements. In this chapter, you will learn about the process for customizing the content model. You will define your own custom properties and custom content to extend the capabilities of your business application.

By the end of this chapter you will have learned how to:

- Configure a custom content model
- Define a custom aspect (set of properties)
- Use a business rule to add this custom aspect to appropriate documents
- Define and use custom content
- Define associated documents for your custom content type
- Preview the content using custom presentation templates
- Enable full auditing of user and system activities

Custom Configuration

The Alfresco repository provides support for the storage, management, and retrieval of content. The content may range from coarse-grained documents to fine-grained snippets of information such as XML elements. The Alfresco repository supports a rich data dictionary where the properties, associations, and constraints of types of content are present to describe the structure of such content.

The Repository Data Dictionary is by default pre-populated with definitions that describe common content constructs such as folders, files, and metadata schemes. However, the data dictionary is extendable allowing the repository to manage new types of content, since each business application will have its own content requirements. This chapter explains the concepts behind the data dictionary, how to define new types of content, and how to use them in an application.

Default Content Model Configuration Files

The core Alfresco configuration files are present in the application WAR file and get expanded out once the server starts. This location, referred to as `<configRoot>`, varies depending on the environment that Alfresco runs in.

JBoss: `<JBOSS_HOME>/server/default/tmp/deploy/tmp*alfresco-exp.war/WEB-INF/classes`

Tomcat: `<TOMCAT_HOME>/webapps/alfresco/WEB-INF/classes`

A Content Model is a collection of related content types and aspects. The default configuration files for the content model maintained by Alfresco are contained in the **<configRoot>| alfresco | model** folder as shown below:

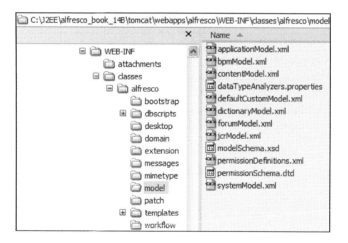

The Alfresco repository is also primed with several models that are described below:

- `contentModel.xml`: This model describes the `Content Domain Model` such as Folder, File, Person, Category, and Dublin Core.

- `systemModel.xml`: This model describes `system-level Repository` concepts.

- `applicationModel.xml`: This model describes the `Alfresco Application` Model.
- `dictionaryModel.xml`: This model describes the `Dictionary Meta-model`.

Several other models to support the implementation of services are defined by the repository such as user management, versioning, actions, and rules. You can examine the other configuration files in the `<configRoot>/alfresco` folder.

Custom Content Model Configuration Files

You can override or extend the Alfresco content model by placing custom configuration files in a folder. This location, referred to as `extension`, varies depending on the environment that Alfresco runs in.

JBoss: `<JBOSS_HOME>/server/default/conf/alfresco/extension`

Tomcat: `<TOMCAT_HOME>/shared/classes/alfresco/extension`

When you install Alfresco, the sample custom-content files are copied to the `extension` folder for your reference. You can also examine the sample custom-configuration files in the `extension` folder.

The steps to define a custom model in `extension` folder are as follows:

- Create a custom model context file
- Create a custom model file
- Create a custom web client configuration file

The custom model context file lists the custom model files. The custom model files define the custom content types, aspects, and associations. The custom web client configuration file contains information to display these custom content types, aspects, and associations. The relationship between these files is shown below:

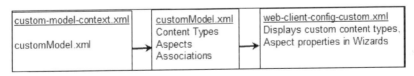

Custom Model Context File

The custom model context file lists one or more custom model files. Create a custom model context file and name the file `<your-custom-model-name>-context.xml`, for example `intranetModel-context.xml`. It is very important for you to note that the Alfresco server recognizes context files that end with `-context.xml`.

The following is the content of the `custom-model-context.xml.sample` file in the `extension` folder. Note that the custom model context file defines `customModel.xml` as the custom model file.

```xml
<?xml version='1.0' encoding='UTF-8'?>
<!DOCTYPE beans PUBLIC '-//SPRING//DTD BEAN//EN'
    http://www.springframework.org/dtd/spring-beans.dtd'>

<beans>

    <!-- Registration of new models -->
    <bean id="extension.dictionaryBootstrap"
        parent="dictionaryModelBootstrap"
        depends-on="dictionaryBootstrap">
      <property name="models">
        <list>
            <value>alfresco/extension/customModel.xml</value>
        </list>
      </property>
    </bean>

</beans>
```

Custom Model File

The custom model file contains the definitions for the custom content types, aspects, and content associations.

A copy of a `customModel.xml` file already exists in `extension` folder. If you examine the `customModel.xml` file, you will notice a custom namespace for all the variables called `custom`. Hence every `custom` variable will have a prefix `custom` in this file as shown below:

```xml
<namespace uri="custom.model" prefix="custom"/>
```

Custom Web Client Configuration File

A copy of web client configuration file `web-client-config-custom.xml` already exists in the `extension` folder. This web client configuration file ensures that the custom content types and aspects are visible in the Alfresco Web Client application. In this file, you can also override the default web client configuration provided out of the box.

In Chapter 3, you have already extended the Alfresco content model for defining language support. You can refer to Chapter 3 to understand the concepts of the custom content model and the folder structure.

Hierarchy of Configuration Files

The hierarchy of configuration files is shown below:

```
<configRoot>/alfresco          <extension>
  xxx-context.xml files          xxx-context.xml files
  web-client-config-xxx.xml files  web-client-config-custom.xml
  model                          xxxModel.xml files
    xxxModel.xml files
```

During the start up, the Alfresco server reads the configuration files in the following order:

1. Context files and then the model files in the `<configRoot>/alfresco` folder

2. Context files and then the model files in the `<extension>` folder

3. Web client configuration files in the `<configRoot>/alfresco` folder

4. Web client configuration files in the `<extension>` folder

A Custom Aspect

Let us assume that your sales people would like to track all their proposals related to a customer. They would like to search the documents and execute a business rule based on the customer details. They would like to capture the following customer details for all the documents in the sales department space:

*   Name of the Customer

*   Contact Name at customer location

*   Contact Person's Phone number

*   Project Identification number internally allocated

*   Is this a New Customer?

You can extend the Alfresco content model to include the properties listed above as an aspect. Then you can apply this aspect to be part of all your documents in the sales department space.

When Do You Need a Custom Aspect ?

The Alfresco content model is extensible. You can provide a solution with custom properties in two different ways. One way is to create custom aspect called `Customer Details` and dynamically attach it to the documents in a specific space. The other way is to create a custom content type called `Proposal Document` and define all the required properties. The process of creating a custom content type is explained in detail in the next section of this chapter.

Choosing a custom aspect over a custom content type is up to you, based on your business requirements.

The following are the advantages of having a custom aspect over a custom content type:

- Flexibility: You will have more flexibility. Having a custom aspect will give you flexibility to add the additional set of properties to the documents in specific spaces. For example, you can define these additional properties to the documents in the **Sales Department | Proposals** and **Finance Department | Customer Checks spaces**.

- Efficiency: Since these properties are applied selectively to certain documents in certain spaces only, you will consume limited storage in the relational database for these properties.

The following are the disadvantages of having a custom aspect over a custom content type:

- High Maintenance: Since the custom aspect (additional properties) is added to documents based on business rules, you need to define it at every space wherever it is required.

- Dependency: You can not define a dependency with other aspects. For example if you want the `effectivity` aspect to always be associated with the `customer details` aspect, you need to make sure you attach both the aspects to the documents.

Steps to Add a Custom Aspect

The following process needs to be followed to add a custom aspect to the Alfresco content model:

- Define the custom properties and type of properties
- Extend the Alfresco Content Model with the custom aspect
- Configure the Web Client application for the custom aspect
- Restart Alfresco to make sure the new changes are effective
- Use the Custom Aspect in a business rule

Each one of these steps is explained in detail in the following sections.

Define the Custom Aspect

You need to define the name of the custom aspect and the properties. For each property you need to define the type of the property. Some of the property types are listed in the following table:

Property Type	Description
text	Any string or name
content	Binary Document
int	Integer or Number
long	Big integer
float	Number with decimal values such as interest rate 7.5
date	Year, Month, and Day
datetime	Timestamp
boolean	Yes or No
category	Reference to a category within a classification
path	URL Path

You may consider calling your custom aspect `Customer Details` with the following properties:

Property Type	Property Name	Property Label
text	CustomerName	Customer Name
text	CustomerContactName	Customer Contact Name
text	CustomerContactPhone	Customer Contact Phone
Int	CustomerProjectID	Customer Project ID
boolean	NewCustomer	New Customer

Extend the Content Model with the Custom Aspect

Now that you have identified your custom aspect and the properties, the next step is to extend the Alfresco content model with the XML representation of your custom aspect.

Go to the `extension` folder and rename the `custom-model-context.xml.sample` file as `custom-model-context.xml`. Now examine the contents of the `custom-model-context.xml` file that includes the name of the custom content model file—`customModel.xml`.

Open the `customModel.xml` file and add your custom aspect as shown below before the last line `</model>`.

```xml
<aspects>

    <!-- Definition of new Content Aspect: Customer Details -->
    <aspect name="custom:CustomerDetails">
        <title>Customer Details</title>
        <properties>
            <property name="custom:CustomerName">
                <title>Customer Name</title>
                <type>d:text</type>
            </property>
            <property name="custom:CustomerContactName">
                <title>Customer Contact Name</title>
                <type>d:text</type>
            </property>
            <property name="custom:CustomerContactPhone">
                <title>Customer Contact Phone</title>
                <type>d:text</type>
            </property>
            <property name="custom:CustomerProjectID">
                <title>Customer Project ID</title>
                <type>d:int</type>
            </property>
            <property name="custom:NewCustomer">
                <title>New Customer</title>
                <type>d:boolean</type>
            </property>
        </properties>
    </aspect>

</aspects>
```

Configure the Web Client for the Custom Aspect

The content model is extended with a custom aspect called `Customer Details`. You need to make sure the web client program recognizes this new custom aspect and displays it in the web-based interface. In order to make this happen you need to configure the web client file `web-client-config-custom.xml` in the `extension` folder.

Open the `web-client-config-custom.xml` file and add the following XML code before the last line `</alfresco-config>`.

```
<!-- Lists the custom aspect in business rules Action wizard -->
<config evaluator="string-compare" condition="Action Wizards">
   <aspects>
      <aspect name="custom:CustomerDetails"/>
   </aspects>
</config>
```

This code ensures that the new aspect called `Customer Details` is listed in the business rules **Set action values** page as shown in the screenshot under the section *Use the Custom Aspect in a Business Rule.*

Open the `web-client-config-custom.xml` file and add the following XML code before the last line `</alfresco-config>`.

```
<!-- Displays the properties in view details page -->
<config evaluator="aspect-name" condition="custom:CustomerDetails">
   <property-sheet>
      <separator name="sepCust1" display-label="Customer Details"
                  component-generator="HeaderSeparatorGenerator" />
      <show-property name="custom:CustomerName"/>
      <show-property name="custom:CustomerContactName"/>
      <show-property name="custom:CustomerContactPhone"/>
      <show-property name="custom:CustomerProjectID"/>
      <show-property name="custom:NewCustomer"/>
   </property-sheet>
</config>
```

This code ensures that the properties added to the content due to the `Customer Details` aspect will be displayed in the content's view details page as shown in the screenshot under the section *Use the Custom Aspect in a Business Rule.*

Now, restart Alfresco to make sure the changes are effective.

Use the Custom Aspect in a Business Rule

Now that the `Customer Details` aspect is available you can use it to add to your documents as if this aspect was available to you out of the box.

You can define a business rule to include customer details dynamically to all the documents in a space. Consider the example provided earlier where the Sales Department needs to maintain the customer details for all its proposals. Follow the steps provided below to add the `Customer Details` aspect to all the documents in the **Sales Department | Proposals space**.

1. Go to the **Company Home | Intranet | Sales Department** space and create a sub-space for proposals called **Proposals**.

2. Ensure that you are in the **Company Home | Intranet | Sales Department | Proposals** space.

3. In the **Proposals** space click the **More Actions | Manage Content Rules**.

4. Click on the **Create Rule** link and you will see the **Create Rules Wizard**.

5. In **Step One, Select Condition** drop-down list, select **All Items** and click on the **Add to List** button. Then click on the **Next** button.

6. In **Step Two, Select Actions** drop-down list, select **Add aspect to item** and click on the **Set Values and Add** button.

7. In the **Set action values** pane, select the **Customer Details** aspect as shown below and then click **OK**. Finally click the **Next** button.

8. In **Step Three**, select the **Inbound** option from the **Type** drop-down list, and provide appropriate name and description for this rule.

9. Check **Apply rule to sub spaces option** and then click **Finish** to apply the rule.

Test this business rule by adding a document in the Proposals space. You will notice five additional properties dynamically added to the document as shown in the screenshot on the next page. Add some meaningful customer data and click the **OK** button.

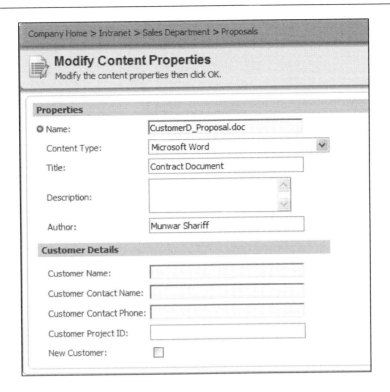

Navigate to the document and click on the **View Details** icon to view the details page. You will notice that the properties added to the document due to the custom aspect are visible in the details page of the document as shown overleaf:

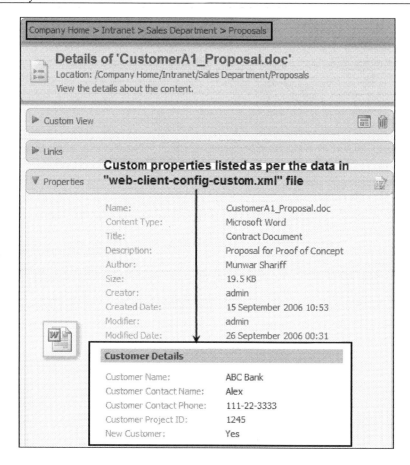

Similarly create a business rule on the **Company Home | Intranet | Financial Department | Customer Checks** space to add customer details to all the incoming checks as shown on the next page. Add an image file (scanned customer check) to this space and notice that the check has additional properties as per the customer details aspect.

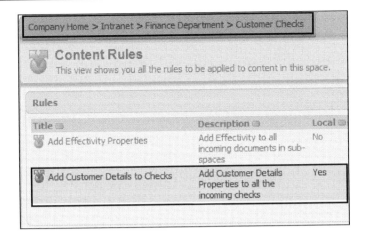

Custom Content

Let us say your Corporate Communications group would like to create press releases and execute certain business rules if the content is of type press release. They would like to have the additional properties as listed below:

- PR Person's Name
- PR Person's Email address
- PR Person's Phone address
- PR Released Date
- Content to be automatically versioned for every update

When Do You Need a Custom Content Type?

Earlier in this chapter you have seen the advantages and disadvantages of having a custom aspect over a custom content type. You need a custom content type if that type of content has some significance for you such as in the case of a press release. You will be able to add Press Release content in any space anywhere you like without going through the hassle of applying all kinds of business rules on spaces. Similarly with custom content you will be able to execute business rules based on the content type. For example, you can send notifications to certain people when a Press Release is created.

Steps to Add a Custom Content Type

The following process needs to be followed to add a custom content type to the Alfresco content model:

- Define a custom content type, with properties and mandatory aspects
- Extend the Content Model with the custom content
- Configure the Web Client for the custom content type
- Restart Alfresco to make sure the new changes are effective
- Add custom content

Define the Custom Content Type

You may consider calling your custom content type `Press Release` with the properties as shown in the table below:

Property Type	Property Name	Property Label
text	PRName	PR Person Name
text	PREmail	PR Person Email
text	PRPhone	PR Person Phone
Int	PRDate	PR Released Date

You may consider reusing the existing aspect called `versionable` to maintain various versions of `Press Release` automatically whenever it is being edited.

Extend the Content Model with the Custom Content Type

Now that you have identified your custom content and the properties, the next step is to extend the Alfresco content model with the XML representation of your custom content.

Open the `customModel.xml` file and add the following XML code before the `aspects` block:

```
<types>

    <!-- Definition of new Content Type: Press Release -->
    <type name="custom:pressrelease">
        <title>Press Release</title>
        <parent>cm:content</parent>
        <properties>
            <property name="custom:PRName">
                <title>PR Person Name</title>
                <type>d:text</type>
            </property>
```

```
        <property name="custom:PREmail">
            <title>PR Person Email</title>
            <type>d:text</type>
        </property>
        <property name="custom:PRPhone">
            <title>PR Person Phone</title>
            <type>d:text</type>
        </property>
        <property name="custom:PRDate">
            <title>PR Released Date</title>
            <type>d:date</type>
        </property>
    </properties>
    <mandatory-aspects>
        <aspect>cm:versionable</aspect>
    </mandatory-aspects>
    </type>

</types>
```

Configure the Web Client for the Custom Content Type

You need to make sure the web client program recognizes this new custom content and displays various dialog screens in the web-based interface. In order to make this happen you need to configure the web client file `web-client-config-custom.xml` in the extension (`<alfresco_install_folder>\tomcat\shared\classes\alfresco\extension`) folder.

Open the `web-client-config-custom.xml` file and add the following lines of code that are highlighted.

```
<!-- Lists the custom aspect in business rules Action wizard -->
<config evaluator="string-compare" condition="Action Wizards">
    <aspects>
        <aspect name="custom:CustomerDetails"/>
    </aspects>
    <subtypes>
        <type name="custom:pressrelease"/>
    </subtypes>
</config>
```

This code ensures that the `Press Release` content is shown in the Business Rules Action wizard.

Add the following XML code just before the block shown above. This code ensures that the press release content type is listed when you create new content.

```
<config evaluator="string-compare" condition="Content Wizards">
   <content-types>
      <type name="custom:pressrelease" />
   </content-types>
</config>
```

Add the following XML code just before the block shown above. This code ensures that the properties are available to edit in the **edit properties** window for press release content.

```
<config evaluator="node-type" condition="custom:pressrelease">
   <property-sheet>
      <show-property name="mimetype"
        display-label-id="content_type"
        component-generator="MimeTypeSelectorGenerator" />
      <show-property name="size"
        display-label-id="size"
        converter="org.alfresco.faces.ByteSizeConverter"
        show-in-edit-mode="false" />
      <show-property name="custom:PRName" />
      <show-property name="custom:PREmail" />
      <show-property name="custom:PRPhone" />
      <show-property name="custom:PRDate" />
   </property-sheet>
</config>
```

After making these changes to the configuration files, restart Alfresco.

Add Custom Content

The new content type called Press Release is now available to add anywhere you like. On your personal computer, create a sample press release in HTML format and save it as PressRelease1.html. Follow the steps given below to upload your Press Release content:

1. Go to the **Company Home | Intranet | Press and Media** space and create a sub-space called **Press Releases**.

2. Ensure that you are in the **Company Home | Intranet | Press and Media | Press Releases** space.

3. In the space header, click the **Add Content** link. The **Add Content** dialog appears.

4. To specify the file that you want to upload, click the **Browse** button. In the **File Upload** dialog box, browse to the file you have created earlier on your personal computer (PressRelease1.html) and click the **upload** button.

5. A message informs you that your upload was successful as shown in the screenshot below.

6. Select **Press Release** as **Type** from the drop-down list.

7. Click the **OK** button to confirm.

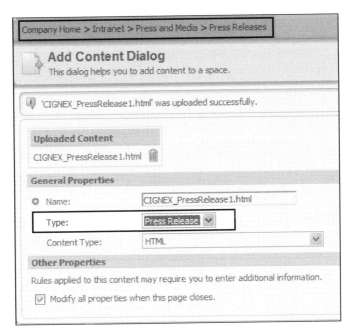

8. A **Modify Content Properties** dialog box appears as shown in the screenshot on the next page.

9. The **Name, Tile, Description**, and **Author** properties are basic properties populated by default. **Auto Version** is a mandatory aspect that was attached to the press release content. The properties **PR Person Name, PR Person Email, PR Person Phone**, and **PR Released Date** are part of press release content. Also notice that **Edit Inline** is checked for HTML content. Fill out appropriate data for these properties.

10. Click the **OK** button to save and return to the **Press Releases** space.

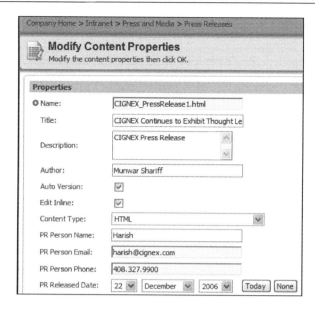

Create a Press Release as HTML Content

You can also create a `Press Release` as HTML content in the web client directly without uploading the file from your personal computer. To create an HTML file in a space, follow the steps given below:

Ensure that you are in the **Company Home | Intranet | Press and Media | Press Releases** space. In the header, click **Create | Create Content**. The first pane of the **Create Content Wizard** appears as shown in the screenshot below:

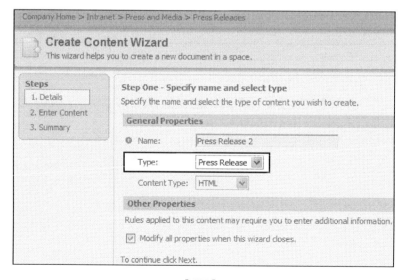

You need to provide **Name** of the HTML file, select **HTML** as **Content Type**, and click the **Next** button. The **Enter Content** pane of the wizard appears as shown in the screenshot below:

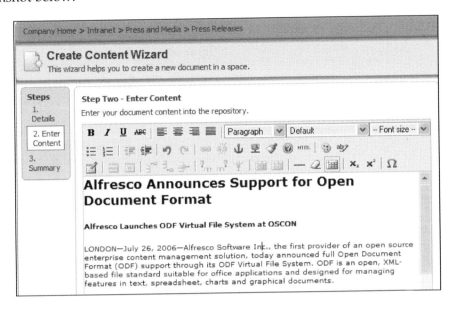

You can enter some sample press release text using the text formatting features. After the content is entered and edited in the **Enter Content** pane, click **Finish**. You will see the **Modify Content Properties** screen to update metadata associated with the content as shown in the screenshot at the top of the page opposite. You can modify properties as required and click the **OK** button. You can preview the newly created **Press Release** by clicking it.

Create Business Rules Targeting a Custom Content Type

You can create a business rule targeting a custom content type. For example you can send notifications to concerned people when a press release is added. While creating the business rule select **Items of a specified type or its sub-types** as condition as shown in the screenshot on the next page.

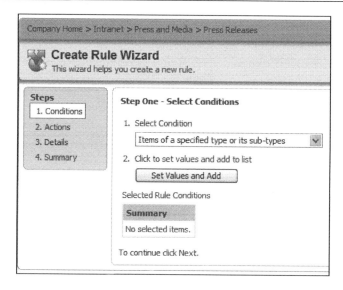

Click the **Set Values and Add** button to set the condition. This will pop up a dialog box for setting condition values as shown below: select the **Press Release** option as **Type**.

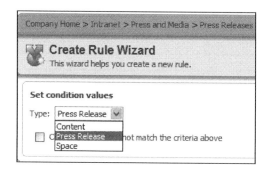

Custom Associations

You can associate content within the Alfresco repository with one or more content items.

Alfresco supports two types of associations. The first type is **reference association** where you refer to other content items within a content item. An example of this kind of association is the `translatable` aspect. When you add the `translatable` aspect to your content, it creates a reference association with other translated documents.

The second type of association is **child association** where content (such as a space) contains other content items.

You can create your own custom associations as per your business requirements. The process of creating and using custom associations is explained in this section.

When Do You Need an Association?

Reference associations are very useful in various business applications. For example, in your engineering department space, if you have a `testing document` you might want associate it with an appropriate `requirements document`. Similarly you might want to refer to some documents in your `Press Release`. Association is required if you want to refer to or contain some other content within your content.

Define Custom Associations

As an example, we will create two associations to the `Press Release` custom content. The first one is a reference association called `Press Release Image`, which refers to an image within the Alfresco repository. The second is an association called `Press Release Files`, which refers to one or more files within the Alfresco repository.

In order to define these associations in the content model, open the `customModel.xml` file and insert the highlighted XML code within the Press Release content type definition as shown below. For the `Press Release Files` association, the option `<many>` is set to `true` to indicate more than one file can be referenced.

```
<!-- Definition of new Content Type: Press Release -->
<type name="custom:pressrelease">
    <title>Press Release</title>
    <parent>cm:content</parent>
    <properties>
        <property name="custom:PRName">
            <title>PR Person Name</title>
            <type>d:text</type>
        </property>
        <property name="custom:PREmail">
            <title>PR Person Email</title>
            <type>d:text</type>
        </property>
        <property name="custom:PRPhone">
            <title>PR Person Phone</title>
            <type>d:text</type>
        </property>
        <property name="custom:PRDate">
            <title>PR Released Date</title>
            <type>d:date</type>
        </property>
```

```
                </properties>
                <associations>
                    <association name="custom:PRImage">
                        <title>Press Release Image</title>
                        <target>
                            <class>cm:content</class>
                            <mandatory>false</mandatory>
                            <many>false</many>
                        </target>
                    </association>
                    <association name="custom:PRFiles">
                        <title>Press Release Files</title>
                        <target>
                            <class>cm:content</class>
                            <mandatory>false</mandatory>
                            <many>true</many>
                        </target>
                    </association>
                </associations>
                <mandatory-aspects>
                    <aspect>cm:versionable</aspect>
                </mandatory-aspects>
            </type>
```

 It is very important to follow a specific sequence while defining the content model. First define the parent, followed by the properties, associations, and then mandatory aspects.

You need to make sure the web client program recognizes these new custom associations in the web-based interface. Open the web-client-config-custom.xml file and insert the following lines of code that are highlighted:

```
<config evaluator="node-type" condition="custom:pressrelease">
    <property-sheet>
        <show-property name="mimetype"
          display-label-id="content_type"
          component-generator="MimeTypeSelectorGenerator"/>
        <show-property name="size" display-label-id="size"
          converter="org.alfresco.faces.ByteSizeConverter"
          show-in-edit-mode="false" />
        <show-property name="custom:PRName" />
        <show-property name="custom:PREmail" />
        <show-property name="custom:PRPhone" />
        <show-property name="custom:PRDate" />
```

```
        <show-association name="custom:PRImage"/>
        <show-association name="custom:PRFiles"/>
    </property-sheet>
</config>
```

Use the Custom Associations

Go to the **Company Home | Intranet | Press and Media | Press Releases** space and upload an image and two text files to test the custom associations. Click the **view details** icon of one of the press releases (HTML files) in the space that you created earlier. Click the **edit properties** icon to select the associations as shown in the screenshot below:

For the `Press Release Image` association, select the image you uploaded earlier. Similarly for the `Press Release Files` association, select both the text files you uploaded earlier. Click the **OK** button to update the properties. In the view details page you will notice the files associated with the press release.

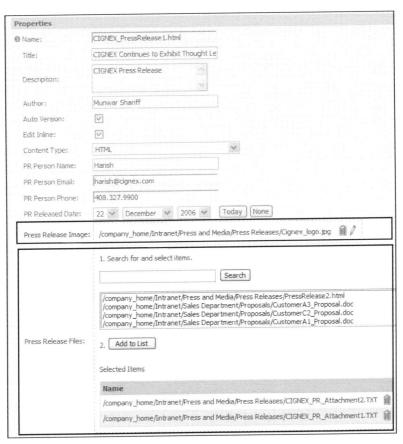

Presentation Template for Custom Content Type

The space **Company Home | Data Dictionary | Presentation Templates** contains presentation templates that are useful to consolidate and view content in various different ways. The presentation templates are written in FreeMarker template language and will have the `.ftl` extension.

You have created your own custom content type called `Press Release`, which has following things:

- Press release content in HTML format
- Properties about PR person details such as PRName, PREmail
- Press Release Image
- Related Files

You can create your own custom presentation template to preview the press release in a specific format as per your business requirements. The following are the steps to create your custom presentation template:

Step1: Create a file called `chapter7_PressReleaseTemplate.ftl` in your personal computer with the following code. This is FreeMarker template code to display press release information in two columns. First column displays the image associated with this press release followed by the actual press release content in HTML format. The second column displays the properties (PR Contact details) followed by the list of associated files.

```
<#-- Shows Press Release content with Custom Properties, Associated
Image and Files -->

<H3> ${document.properties.name} </H3>
<HR>

<#if document?exists>
   <table>
      <tr>
        <td valign="top">
        <#if document.assocs["custom:PRImage"]?exists>
          <#list document.assocs["custom:PRImage"] as t>
               <img src="/alfresco${t.url}">
          </#list>
        </#if>

        <BR><BR>
```

```
        ${document.content}
        </td>
        <td valign="top">

            <B> PR CONTACT :</B> <BR>
            Contact: ${document.properties["custom:PRName"]} <BR>
            Email: ${document.properties["custom:PREmail"]} <BR>
            Phone: ${document.properties["custom:PRPhone"]} <BR>

        <BR>

            <B> Associated Files: </B>
        <#if document.assocs["custom:PRFiles"]?exists>
            <#list document.assocs["custom:PRFiles"] as t>
                <a href="/alfresco${t.url}"> ${t.name} </a> <BR>
            </#list>
        </#if>
        </td>
    </tr>

    </table>
<#else>
    No document found!
</#if>
```

Step 2: Go to the **Company Home | Data Dictionary | Presentation Templates** space and click the **Add Content** link and upload the `chapter7_PressReleaseTemplate.ftl` file that you created earlier as a new presentation template.

Step 3: Go to the **Company Home | Intranet | Press and Media | Press Releases** space and make sure the content item you created earlier as `Press Release` has all the properties filled out.

Step 4: Use the **Preview in Template** button and select the `chapter7_PressReleaseTemplate.ftl` template from the drop-down list to display the press release as shown below:

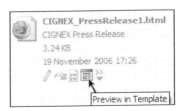

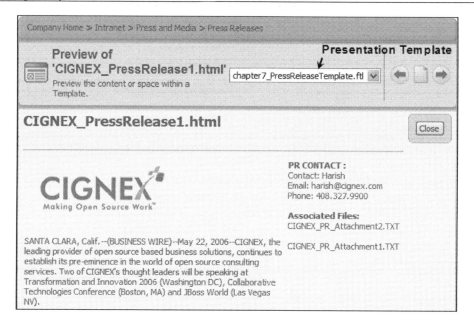

Sample Extensions

You can create various custom content types, aspects, and associations as per your business requirements.

Handling Publishing Material

Let us say you belong to training department and would like to maintain the training material in the Alfresco repository.

As an example, create custom content types called the Book and the Chapters. In the content model, define the Book content type to have chapters as child associations.

Chapters are the actual text or HTML or XML documents, which are version controlled. The Book content type logically groups all the chapters using the child-association property. Create a presentation template for Book content to display all the associated chapters.

Handling Translations

Try adding the Translatable aspect to your content. The Translatable aspect creates a multi-document association to your content for translations. There is an existing presentation template called translatable.ftl to display multiple translations of a document.

Full Auditing

In the earlier chapters, you have learned how to enable content versioning to be automatically built into the system. You can quickly access any previous version, to republish it as is, or with edits. You can also recover deleted content.

Your content could be one of your most valuable assets. Based on the regulatory and compliance requirements, you might want to have a full audit trail and accountability of user activities in your content management system.

While content may be removed from the site, a full audit trail is always recoverable. That audit trail includes the content itself, all edited versions of the content, and a full record of exactly who did what and when.

In Alfresco, the auditing is carried out at the service layer of the repository. This captures both user and application interaction with the repository. All user and system activities are logged and made available through the server auditing system. The date, time, user, comments, and the actual content changes are stored and are accessible by the users.

Controlling Audit Information

Auditing is disabled by default. To enable the default audit configuration, change the `enabled` attribute, highlighted in bold, in the following code to `true`.

For auditing to be enabled for a method it must be enabled or unset on the method, enabled or unset on the service, and enabled on the top-level audit element. If it is marked as `enabled="false"` anywhere in the stack then auditing will be disabled.

The audit configuration file is located at `<configRoot>\auditConfig.xml`. The following are some of the important parameters in the audit configuration file.

```
<!-- Default Audit Configuration -->

<Audit xmlns="http://www.alfresco.org/model/audit/1.0" xmlns:
xsi="http://www.w3.org/2001/XMLSchema-instance" enabled="false"
auditInternal="false" mode="all">

    <!-- The File/Folder Service -->

    <Service name="FileFolderService" mode="none">
        <Method name="rename" mode="all"/>
        <Method name="move" mode="all"/>
        <Method name="copy" mode="all" auditInternal="true"/>
        <Method name="create" mode="all"/>
        <Method name="delete" mode="all"/>
```

```
        <Method name="makeFolders" mode="all"/>
        <Method name="getWriter" mode="all"/>
    </Service>

    <Service name="NodeService" mode="none">
        <Method name="createStore" mode="all"/>
        <Method name="createNode" mode="all"/>
        <Method name="moveNode" mode="all"/>
        <Method name="setChildAssociationIndex" mode="all"/>
        <Method name="setType" mode="all"/>
        <Method name="addAspect" mode="all"/>
        <Method name="removeAspect" mode="all"/>
        <Method name="deleteNode" mode="all"/>
        <Method name="addChild" mode="all"/>
        <Method name="removeChild" mode="all"/>
        <Method name="setProperties" mode="all"/>
        <Method name="setProperty" mode="all"/>
        <Method name="createAssociation" mode="all"/>
        <Method name="removeAssociation" mode="all"/>
        <Method name="restoreNode" mode="all"/>
    </Service>

    <Service name="PersonService" mode="none">
        <Method name="setCreateMissingPeople" mode="all"/>
        <Method name="setPersonProperties" mode="all"/>
        <Method name="createPerson" mode="all"/>
        <Method name="deletePerson" mode="all"/>
    </Service>

    <Service name="VersionService" mode="none">
        <Method name="createVersion" mode="all"/>
        <Method name="revert" mode="all"/>
        <Method name="restore" mode="all"/>
        <Method name="deleteVersionHistory" mode="all"/>
    </Service>


</Audit>
```

Simple Audit Template to Display Audit Information

To enable auditing, open the `<configRoot>\auditConfig.xml` file and change the `enabled` attribute value to `true`. Now restart the Alfresco server to apply the changes.

Go to the **Company Home | Intranet | Press and Media | Press Releases** space and edit one of the press release documents. For the same press release document, use the **Preview in Template** button (as shown before) and select the **show_audit. ftl** template from the drop-down list. You will see the audit information as shown in the screenshot below. Notice the column titled **Method** in the audit report, which captures all the actions that happened on the document.

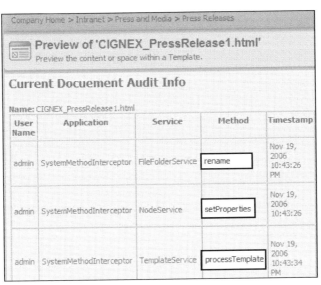

Go to the **Company Home | Data Dictionary | Presentation Templates** space and examine the code in the show_audit.ftl file. This is a simple audit template provided to display the audit information. You can either edit this template or create another one as per your audit reporting requirements.

Summary

The Alfresco content model is highly extensible. The custom aspects provide you with the flexibility to add additional sets of properties to the documents in specific spaces. You can customize the content model to handle the data and business rules in a way to suit your business needs. Similarly, with custom content types you will be able to execute business rules based on the content type. Using content associations you can associate and logically group the content as one entity. You can preview the content using custom presentation templates.

You can enable full auditing on your content. Your content may be removed from the site, but a full audit trail is always recoverable. The audit trail includes the content itself, all edited versions of the content, and a full record of exactly who did what and when.

8
Search

The success of content management systems depends on their ability to locate the required content with fewer clicks. The way you choose the content name, the way you categorize the content, the location where you place the content, and the property values you provide will help you to easily locate the content and generate reusable reports. You will realize the benefits of having a powerful search engine, when you have a lot of files in your content management system. In this chapter, we will examine the advanced search features and extend the capabilities of search.

By the end of this chapter you will have learned how to:

- Use the advanced search form
- Extend search capabilities
- Define and save search criteria as reusable reports
- Configure Alfresco's search engine

Search Overview

Using Alfresco, you will be able to search both content and properties. You can do a full-text search on any word in content, regardless of the format. You can search for content in a particular space. You can also search for content belonging to certain categories or of a specific type. You can search for content created or modified between certain dates, created by a specific person, and so on. You can extend the search capabilities to search on custom content types and custom property values.

Full-Text Search

By default the content in Alfresco is full-text searchable. Any content uploaded to Alfresco, such as the following types will be internally converted to text, indexed, and searchable:

- Microsoft Office documents: MS Word, Excel, PowerPoint
- Open Office documents
- XML/HTML
- PDF
- Emails
- Content in foreign languages

Boolean Search

Doing a search on Alfresco is easy. Simply type one or more search terms (the words that best describe the information you want to find) into the search box and hit the *Enter* key or click on the search icon.

You can use the Google-style query syntax to search the content stored in the Alfresco repository. The following table lists various items of search syntax with description:

Search String	Description
Customer	Returns all documents that contain the text "Customer" (as file name or file content)
-Customer	Returns all documents that do not contain text "Customer"
Customer Alfresco	Returns all documents that contain "Customer" or "Alfresco". Equivalent to Customer +Alfresco
Customer +Alfresco	Returns all documents that contain "Customer" or "Alfresco"
Customer -Alfresco	Returns all documents that contain "Customer" and do not contain "Alfresco"
inter	Returns all documents that contain "inter" as any portion of a word such as International, Interest. This is known as a wild card search.

Search File Names Only

It is faster to search the content by file names if you know the file name or some portion of the file name. When you click on the search options icon you will see the list of options available to you as shown in the screenshot on the next page:

You can select an option by clicking on its radio button as shown in the above screenshot. You have the following options:

- **All Items**: Search the entire content and all the properties
- **File names and contents**: Search the entire content and file name property
- **File names only**: Search only the name property of file content
- **Space names only**: Search only the name property of space content

Advanced Search

You can view the advanced search form by clicking on the **Advanced Search** link provided in the search drop-down options as shown in the above screenshot. Using the advanced search form (shown in the screenshot overleaf) you can search content:

- Within a space, optionally its sub-spaces
- Matching a given category, optionally sub-categories
- Of a specific content type or a MIME type
- Matching properties such as title, description, or author
- Created or modified within certain date ranges
- Matching custom properties

The menu bar of the advanced search form contains the **Reset All** button (refer to the screenshot overleaf), which is useful to clear all the options selected in the form. You can save the search options and execute the saved searches as reports. More information about saved searches is provided in later sections of this chapter.

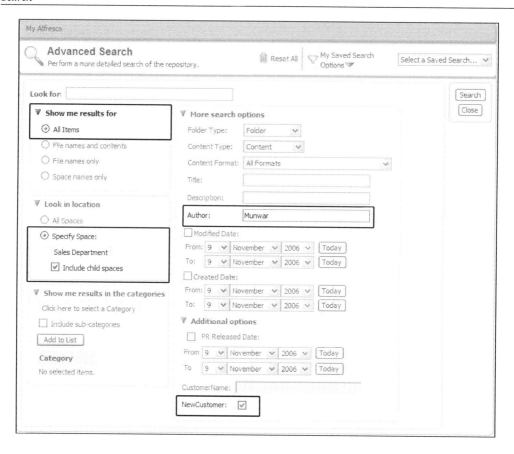

Search by Content Location

Options provided in the **Look in location** block of the advanced search form will allow you to search content by its location. Clicking on the **Specify Space** radio button will list the spaces for you to choose as shown in the screenshot opposite. From the list of a spaces, click on space name to browse to sub-spaces. You can click on the radio button to select a space and optionally choose to search in all sub-spaces by checking the **Include child spaces** option. You can choose only one space and its sub-spaces at a time to search the content.

Search by Content Category

Options provided in the **Show me results in the categories** block of the advanced search form will allow you to search content belonging to one or more categories. Clicking on the **Select Category** link will list the categories as shown in the screenshot on the next page. From the list of categories, click on a category name to browse the sub-categories. You can click on the radio button to select a category and optionally choose to search in all sub-categories by checking the **Include sub-categories** option. Click on the **Add to List** button to add the category to the list of selections. You can choose as many categories as you want to search the content.

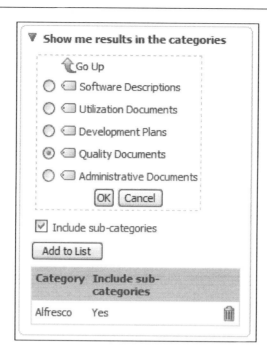

Search by Content Properties

Options provided in the **More search options** block of the advanced search form will allow you to search content based on property values. You can search for content that belongs to a specific content type by selecting the **Content Type** drop-down option. You can search for the content created by a specific author by providing the full or partial name of the author in the **Author** text box as shown in the following screenshot. You can search for the content created within a certain date range by selecting the **Created Date** checkbox and by providing the **From** and **To** dates.

If you choose more than one option, then the content that satisfies all the conditions will be listed as search result. For example, if you have provided author's name and **Created Date** range, then the content created within that date range and authored by that specific person will be listed. This is equivalent to logical AND criteria to select the content. The current limitation with the advanced search form is that you can not provide OR criteria. For example, you can not search for content within a date range or that is created by a specific person.

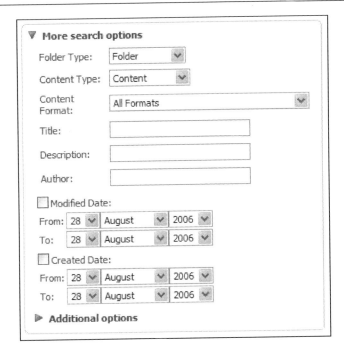

Extending the Search Form

In the previous chapter titled *Extending the Alfresco Content Model*, you have created a custom content called *Press Release* and a custom view called *Customer Details*. You can search for content of press release type. You can search for content having a specific custom property value.

For the advanced search form to recognize and list the custom content types and custom aspects, you need to customize the web client.

Configure the Web Client User Interface

Edit `web-client-config-custom.xml` file in the extension folder (`<alfresco_install_folder>\tomcat\shared\classes\alfresco\extension`) and add the following XML code to extend the advanced search form:

```
<config evaluator="string-compare" condition="Advanced Search">
  <advanced-search>
    <content-types>
      <type name="custom:pressrelease" />
    </content-types>
    <custom-properties>
```

```
        <meta-data type="custom:pressrelease"
                                    property="custom:PRDate" />
        <meta-data aspect="custom:CustomerDetails"
                                property="custom:CustomerName" />
         <meta-data aspect="custom:CustomerDetails"
                                property="custom:NewCustomer" />
      </custom-properties>
    </advanced-search>
  </config>
```

The code in the `<content-types>` block will list this content type in the advanced search form. The code in the `<custom-properties>` block will list the given custom properties in advanced search form.

After making changes to the configuration file, restart Alfresco.

Search Custom Content and Properties

After you log in to Alfresco, open the advanced search form, and click on the **Additional options** block, you will notice the custom properties as highlighted in the next screenshot. Similarly, when you click on the **Content Type** drop-down list, you will notice the custom content type listed as shown in the same screenshot.

You can search content by providing various values in **Additional options** block. For example, you can list the documents belonging to new customers by selecting the **NewCustomer** checkbox and clicking the *Enter* button on your keyboard or by clicking on the **Search** button in the advanced search form.

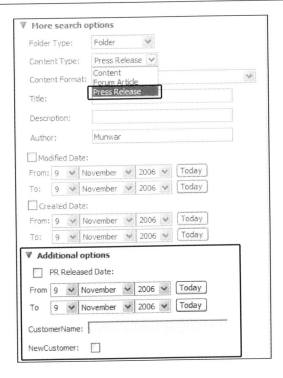

Using a Saved Search as a Report

Sometimes, you will have to repeatedly search for some content, that satisfies specific search criteria. Instead of typing or selecting the same options in the advanced search form again and again, you can save the search criteria to reuse. This is like a personalized report for you. You can choose to share this report with others by making the saved search as **Public**. You can keep certain reports to yourself by not sharing them with others and these reports will be listed for you as private reports.

Define Complex Search Criteria

As an example, generate a report to list all sales documents authored by Munwar for new customers.

In order to define these search criteria, open the **Advanced Search** form. Under the **Look in location** block, select the **Company Home | Intranet | Sales Department** space and select sub-spaces. Under the **More search options** block, type Munwar for **Author**. Under the **Additional options** block, select the **NewCustomer** checkbox.

You can further complicate the search criteria by selecting a date range for **Created Date**.

Once you are done with your search criteria, click the **Search** button to display the search results.

Save Search Criteria as a Public or Private Report

The Search Results page is shown in the following screenshot. You can save the search criteria by clicking on the **More Actions | Save New Search** option as shown in the screenshot.

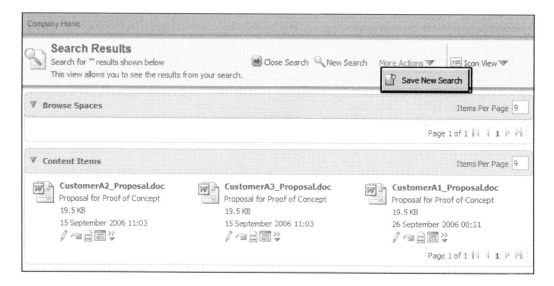

Clicking on the **Save New Search** link will open up the **Save New Search** dialog as shown in the screenshot below:

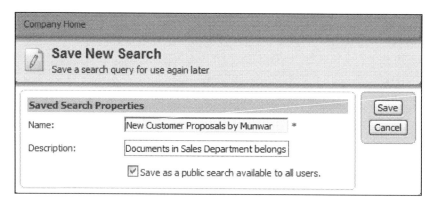

In the **Save New Search** dialog, give some meaningful **Name** and **Description** to your custom report (saved search).

If you select the **Save as a public search available to all users** option then this report becomes a public report and visible to all other users in the advanced search form. If you have not selected this option, then the report is visible only to you as a private report.

All saved searches can be located at the **Company Home | Data Dictionary | Saved Searches** space.

Reuse the Saved Search

You can reuse the search criteria that were saved earlier by selecting them in the **Advanced Search** form. In the **Advanced Search** form, click on the **My Saved Search Options** and then on **Public Searches**. The right side drop-down box will list all the available public reports (saved searches).

Selecting a saved search will automatically create the search criteria by selecting the options in the advanced search form. Similarly, you can reuse **Your Searches**, which are a kind of private reports for you.

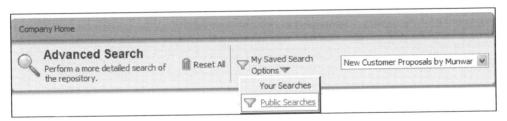

Configuring the Alfresco Search Engine

The Alfresco search engine is configurable and highly scalable. This section provides information about the underlying search engine and the process to configure it.

The Theory behind the Search Engine

Alfresco supports full-text search capabilities, using Apache's powerful Lucene search engine (`http://lucene.apache.org`). Lucene is an open-source, highly scalable, and fast search engine. Lucene powers searching in discussion groups at Fortune 100 companies, in commercial issue trackers, email search from Microsoft, and the Nutch web search engine (which scales to billions of pages).

Lucene's logical architecture is such that it performs a search on a document based on the fields of text. This helps Lucene to be independent of the file format. So any kind of text (PDF, HTML, Microsoft Word documents, etc.) can be indexed as long as the textual information can be extracted.

Lucene stores the search indexes and related data in the back-end file system, similar to Alfresco binary files. You can locate the search-index files in your `<alfresco_installation>\alf_data\lucene-indexes` folder. Lucene also supports federated searches by combining various data sources.

Currently Alfresco supports two languages, Lucene and XPath, to search the content in the Alfresco repository.

Limit Search Results

By default a search returns all the results that match the search criteria. Let us say you have millions of documents in your repository. If a particular search results to thousands of documents, the web client creates pagination to display the search results in multiple pages. Quite often we never see the search results in later portions of the page. Do you ever remember clicking on page number 10 (or more) in a search results page to locate content? It is very inefficient to get all the search results and display them in pages.

You can limit the search results by customizing your web-client configuration file `web-client-config-custom.xml` in the extension folder (`<alfresco_install_folder>\tomcat\shared\classes\alfresco\extension`).

Edit the `web-client-config-custom.xml` file and add the following XML text after the first line `<alfresco-config>`. If you have already created this XML block in your `web-client-config-custom.xml` file, then insert the lines which are highlighted.

```
<config>
  <client>
    <!-- Override the from email address -->
      <from-email-address>munwar@cignex.com</from-email-address>
      <!-- the minimum number of characters required for a valid
                                          earch string -->
        <search-minimum>3</search-minimum>
      <!-- set this value to true to enable AND text terms for
                      simple/advanced search by default -->
        <search-and-terms>false</search-and-terms>
      <!-- Limit search results. -1 for unlimited. -->
        <search-max-results>100</search-max-results>
  </client>
</config>
```

The code ensures that the search engine will return a maximum of 100 results. The minimum search string length is set to 3 characters. The Boolean AND search option is disabled by default to improve search performance.

Restart Alfresco to make sure the above changes are effective.

Indexing Properties

In the Alfresco content model, the data dictionary settings for properties determine how individual properties are indexed in the search engine. Refer to the `contentModel.xml` file in your `config\model` folder. For a Tomcat installation on Windows, the file can be located in your `<alfresco_install_folder>\tomcat\webapps\alfresco\WEB-INF\classes\alfresco\model` folder.

In the `contentModel.xml` file, refer to the highlighted code to understand how the indexing for a content property is controlled.

```
<type name="cm:content">
   <title>Content</title>
   <parent>cm:cmobject</parent>
     <properties>
        <property name="cm:content">
           <type>d:content</type>
           <mandatory>false</mandatory>
           <index enabled="true">
              <atomic>true</atomic>
              <stored>false</stored>
              <tokenised>true</tokenised>
           </index>
        </property>
     </properties>
   </type>
```

If the attribute `enabled` for `index` is set to `true`, then this property will be indexed in the search engine. If this is false, there will be no entry for this property in the index.

If the option `Atomic` is set to `true`, then the property is indexed in the transaction. If not, the property is indexed in the background.

If the option `Stored` is set to `true`, then the property value is stored in the index and may be obtained through the Lucene low-level query API.

If the option `Tokenized` is set to `true`, then the string value of the property is tokenized before indexing; if it is set to false, then it is indexed as it is, as a single string. The token is determined by the property type in the data dictionary. This is locale sensitive as supported by the data dictionary. So, you could switch to **tokenize** all your content in German. At the moment you can not mix German and English tokenization.

In the previous chapter, you created custom properties in custom aspects and custom content types. If you have not specified any indexing values have your custom properties, then Alfresco assumes default values have your properties.

By default, the properties are indexed atomically. The property value is not stored in the index, and the property is tokenized when it is indexed.

Configuring Lucene in Alfresco

The `repository.properties` file in your `config` folder defines a number of properties that influence how all indexes behave. You can improve the search performance by setting appropriate values in properties file.

 Do not change the `repository.properties` values without knowing your application needs. If you have to make changes to the `.properties` file, take a backup before making changes.

The following are the default search-index properties.

- `lucene.query.maxClauses=10000`
- `lucene.indexer.batchSize=10000`
- `lucene.indexer.minMergeDocs=1000`
- `lucene.indexer.mergeFactor=10`
- `lucene.indexer.maxMergeDocs=100000`

Max Clauses (Lucene standard parameter): Lucene queries limit the number of clauses in a Boolean query to this value. Some queries are expanded into a whole set of Boolean queries with many clauses under the covers. For example, searching for `luc.*` will expand to a Boolean query containing an OR for every token the index knows about that matches `luc.*`.

Batch size (Alfresco indexing parameter): The indexer stores a list of what it has to do as the changes are made using the node service API. Typically, there are many events that would cause a node to be re-indexed. Keeping an event list means that the actions can be optimized. The algorithm limits re-indexes to one per batch size, and it will not index if a delete is pending, etc. When the list of events reach this size, the whole event list is processed and documents added to the delta index.

Min Merge Docs (Lucene standard parameter): This determines the size of the in-memory Lucene index used for each delta index. A higher value of Min Merger Docs would mean that we have more memory but less IO writing to the index delta. The in-memory information will be flushed and written to the disk at the start of the next batch of index events; as the process progresses, the event list requires reading against the delta index. This does not affect the way information is stored on disk, just how it is buffered before it gets there.

Merge Factor (Lucene standard parameter): This determines the number of index segments that are created on the disk. When there are more than this number of segments some segments will be combined.

Max Merge Docs (Lucene standard parameter): This value determines the maximum number of documents that could be stored in an index segment. When this value is reached in a segment it will not grow any larger. As a result there may be more segments than expected from looking at the merge factor.

Summary

Alfresco supports full-text search capabilities using an open-source-based, highly scalable, and fast search engine called Lucene. The content as well as content properties will be indexed in the search engine automatically. You can use the advanced search form to create complex search criteria to search your content. You can save the searches as reusable reports. You can extend the advanced search form to include your custom content types and custom properties.

9
Implementing Workflow

Workflow is an automation of a business process, during which documents are passed from one participant to another for action, according to a set of procedural rules. Every content management system implementation will have workflow requirements. For some companies workflow could be a simple approval process and for some companies it could be a complex business process management. Workflow provides ownership and control on the content and processes. In this chapter, you will learn about the basic out-of-the-box workflow capabilities of Alfresco and ways to extend it as per your business requirements.

By the end of this chapter you will have learned how to:

- Enable simple workflow on documents
- Create email templates and set email notifications
- Extend workflow with multiple approval steps
- Implement a complex workflow scenario for digital asset management
- Start an advanced workflow from the list of predefined workflows
- Assign priority, due date, reviewer, and documents to the workflow
- Take ownership of a task
- Reassign a task
- Change the workflow state
- List tasks assigned to you and tasks completed by you
- Cancel or abort the workflows you have started
- Create your own custom advanced workflow

Introduction to the Alfresco Workflow Process

Alfresco includes two types of workflows out of the box. One is the **Simple Workflow**, which is content-oriented, and the other one is the **Advanced Workflow**, which is task-oriented.

The Simple Workflow process in Alfresco is the movement of documents through various spaces. It's simple in that each workflow definition is restricted to a single state. Multiple states are represented by loosely tying multiple workflow definitions. Loose coupling is achieved by attaching a workflow definition to a space and a workflow instance to a content item. A content item is moved or copied to a new space at which point a new workflow instance is attached based on the workflow definition of the space. A workflow definition is unaware of other related workflow definitions.

The Advanced Workflow process is task-oriented, where you create a task, attach documents to be reviewed, and assign it to appropriate reviewers. You can track the list of tasks assigned to you and the tasks initiated by you. You can change the status of the tasks, reassign the tasks to other users, and cancel a task. You can send various notifications to all the parties involved and track the tasks to closure.

You can use out-of-the-box features provided by both the workflows or you can create your own custom advanced workflow as per the business processes of your organization.

Simple Workflow

For example, consider a purchase order that moves through various departments for authorization and eventual purchase. To implement a simple workflow in Alfresco, you will create spaces for each department and allow documents to move through various department spaces. Each department space is secured allowing only users of that department to edit the document and to move it to the next departmental space in the workflow process.

The workflow process is so flexible that you could introduce new steps for approval into the operation without changing any code.

Out-of-the-Box Features

The simple workflow is implemented as an aspect which could be attached to any document in space through business rule. Workflow can also be invoked on individual content items as actions.

The workflow has two steps—one is an approve step and the other is a reject step. You can refer to the screenshot below where the workflow is defined for the documents in a space called **Review Space**. Users belonging to the **Review Space** can act upon the document. If they reject it then the document moves to a space called **Rejected Space** and if they approve it then the document moves to a space called **Approved Space**. You can define the names of the spaces and the users on the spaces as per your business requirements.

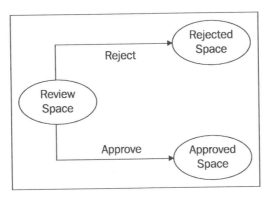

Define and Use a Simple Workflow

The process to define and use a simple workflow in Alfresco is as follows:

- Identify spaces and set security on those spaces.
- Define your workflow process.
- Add workflow to content in those spaces accordingly.
- Select the email template and people to send email notifications.
- Test the workflow process.

As an example, let us define and use a simple workflow process to review and approve the engineering documents in your intranet. Go to the **Company Home | Intranet | Engineering Department** space and create the **ProjectA** space using an existing **Software Engineering Project** space template. For more information about creating a space using an existing space template refer to Chapter 5.

Identify Spaces and Security

If you go to the **Company Home | Intranet | Engineering Department | ProjectA | Documentation** space, you will notice the following sub-spaces:

- **Samples**: This space is to store sample project documents. Set the security on this space so that only managers can edit the documents and others can copy the documents from this space.

- **Drafts**: This space contains initial drafts and documents of **ProjectA** that are being edited. Set security in such a way that few selected users (such as **Engineer1** and **Engineer2** as shown in the screenshot below) can add and edit documents in this space.

- **Pending Approval**: This space contains all the documents under review. Set security so that only the Project Manager of **ProjectA** can edit the documents.

- **Published**: This space contains all the documents that are approved and visible to others. Nobody should edit the documents while they are in the **Published** space. If you need to edit a document, you need to retract it to the **Drafts** space and follow the workflow process as shown below:

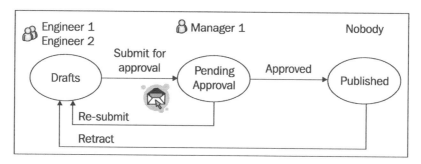

Set the security on these sub-spaces as required. For more information about securing spaces, refer to Chapter 4.

Define Workflow Process

Now that you have identified the spaces, the next step is defining your workflow process. The screenshot above illustrates the spaces and the workflow.

We will add workflow to all the documents in the **Drafts** space. When a user selects the approve action called **Submit for Approval** on a document, the document moves from the **Drafts** space to the **Pending approval** space.

We will add workflow to all the documents in the **Pending Approval** space. When the user selects the approve action called **Approved** on a document, the document moves from the **Pending Approval** space to the **Published** space. Similarly, when the user selects the reject action called **Re-submit** on a document, it moves from the **Pending Approval** space to the **Drafts** space.

We will add workflow to all the documents in the **Published** space. When a user selects the reject action called **Retract** on a document, it moves from the **Published** space to the **Drafts** space.

You can have as many review steps (spaces) as needed and you can choose the workflow action names as per your business requirements.

Add Simple Workflow to Items

Now that you have defined your workflow process, the next step is to add workflow to the documents in these spaces.

To add workflow to the **Drafts** space follow the steps provided below:

1. Ensure that you are in the **Company Home | Intranet | Engineering Department | ProjectA | Documentation | Drafts** space.
2. Click on **More Actions | Manage Content Rules**.
3. Click the **Create Rule** link and you will see the **Create Rules Wizard**.
4. In **Step One**, **Select Condition** drop-down list, select the **All Items** option and click the **Add to List** button. Click the **Next** button.
5. In **Step Two**, **Select Actions** drop-down list, select the **Add simple workflow to item** option and click the **Set Values and Add** button. A **Set action values** dialog window appears as shown in the screenshot on the next page.

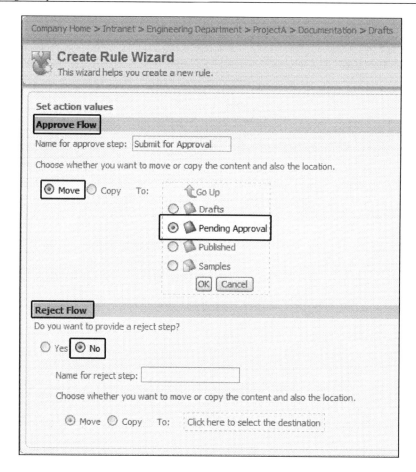

6. In the **Approve Flow** section, provide the workflow step name as **Submit for Approval** and move the content to the **Pending Approval** space. This is as per your workflow design shown in the screenshot under the section *Identify Spaces and Security* for the **Drafts** space.

7. The workflow for the **Drafts** space does not require a reject step. Hence select the option **No** for **Reject Flow**.

8. Click **OK** and then click the **Next** button.

9. In **Step Three**, select **Type** as **Inbound**, and provide an appropriate name and description for this rule.

10. Finish the rule.

Similarly, create the workflow for the **Pending Approval** space as per the design shown in the screenshot under the section *Identify Spaces and Security*. Remember this space has both an approve step and a reject step as shown in the next screenshot:

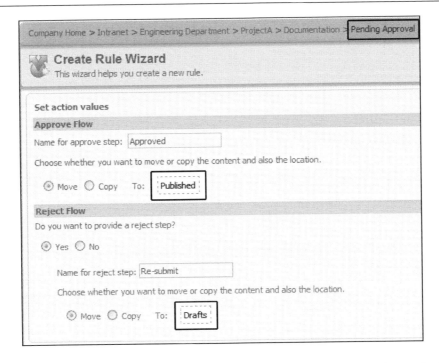

Now create the workflow for the **Published** space as per the design shown in the screenshot under the section *Identify Spaces and Security*. Remember this space has only an approve step that moves the content to the **Drafts** space upon **Retract**. Provide **Retract** as the name for the approve step.

Send Notification to the Manager for Approval

You can send notification by email to the Project Manager whenever a document is pending approval. Follow the steps below to send email notification to the Project Manager of **ProjectA** when a document gets into the **Pending Approval** space:

1. Ensure that you are in the **Company Home | Intranet | Engineering Department | ProjectA | Documentation | Pending Approval** space.

2. Click on **More Actions | Manage Content Rules**.

3. Click the **Create Rule** link and you will see the **Create Rule Wizard**.

4. In **Step One**, from the **Select Condition** drop-down list select the **All Items** option and click the **Add to List** button. Then click the **Next** button.

5. In **Step Two**, from the **Select Actions** drop-down list select **Send an email to specified users** and click the **Set Values and Add** button.

6. You will notice a **Set action values** dialog box as shown in the screenshot on the next page.

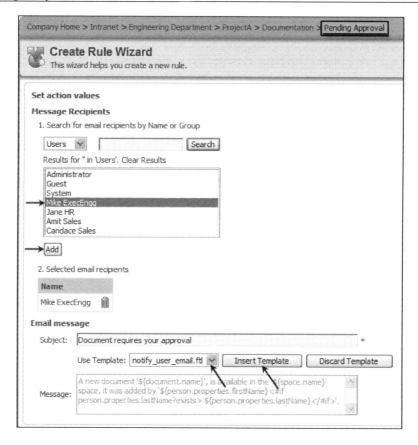

7. Search and select the Project Manager's name as email recipient and click the **Add** button. Provide an appropriate subject for the email. As an email message, you can either provide your own text or use a built-in email template (`notify_user_email.ftl`) as shown in the screenshot above.

8. Click **OK** and then click the **Next** button.

9. In **Step Three**, select the **Type** as **Inbound**, and provide an appropriate name and description for this rule.

10. Finish the rule.

Test Simple Workflow

To test the workflow process, go to the **Drafts** space and upload a sample document. You will see the available workflow actions in the **more actions** drop-down menu as shown on the next page. When you click the **Submit for Approval** action, the document will be moved automatically to the **Pending Approval** space as per the workflow rule.

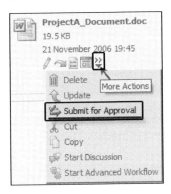

When the document moves into the **Pending Approval** space two business rules will be applied.

One business rule is to send email notification to the Project Manager indicating to him or her that the document is pending approval. If your email server is configured right, then the Project Manager will receive an email notification with information about the document.

The second business rule is the workflow on all the incoming documents to this space. When the Project Manager logs in he or she will see the workflow actions in the **more actions** drop-down menu as shown in the screenshot below:

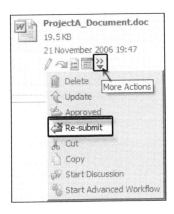

If the Project Manager is satisfied with the document, then he or she can click the **Approved** action and the document will be moved to the **Published** space automatically. If the project manager requires more details or not satisfied with the document, then he or she can click the **Re-submit** action to send the document to the original author to edit and re-submit. In this situation the document will be moved to the **Drafts** space automatically. Once the document is in the **Drafts** space, the workflow process starts all over again.

Select the **Approved** action and notice that the document is moved to the **Published** space. When the document is in the **Published** state, it is typically visible to all the required employees as it is already reviewed and approved. You can retract the document to the **Drafts** space (as shown in the screenshot below) for further edit and approval.

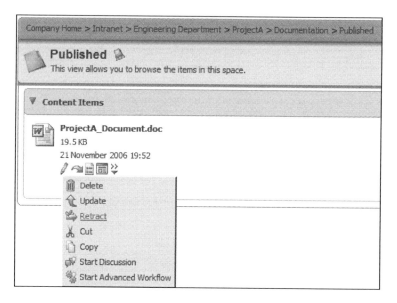

Email Notification Templates

For email notifications, you can either use your own email message or use a standard email notification template (as shown in the screenshot under the section *Send Notification to the Manager forApproval*). You can also create your own email templates to reuse wherever required.

The space **Company Home | Data Dictionary | Email Templates** contains various email templates. The email templates are written in the **free marker template language** and will have the .ftl extension. The following are the steps to create your own email template.

Create a file chapter9_notify_pending_approval_email.ftl in your personal computer with the following code. This is free marker template code, which includes the details of the document and the author to send to the reviewer. Replace your title, company name, and other details as required.

```
<#-- Sends email to people when a document is pending approval -->

A document titled '${document.name}' is pending your approval in the
'${space.name}' space.
```

```
You can view it through this link:
http://localhost:8080/alfresco${document.url}

Please review and approve it as soon as possible.

Best Regards

'${person.properties.firstName}<#if person.properties.lastName?exists>
${person.properties.lastName}</#if>'
Your Title
Your Company Name
Your Signature
```

Go to the **Company Home | Data Dictionary | Email Templates** space and click the **Add Content** link and upload the chapter9_notify_pending_approval_email. ftl file that you have created.

The email template is ready to be used. You can go back to the email notification business rule created on the **Pending Approval** space and edit it to include the new email template that you have created.

Implementing Complex Workflows

You can implement some complex workflows by chaining spaces with business rules as long as each step in the workflow results in an approve or reject type of decision. Once such a workflow is clearly defined and identifies the various steps (spaces), people, and business rules involved, it is easy to implement using Alfresco.

Consider a sample workflow shown in the screenshot on the next page for a **Digital Asset Management System**, where a digital asset goes through multiple approval steps. The digital assets can be in electronic media form such as MP3 files or AVI files, or in physical media form such as video cassettes, audio cassettes, photos, and paper documents.

In the screenshot on the next page, the **Pending Asset** space holds the document till you receive a physical copy of the digital media. After that you can define review, approval, and archive steps for digital assets as per your business requirements. You can consider sending notifications to various parties when a document arrives in a space and when a document leaves a space.

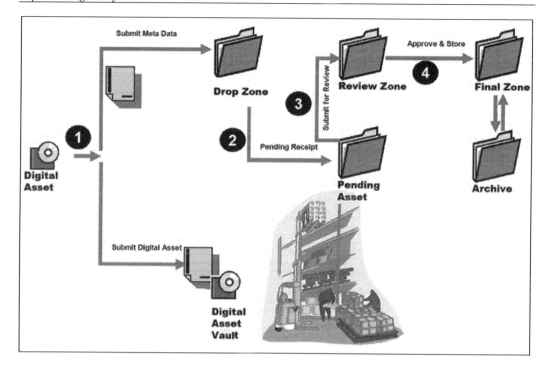

Advanced Workflows

Simple workflows are good to implement content-oriented workflow processes. However, there are certain limitations of the simple workflow that are as follows:

- Unable to create multi-state workflow definitions
- Restricted to one or two exit transitions (approve, reject)
- Unable to define parallel workflows
- Reliance on folder structure for multi-stage workflow and action triggering
- No notion of a task or assignment

To resolve these limitations, Alfresco has embedded the JBPM (JBoss Business Process Management) engine into its core. With JBPM, the Alfresco platform is extended to support complex task-oriented processes.

JBoss jBPM is a flexible, extensible workflow management system with an intuitive process language to express business processes graphically in terms of tasks, wait states for asynchronous communication, timers, and automated actions.

Out-of-the-Box Features

The Advanced Workflow process is task-oriented, where you create a task, attach documents to be reviewed, and assign it to appropriate reviewers.

There are two advanced workflows available out of the box.

- **Adhoc Task** workflow: Assign tasks to your colleague on an ad-hoc basis.
- **Review and Approve** workflow: Assign tasks to your colleague for review and approval.

The figure below explains the process of creating an advanced workflow. An **initiator** starts the workflow task by providing the important information such as due date to complete the task, priority of the task, and notification information. The initiator then selects one or more documents to be reviewed as per the workflow process and assign the users to work on the tasks.

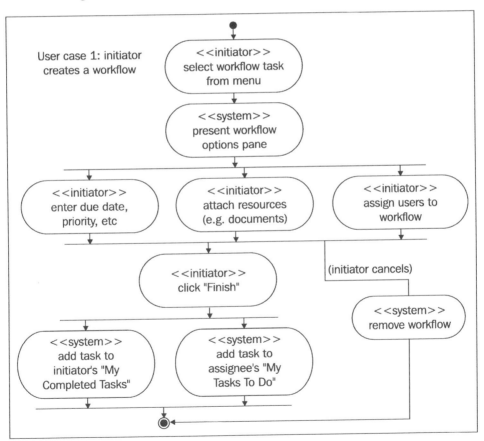

Once the **initiator** assigns the tasks to a user (assignee), the assignee then owns and manages that task. All the tasks assigned to a person are listed in the **My Tasks To Do** window of the **My Alfresco** page. The process flow diagram is shown in the figure below. The assignee can change the status of the task, reassign the task to somebody else, reject, or approve the task.

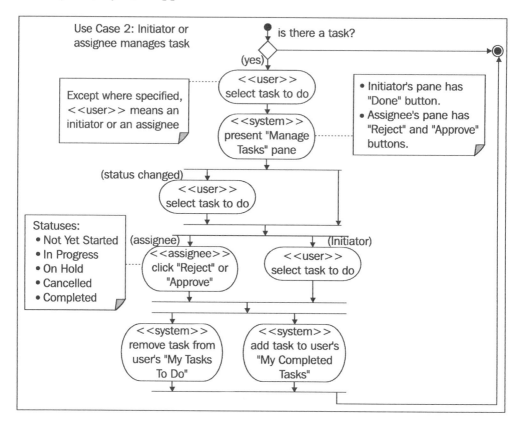

Workflow User Interactions

As a user you will be able to perform the following interactions using the Alfresco web client interface (i.e. Web Browser):

- Start a workflow
  - ○ Select from list of pre-defined workflows
  - ○ Attach resources (additional related documents)
  - ○ Assign users to workflow
- List my tasks (what have I got to do?)

- List tasks I could assign to myself
- Perform task
    - View associated task resources (if any)
    - Change task state
    - Mark task done (or other outcome)
- Look back (trail of steps up to my task assignment)
- Look forward (why hasn't something happened yet?)
- Re-assign task to someone else
- Take ownership of task (if it is assigned to my group)
- Cancel / abort workflow I've started

Adhoc Task-Based Workflow

Let us consider an example where sales people in your organization review and approve proposals. This example uses the existing space called the **Sales Department**, which you have already created as a part of your Intranet sample application. As you have secured this space earlier, only the administrator (**admin**) and users belonging to the Sales group (**Amit Sales** and **Candace Sales**) can access content in this space. Refer to Chapter 4 for more information about the sample users and spaces.

The use-case scenario is as follows. **Amit Sales** creates a proposal document in the **Intranet | Sales Department | Proposals** space. He starts an adhoc task workflow on the document by specifying the due date for review and the priority. He then assigns the task to his colleague **Candace Sales**. **Amit Sales** can track the status of the task from his web client interface. If the task is not completed within a specified time or for some other reasons, **Amit Sales** can cancel the workflow request or reassign it to somebody else.

On the other hand, **Candace Sales** receives a notification about the new task in her **My Tasks To Do** window. She examines the task and completes the task. Once the task is completed, it is reassigned to the initiator **Amit Sales** for further action. **Amit Sales** can send the document for further review to some more people or complete the process. Let us follow the steps given in the following sections to test the use-case scenario.

Start an Advanced Workflow

Log in to the Alfresco web client as **Amit Sales.** Go to the **Company Home | Intranet | Sales Department** space and create a subspace called **Proposals** if it doesn't exist.

Upload a document to the **Proposals** space. Click the document's **More Actions** button and click the **Start Advanced Workflow** link as shown in the screenshot below:

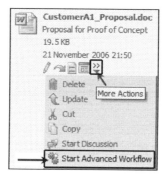

Select Adhoc Task from the List of Predefined Workflows

You will see the **Start Advanced Workflow Wizard** as shown below. This wizard lists all the available workflows including any custom-workflow processes. From the list of available workflows, select the **Adhoc Task** option and click the **Next** button.

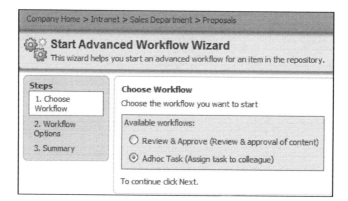

Select Due Date, User, and Resources

You will see the **Workflow options** pane of the **Start Adhoc Task Workflow Wizard** as shown in the screenshot on the next page. Provide a meaningful **Description** for the task; choose the **Priority** and the **Due Date**. Select the **Notify Me** checkbox to receive notifications on various workflow status updates on the document.

From the list of users search for **Candace Sales** and assign her the task. You can also add additional resources (documents) to this workflow task by clicking the **Add Resource** button as shown in the screenshot on the next page. This helps if you want to send a set of documents as one bunch for approval. Once you have filled out the entire relevant information click the **OK** button to start the workflow process.

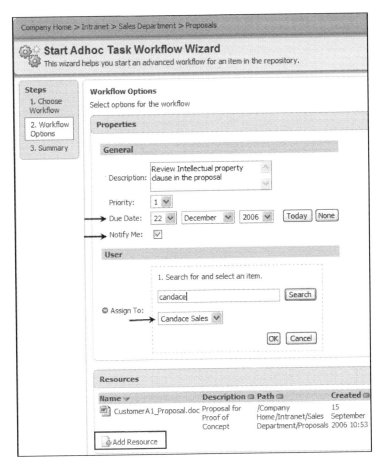

Workflow Information in the Document Details Page

For a specific document in your space, you can find out the workflow details by clicking the document's **View Details** button.

The document's details page also lists the workflow details as shown overleaf. If you have sent this document to multiple people for approval, then all those workflow tasks will be listed here for your reference.

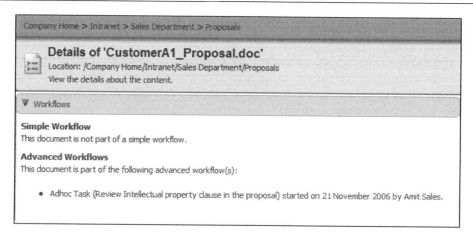

View Status or Cancel Workflow

Click the **My Alfresco** menu link in the toolbar to view your personal dashboard. The dashboard lists all your pending and completed tasks as shown in the screenshot below.

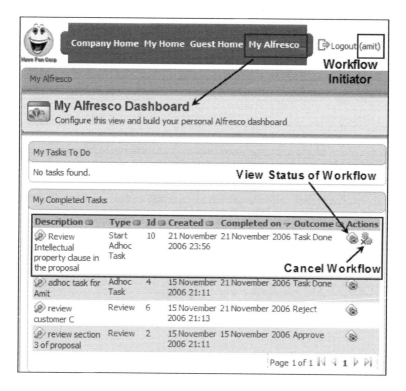

As an initiator you can view the status of the workflow by clicking the **View Status** button. You can cancel the task by clicking the **Cancel Workflow** button.

Adhoc Activities as seen by the Assignee

From your web client user interface log out as **Amit Sales** and log in as **Candace Sales** to work on the adhoc task assigned in the previous section.

List of My Tasks To Do

Click the **My Alfresco** menu link in the toolbar to view your personal dashboard. The dashboard includes your tasks to do as shown in the screenshot below. You may notice that the new task assigned to you by **Amit Sales** is listed in the **My Tasks To do** window.

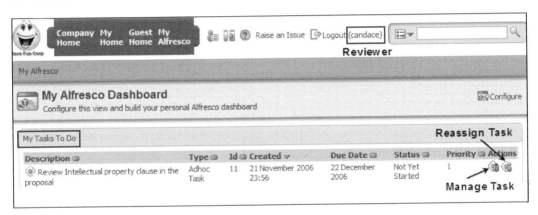

Reassign an Adhoc Task

For various business reasons you can reassign the task by clicking the **Reassign Task** button as shown above. Once you click the **Reassign Task** button, you will see the **Reassign Task** window as shown overleaf. You can search for users and reassign the task to an appropriate user.

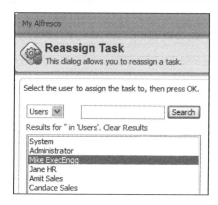

Manage an Adhoc Task

You can manage the task by clicking the **Manage Task** button. Once you click the **Manage Task** button you will see the **Manage Task** window as shown below. You can update the document and update the properties based on the access permissions you have on the document.

To complete the task, choose **Status** as **Completed** and click the **Task Done** button as shown below:

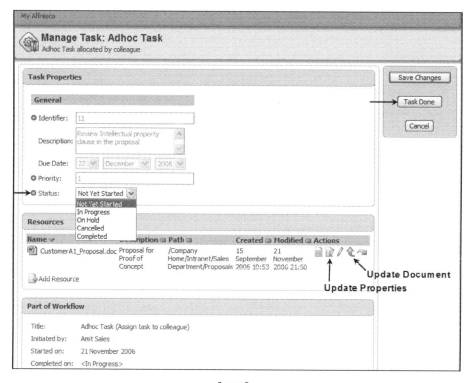

List of My Completed Tasks

Once you are done with the task assigned to you, you will notice that the task is removed from the **My Tasks To Do** window and moved to the **My Completed Tasks** window as shown below:

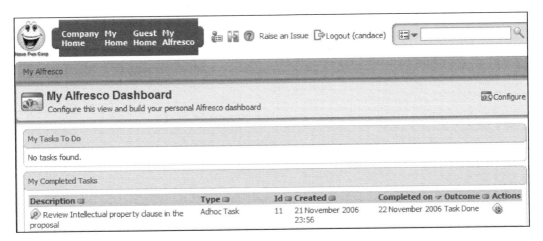

Further Adhoc Activities by the Workflow Initiator

Now log in as **Amit Sales** to track your workflow tasks. Click the **My Alfresco** menu in the toolbar to view your dashboard. You will then notice that the adhoc task you initiated earlier is now completed by **Candace Sales** (as shown in the below). You can complete the process or you can reassign the task to some more people as per the business process.

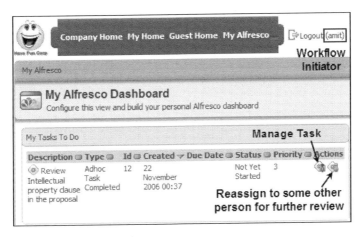

The **initiator** can click the **Manage Task** button (as shown in the previous screenshot) to open the **Manage Task** window and click the **Task Done** button to complete the workflow.

The **initiator** can otherwise reassign the task to somebody else for further review by clicking the **Reassign** button as shown in the previous screenshot.

Review and Approve Workflow

The process of initiating and tracking the Review and Approve advanced workflow is similar to that for the Adhoc Task workflow. However, as the initiator of the task you would expect a decision (either reject or approve) from the assignees using this workflow.

Activities by the Assignee

The assignee can view the task in his or her tasks window and act upon it. The assignee can click the **Manage Task** button for each task to provide appropriate information.

The **Manage Task** pane (as shown in the screenshot below) for the tasks belonging to this workflow process contains **Reject** and **Approve** buttons to convey your decision.

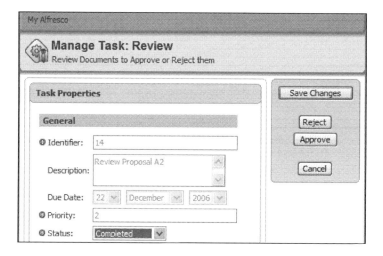

Creating Custom Advanced Workflows

You can define and deploy your own task-oriented workflows in the Alfresco repository. However, you need to follow a particular format to define your workflow and a particular process to deploy it in Alfresco.

A good tutorial about creating and deploying your own custom workflow is provided at `http://wiki.alfresco.com/wiki/WorkflowAdministration`.

The following are the steps you need to follow to create a custom advanced workflow.

Step 1: Create the process definition.

There are two ways of building the process definition (as dictated by JBoss jBPM). One is by hand i.e. create a jPDL XML document. The second option is using a designer i.e. using a tool to generate the jPDL XML document.

The JBoss jBPM also includes a graphical designer tool for authoring business processes. The most important feature of the graphical designer tool is that it includes support for the tasks of the business analyst as well as those of the technical developer. This enables a smooth transition from business process modeling to the practical implementation. A sample screenshot of the graphical designer tool is provided below for your reference.

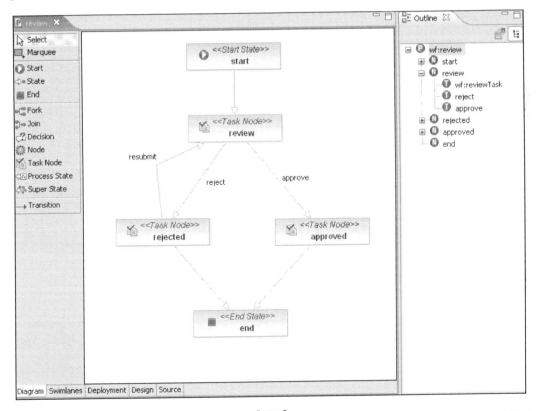

Step 2: Create and deploy the task model.

For each task in the process definition (as defined by `<task>` elements in jPDL) it is possible to associate a task description. The description specifies the information that may be attached to a task i.e. properties (name and data type) and associations (name and type of associated object). A user may view and edit this information in the **Task** dialog within the Alfresco Web Client.

Step3: Add behavior to the process definition.

Write code to handle task assignments, notifications, and data.

Step 4: Create workflow resource bundles.

For localized workflow interaction it is necessary to provide resource bundles containing UI labels for each piece of text that is exposed to the user. With the appropriate resource bundles, a single workflow instance may spawn tasks where the user interface for each task is rendered in a different language based on the locale of the user.

Step 5: Configure the **Web Client Task** dialogs.

The **Start Workflow Wizard** uses the XML configuration to display the relevant controls to collect the data from the user. The **Manage Task** dialog uses the same approach to display the data it needs to collect.

Step 6: Test the workflow.

Custom workflow definitions may be tested using one of the following methods.

- Start the Alfresco Server and test via the Alfresco Web Client.
- Use the Workflow console to interactively step through workflows. You can access the workflow console as administrator using the URL. `http://<host>:<port>/alfresco/faces/jsp/admin/workflow-console.jsp`.

Display of Workflow Definition Diagrams

When developing a workflow definition with the Alfresco Workflow Designer it is possible to create a graphical view (diagram) of the workflow. Deploying the workflow definition directly from the designer into Alfresco will also deploy its diagram.

The diagram may be shown in the **Start Workflow and Manage Task** dialogs. This is achieved by changing the value of the `rendered` attribute to `true` as shown below:

```
<a:panel rendered="true" id="workflow-outline" ...
```

This line of code is available in the following files:

`/jsp/workflow/start-workflow-wizard/workflow-options.jsp`

`/jsp/workflow/manage-task-dialog.jsp`

Summary

Alfresco includes two types of workflows out of the box. One is the Simple Workflow, which is content oriented, and the other one is the Advanced Workflow, which is task oriented.

The simple workflow feature of Alfresco enables you to define a simple approve-reject workflow for your documents. The email templates and notification business rules are helpful to notify all the concerned people involved in the workflow process. You can also implement complex workflows by chaining spaces with multiple approve and reject steps.

The complex task-oriented workflow requirements can be handled by Advanced Workflow features. You can create a task, attach multiple documents, and send it to multiple people for review. Using the dashboard views, you can view all the tasks assigned to you and all the tasks you have assigned to others. You can track the tasks to closure using the web client user interface.

10

Collaboration and Syndication

The fundamental concept behind collaboration is that groups can achieve more than individuals. Collaboration allows individuals with complementary areas of expertise to create better results faster than before. This chapter introduces you to the features available in Alfresco to create a collaborative framework for your business application. Syndication allows you to share content with others. In this chapter you will learn various secure ways to share your content online using the syndication features.

By the end of this chapter you will have learned how to:

- Create and use organizational or departmental discussion forums for collaboration
- Set up interdepartmental collaboration using spaces
- Achieve collaboration on individual content items
- Provide outbound RSS syndication of content

Using Alfresco as a Collaborative Framework

You can use Alfresco to build a collaborative framework, where groups of people can collaborate; to create content within spaces, to review content items through discussions, and to discuss general topics and ideas.

Collaboration technologies enable individual users, such as employees or business partners, to easily create and maintain project teams, regardless of geographic location. These technologies facilitate collaborative, team-based content creation and decision-making. Using collaboration, you can achieve operational objectives like saving time, streamlining processes, cutting costs, and improving time to market.

Alfresco provides a special type of spaces called *Discussion forums* for collaboration. You can leverage the extensive security framework to provide access to these spaces to promote collaboration. You can also set up interdepartmental collaboration using spaces allowing multiple people to work on documents within a particular space.

Using the collaborative features, the author of a document can invite others to work on the document and participate in the general discussions about the document.

Discussion Forums for Collaboration

A discussion forum is a web-based facility for holding discussions. These forums are also commonly referred to as Internet forums, web forums, message boards, discussion boards, discussion groups, bulletin boards, or simply forums.

In Alfresco a *forum space* is special space that can contain other forum spaces or forums (discussion forums). A forum is essentially a space composed of a number of member-written topics. Each topic entails a discussion or conversation in the form of a series of member-written replies. These topics remain saved on the website for future reading indefinitely or until deletion by a moderator.

To summarize, you can have one or more *forum spaces* in Alfresco. Each forum space can have one or more *forums*. Each forum can have one or more *topics*. Each topic can have one or more *replies*. All the forums, topics, and replies are searchable.

You can create more than one forum. These forums are containers for topics started by the various user groups. Depending on the permissions of group members as defined by the administrator, they can post replies to existing topics, or start new topics as they wish. You can allow visitors to post anonymously, or you can secure the forum, so that only registered members can post the topics.

Forum Space

Forum space is a special type of space, which contains discussion forums. As an example, create a forum space in the engineering department space. To create the forum space, follow the steps given below:

1. Log in to the Alfresco web client and go to **Company Home | Intranet | Engineering Department** space.

2. Using the **Create** menu drop-down list, choose **Advanced Space Wizard** as shown in the following screenshot:

3. The **Create space wizard** window will pop up with multiple steps as shown in the following screenshot.

4. From the options, select the **From scratch** option and click on the **Next** button situated at the right-hand side of the screen.

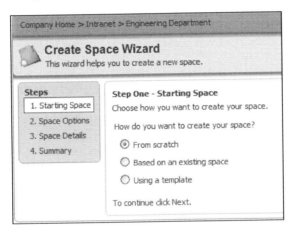

5. You will see a window with step 2 to select space options as shown in the next screenshot.

6. Choose **Forum Space** and click on the **Next** button to view step 3.

7. In step 3, provide a name for your forum (say `Engineering Discussions`) and click on the **Finish** button.

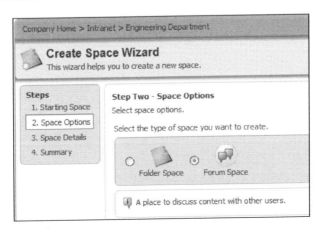

Create Discussion Forums in a Forum Space

You can create other forum spaces within a forum space or you can create discussion forums within a forum space.

Go to the forum space just created named **Engineering Discussions**. When you click on the **Create** drop-down menu at the top, you will notice the options for creating forum spaces or forums within a forum space as shown in the following screenshot:

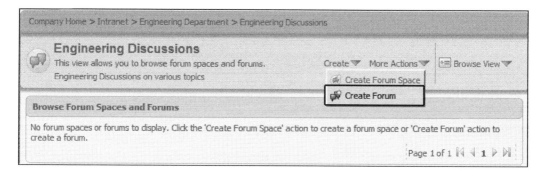

Click on the **Create Forum** action and create few forums as shown in the following screenshot:

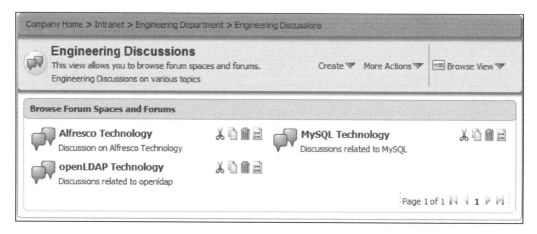

Create Topics in a Forum

You can create various topics within a discussion forum. Topics are a type of content item like a plain-text item.

Click on a forum (say **Alfresco Technology**) and click on the **Create Topic** button to create a topic as shown in the screenshot on the next page:

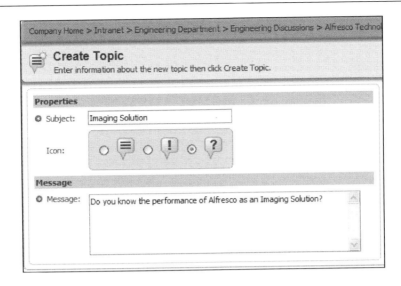

Replying to Topics

Users who have access to this topic can reply with messages as shown in the next screenshot. Users can reply to the replies. There is no limitation on the number of replies.

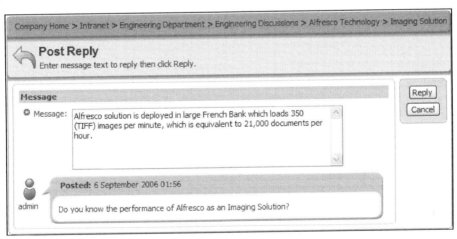

You can create as many topics as you like in a discussion forum. As an administrator you can edit or delete a particular topic or a post (reply). The **Details View** of a discussion forum lists all the available topics and the replies as shown in the screenshot overleaf:

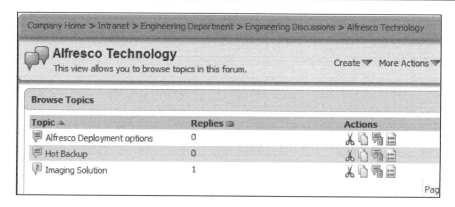

Departmental Forums and Security

Forums and topics are types of spaces and they are governed by the same permissions as all spaces. Users may be invited to forums and topics with certain roles.

The following table explains the roles and permissions with the forums:

Role	Permission
Consumer	Copy/View Details (of forum and its topics)
Editor	Consumer permissions plus may edit posts (within topic) Edit details of forum and topics
Contributor	Consumer permissions plus may create topic with forum post to topic/post reply within a topic
Coordinator	Consumer permissions plus may create topic View/edit details of forum and topics Manage space users of forum and topics Post to topic & cut/delete topic Post reply/edit post

The following table explains the roles and permissions with topics:

Role	Permission
Consumer	Copy/View
Editor	Consumer permissions plus may edit post Edit details of topics
Contributor	Consumer permissions plus may post to topic/post reply within a topic
Coordinator	Consumer permissions plus may post to topic Post reply Edit a post Delete a post

When the option **Inherit parent space permissions** is disabled, no user can view the discussions unless explicitly invited. Even Coordinators of the forum cannot see the topic. Those invited have the access rights as above corresponding to their role.

Define Forums for Groups within a Department

By setting the appropriate security, each group within a department can have a discussion forum. Similarly, each project can have a separate discussion forum specific to that project. In Chapter 5, you have created a project (called *ProjectA*) in Engineering Department space, based on the *Software Engineering* project space template.

As a sample exercise, go to **Company Home | Intranet | Engineering Department | ProjectA** space, delete the **Discussions** space and create **Discussions** as a forum space. Create a few project-specific discussion forums and topics. Invite various users to participate in discussions by giving them the **Contributor** role on the discussion forum. Test this by logging in as various users and by participating in discussions.

Interdepartment Collaboration Using Spaces

If you are in charge of a department, then it is very important for you to secure your content. At the same time, you might want to allow certain people to collaborate with your group members in certain spaces.

You can use the existing security framework to allow groups and individuals to access certain spaces and collaborate on content.

Manage Space Users

As an owner of a space, you can invite other users to your space to view, add, or edit content. On any space the **More Actions | Manage Space Users** link shows a list of users that have permission to work on content in that space. You can click on the **Invite** link to invite individual users or groups and assign them appropriate permissions. More details about securing a space are provided in Chapter 4.

The screenshot on the next page lists the users and groups who have access to the **Intranet | Company Policies** space. All the users who belong to the **HR** group and the individual user **Tom FinExec** have read, write, and delete access (coordinator role) on all the content present in **Company Policies** space. Every body else has only read access to the space.

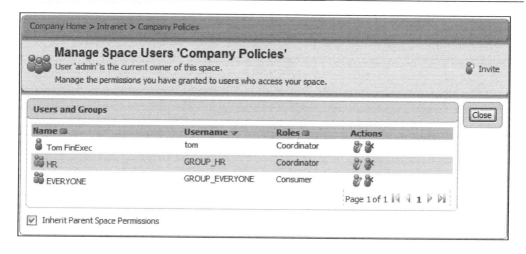

Space Collaboration Using Emails

All users who have access to a space can communicate using emails. In order to send email to the users in a space, click on the **More Actions | View Details** link and click on the **Email Space Users** action as shown in the screenshot below:

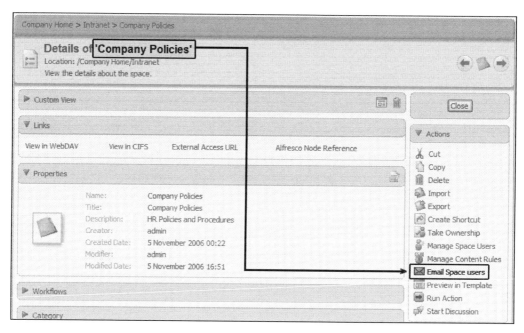

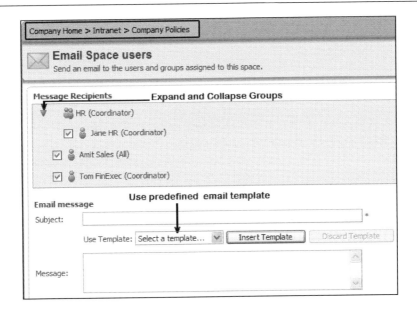

The **Email Space users** pane appears as shown in the above screenshot. Groups and individual users who have access to this space will be listed as email **Message Recipients**.

You can email to the entire group (HR group in this example) by selecting the check box. You can also send email to only certain users in the group by expanding the group icon and by selecting individual users as shown in the above screenshot.

Start a Discussion on a Specific Space

You can start a discussion on a specific space directly by clicking on the **Start Discussion** action provided in the actions menu as shown in the screenshot below:

Once the discussion is started, you will see a discussion forum icon as shown in the screenshot below to view the discussions on the space:

Content Collaboration

Similar to collaboration on a specific space, you can collaborate on individual content items as well.

Start a Discussion on Individual Content

You can start a discussion on a specific document directly by clicking on the **Start Discussion** action provided in the actions menu as shown in the screenshot below:

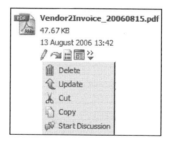

 It is always good practice to start discussion on a document in the workflow process. It enables various people to make and review comments, and capture all the review data as the document goes through various approval steps.

Owner Invites Individuals to Collaborate on Content

As the owner of some content, you can give the **Editor** role to another individual to edit the content. In the content's **View Details** screen, the **Manage content users** action shows a list of users that have permission to work on that content.

The process is similar to that for space collaboration. However, the invited users should have proper roles on the content and the parent space.

RSS Syndication

Often, Alfresco sites present complex user interfaces, but do not provide that same information in a format that a computer can parse and understand. As a sample exercise, go to **Company Home | Intranet | Press and Media** space, create a space called **News** and create a couple of text documents as shown in the next screenshot:

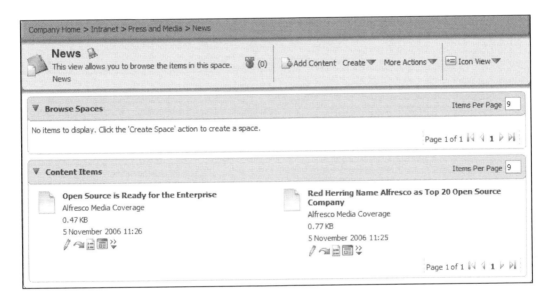

Consider an icon view of the **News** space as shown in the above screenshot. The user can see the title, size, and creation date on the screen, but a computer must translate the intent of the designer. For example, the HTML `<B> Red Herring Name Alfresco as Top 20 Open Source Company </B>` contains an important piece of data about the content, but there is no way for another system to know this. This information is not conveyed in the structure of the data (which is HTML) but instead in the words presented.

Getting a computer to screen-scrape an HTML page for important data is one of the hardest things to do well, and you can never do it perfectly. To make it worse, as soon as you've managed it, the designer is sure to change the layout of his or her HTML. To solve this problem, web engineers have come up with a standard way for communicating information about web resources using a standard XML format that can be easily parsed by any framework. This protocol is **Really Simple Syndication (RSS)**.

Developers generally use RSS to describe a web resource. For example, if you have a document available on the web, you can use RSS to describe that document to another system that can access it.

Web publishers can make their content available through syndication by using RSS to produce what are known as 'feeds' (blog feeds or news feeds). These feeds can either show headlines only, headlines and summary, or full content. As the mainstream media attempt to realize the full potential of RSS, the news media are utilizing RSS by bypassing traditional news sources. By using RSS feeds, consumers and journalists are now able to have news constantly fed to them instead of searching for it. Many browsers have integrated support for RSS feeds as well.

Enabling RSS Syndication

In order to share the information in a space with external systems as RSS feeds, you need to enable **RSS Feed** on that space.

To enable RSS feed on **News** space, go to the details page of the **News** space and click on the enable RSS syndication icon as shown in the following screenshot:

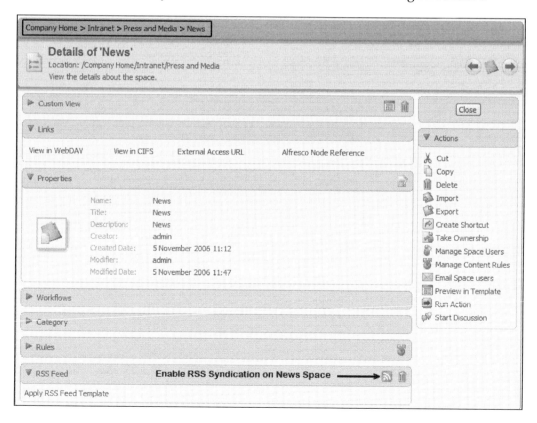

A new window pops up as shown in the screenshot below enabling you to select the RSS template to be applied to the space as an RSS feed. RSS templates are custom scripts that determine the content to be shown as feeds. Alfresco ships with a built-in standard RSS template called **RSS_2.0_recent_docs.ftl,** which renders a valid RSS 2.0 XML document showing the documents in the current space created or modified in the last 7 days. More information is provided in the *RSS Templates* section in this chapter.

Choose the default RSS template from the drop-down menu (shown in the next screenshot) and select the **OK** button.

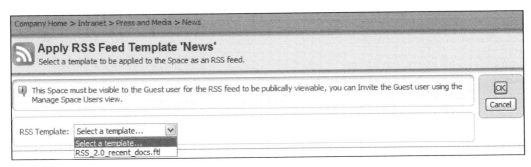

Once RSS feed is enabled on a space, you will notice the link to RSS feeds as shown in the figure below. You can remove the RSS feeds by clicking on the **Remove** icon or you can modify the RSS template by clicking on the **Modify** icon as shown in the following screenshot:

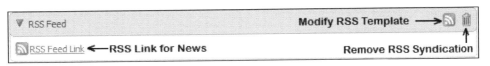

In order for anonymous users to view the news feeds, they must have read permission on the news space. This means the *Guest* (anonymous) user must have the *Consumer* role (READ access) on this space for the RSS feed to be publicly viewable.

This can be achieved using the **Manage Space Users** dialog and inviting the *Guest* user into the **News** space as shown in the screenshot overleaf:

 It is very important to ensure that the guest user has the consumer role on the space to view RSS feeds of that space.

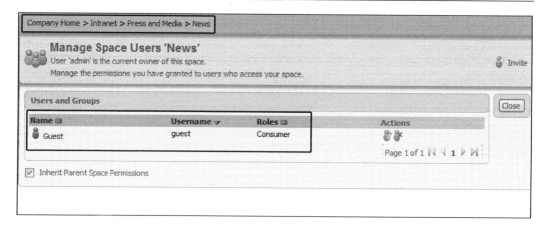

Using RSS Feeds

Let us test the RSS syndication features on the **News** space. Once RSS feeds are enabled on a space, the **RSS Feed Link** icon will be listed as shown in the following screenshot:

By clicking on the **RSS Feed Link**, you can view the RSS feeds of the **News** space in a web browser as shown in the screenshot on the next page:

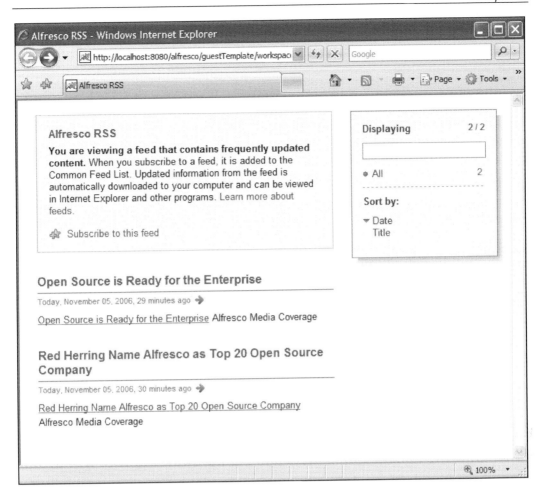

You can view the RSS feeds of the **News** space in any RSS feeds-enabled web browser or RSS browser.

Anyone who is interested to know about the latest Alfresco news can subscribe to this feed to get regular updates.

The recent version 7.0 of Microsoft Internet Explorer has a built-in RSS feeds viewer. You can receive content automatically by subscribing to a web feed. When you subscribe to a web feed, you set the interval at which Internet Explorer will check the website for updates. Once you've set an interval, Internet Explorer will automatically download the most up-to-date web feed list. You view feeds on the feeds tab in the favorites center. To view your feeds, click on the **Favorites Center** button, and then click on the **Feeds** link. This allows you to subscribe to feeds with Internet Explorer and read them in other programs, such as email clients.

RSS Templates

The news information that is displayed as an RSS feed is controlled by the RSS template used. RSS templates are custom scripts written in Freemarker template language. All the RSS templates in Alfresco are located in the **Company Home | Data Dictionary | RSS Templates** space as shown in the screenshot below:

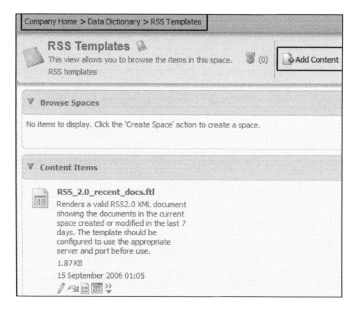

You can either customize the existing template by editing it or add a new RSS template by clicking on the **Add Content** link provided as shown in the above screenshot.

Summary

Alfresco framework is best suited for collaboration. You can define collaboration at organization level or at department level or at a smaller group level. You can also define individuals on a space (on an ad-hoc basis) and allow them to collaborate on content. You can share space as well as content for collaboration. You can leverage the discussion forums to discuss on any topic as per your business requirements. You can use built-in email features to communicate with all the parties involved with a space or content.

It is advisable to start discussion on a document in the workflow process. It helps people to review the content and make comments, also to save the review data during the approval steps.

You can share your content with external systems or users using the outbound RSS syndication features of Alfresco.

11
Customizing the User Interface

The web-client user interface is designed to handle most of the common user interaction scenarios. However, each business application will have some specific user interface requirements. You can configure certain user-interface elements in the web client, such as space icons, menu options, and the custom look and feel of a space. Of course, you can change the entire look and feel of the application using Java programming.

For each user of the system, you can provide a personalized dashboard view. In this chapter, you will examine various options to customize the user interface including custom dashlets (dashboard components). You will experience the power of FreeMarker templating language in consolidating content information and presenting it to the end users.

By the end of this chapter, you will have learned how to:

- Configure space portal views
- Add custom icons to spaces
- Extend the action menu items
- Configure personal dashboard wizard
- Write custom dashlets
- Write dashboard components
- Write custom templates to preview content

Configuring the Web Client

You can configure the look and feel of the web client by simply editing the XML configuration file without programming. You can change the way the web client looks and operates, you can change the navigation elements, and you can modify the space views as per your organizational or departmental requirements.

Configuring Space Views

Every space can be viewed in the following four different ways as follows:

- Details view provides detailed information about documents as rows.
- Icon view provides an icon, description, and the modification time properties of the documents.
- Browse view provides information about sub-spaces.
- Custom view provides the custom view selected by the user for that space.

For Windows users, this is similar to having various view options on folders in Windows Explorer. The **Details View**, **Icon View**, and **Browse view** are provided out of the box. **Custom View** is a customized view of that space, which is selected by the user.

The default view for a space is the **Icon View**. You can choose a specific view (say the **Details View**) by selecting from the drop-down list as highlighted in the screenshot below. However, the selection is going to be saved only for that session and the next time you log in to the Alfresco web client, you will see the default view on the space. You can configure the default view for spaces, and you can also specify the number of items to be displayed in a page.

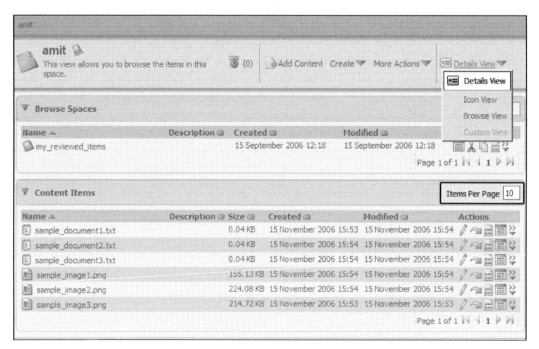

You can find the details about the default configuration in the `web-client-config.xml` file located in your configuration folder. To customize the default view, you need to update the `web-client-config.xml` file in the `extensions` folder. Go to the `extensions` folder (for Tomcat installation it is in the following folder: `<alfresco_install_folder>\tomcat\shared\classes\alfresco\extension`. Here you will have to edit the `web-client-config-custom.xml` file and add the following XML block. If you want to display the details of all documents in your space (as shown in the screenshot on the previous page), then you can choose **Veiw Details** as default. If you want to see more documents in a page, you can increase the number of documents displayed per page from 10 to 25.

```
<config evaluator="string-compare" condition="Views">
      <!-- the views available in the client -->
  <views>
      <!-- default values for the views available in the client -->
    <view-defaults>
      <browse>
      <!-- allowable values: list|details|icons -->
       <view>details</view>
       <page-size>
       <list>10</list>
       <details>25</details>
       <icons>9</icons>
       </page-size>
      </browse>
    </view-defaults>
  </views>
</config>
```

> Whenever you make changes to the `web-client-config-custom.xml` file you always have to restart Alfresco.

Applying a Custom View on a Space

The **Custom View** is a portal window, which appears at the top of each space, when a **Custom View** option is selected. This is useful to represent the content in a space in a specific manner such as showing the recent documents, and the summary of documents. For example, you can apply a custom view on the **Finance Department | Checks** space to display the list of checks received in the past week.

This enables you to have an alternative view of spaces using templates. Other examples include:

- Show the space and its sub-spaces (collapse the tree)
- Traverse the entire repository displaying content whose date is effective
- Show file names of all images, their thumbnails, and HTML links to the actual images
- Display summaries of information within a space such as the total number of documents, number of documents under review, number of documents belong to a category, and number of documents published or approved.

Let us say you would like to see all the documents in your home space that were either created or modified in the past one week. Follow the steps given below to apply a custom view on your home space.

1. Go to the space on which you would like to apply the custom view. For example, go to your home space by clicking on the **My Home** menu link in the tool bar.

2. Using the **More Actions | View details** menu option, go to the details page.

3. Click on the **Add Custom View** icon as shown in the following screenshot to select a custom view. The **Remove Custom View** icon (also shown in the following screenshot) is useful to remove an existing custom view on a space.

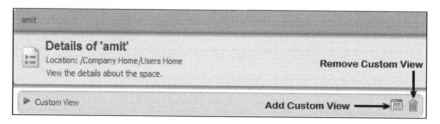

4. Clicking on the **Add Custom View** icon will open an **Apply Template** window as shown in the screenshot on the next page. You can select a template to be applied on the space as a **Custom View**. There are already some built-in templates provided for you for most generic use cases. You can also apply your own custom templates to this space. The process of adding a custom template is explained later in this chapter.

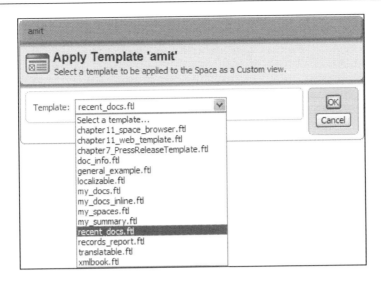

5. From the list of presentation templates, select the **recent_docs.ftl** template, which displays the list of documents in the current space that were either created or updated in the past week.

6. Once you have selected the presentation template, click on the **OK** button and close the **View Details** page. You will notice that the presentation template you have chosen is applied to the space as **Custom View** (refer to the screenshot below):

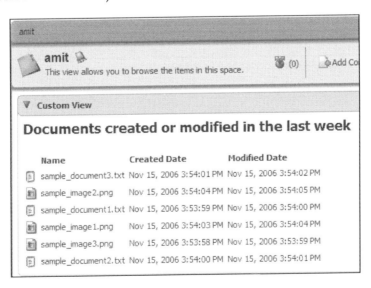

Configuring Forum Topics Sort Direction

By default, the topic view in the forums functionality lists the posts in descending order i.e. the last post is at the top of the list. If you wish to change this, add the following XML text to the `web-client-config-custom.xml` file. Also, you can define the number of posts listed per page.

```
<topic>
        <!-- allowable values: details|bubble -->
    <view>bubble</view>
    <sort-column>created</sort-column>
        <!-- allowable values: ascending|descending -->
    <sort-direction>ascending</sort-direction>
    <page-size>
      <bubble>5</bubble>
      <details>20</details>
    </page-size>
</topic>
```

Adding a Custom Icon to a Space

To add another space icon to the list to choose from when creating a space add the following to the `web-client-config-custom.xml` file.

```
    <!-- Example of adding a custom icon to the Create Space dialog -->
    <config evaluator="string-compare" condition="cm:folder icons">
      <icons>
        <icon name="space-icon-custom" path="/images/icons/
                                        space-icon-custom1.gif" />
      </icons>
    </config>
```

A similar approach can be used to add icons for the forums space types (`fm:forums`, `fm:forum`, and `fm:topic`).

Once you have added the custom icon names in the `web-client-config-custom.xml` file, you need to make sure the icons with the same file name are copied to the file system icons folder. For a Tomcat installation the icons folder is at `<install_folder>\tomcat\webapps\alfresco\images\icons`. Also, for uniformity, ensure that all the icons are of 32 x 32 pixels size.

As per the example, create a `.gif` file icon named `space-icon-custom1.gif` (32 x 32 pixels size) and copy it to the icons folder. Once you restart Alfresco, you will see the new icon while creating a space, as shown in the screenshot on the next page:

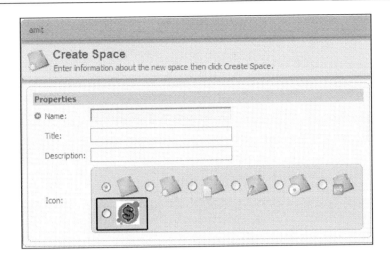

Configuring HTML Links to Appear in the Web Client

You can control certain HTML links that appear in the web client. For example, there is a small help icon in the top menu, by clicking on which, you can navigate to Alfresco's website. You can update the following lines in the web client configuration file to point the help icon to your internal *online help guide* (if you have one). The URL to the client Help file is:

```
<help-url>http://www.alfresco.org/help/webclient</help-url>
```

Adding Custom Menu Items

You can add your own menu items. For example, to launch a fictional *addAspect* dialog from the **More Actions** menu associated with each document, add the following to the `web-client-config-custom.xml` file.

```
<config>
  <actions>
        <!-- Launch Add Aspect Dialog -->
    <action id="add_aspect">
      <label>Add Aspect</label>
      <image>/images/icons/add.gif</image>
      <action>dialog:addAspect</action>
    </action>
        <!-- Add action to more actions menu for each document -->
    <action-group id="document_browse_menu">
      <action idref="add_aspect" />
```

```
        </action-group>
      </actions>
   </config>
```

Each document will now have an **Add Aspect** menu item as shown in the screenshot below:

User Configurable Dashboards

In the web client user interface, the **My Alfresco** area is known as the Dashboard. It can be configured by the user, and they can construct their own page from a list of pre-configured components. As a developer, you can configure new components and make them available for selection by users when they are configuring their pages.

Choosing My Alfresco Dashboard as Start Location

The start location is the first page that will be displayed immediately after you log in to the web client. You can choose your start location using the user options icon as shown in the screenshot on the next page. Once you log in to the web client, the first page you will see is the page that you have chosen as start location.

To select the My Alfresco dashboard as your starting page, click on the user options icon in the top menu and select **My Alfresco** as your start location. Next time, when you log in, the My Alfresco dashboard will be displayed as your personal home page. You can also view this dashboard page by clicking on the **My Alfresco** menu item at the top.

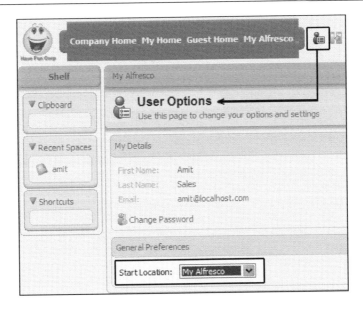

Configuring Your Personal Dashboard Using the Wizard

If you click on the **My Alfresco** link provided in the tool bar menu, you will see a default dashboard, which contains useful information for the beginners. Using the dashboard wizard, you can configure the dashboard layout and dashboard components (also known as dashlets). The dashboard configuration is very specific to your personal requirements. The dashboard configuration settings you choose will be stored in the database. Every time you log in to the Alfresco web client, you will see your personal dashboard as the home page.

To start configuring your dashboard, click on the **Configure** icon given in **My Alfresco Dashboard** as shown in the screenshot below. The **Configure Dashboard Wizard** will open up (as shown in the screenshot on the next page) allowing you to select the dashboard layout and dashlets.

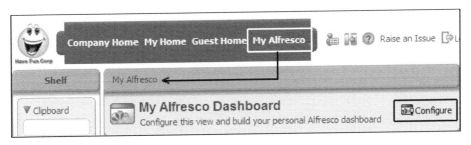

Step One — Select Layout

The first step is to choose the layout and number of columns for your dashboard view. There are four styles given to display your dashlets. The options are pictorially represented in the screenshot below:

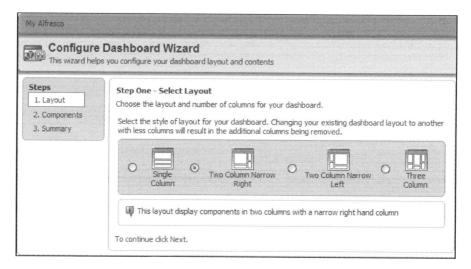

Select the style of layout for your dashboard. Changing your existing dashboard layout to another with less columns will result in the additional columns being removed.

As an example, select the **Two Column Narrow Right** option, to display your dashboard components in two columns with a narrow right-hand column. Click on the **Next** button to move to the next step of selecting dashboard components.

Step Two — Select Components

Based on the number of columns you selected in the previous step, you need to add components to each column as shown in the screenshot on the next page. Notice the list of available dashboard components. These dashboard components are also called dashlets as they display certain information in small windows similar to portal's portlets. Also, you can sequence the dashlet using + and - buttons given.

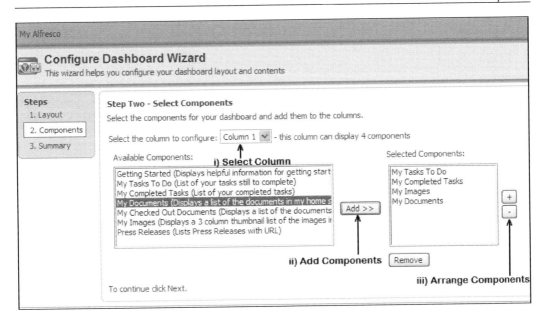

Select the following components for Column 1:

- My Tasks To Do: Lists all the tasks assigned to you and are pending
- My Completed Tasks: Lists all the tasks completed by you
- My Images: Lists the images in your home space
- My Documents: Lists the documents in your home space

Select the following component for Column 2:

- My Checked Out Documents: Lists all the documents checked out and locked by you

Click on the **Next** or **Finish** button to save your selection. The selection is effective immediately as you can see the dashboard with your selections as shown in the screenshot on the next page:

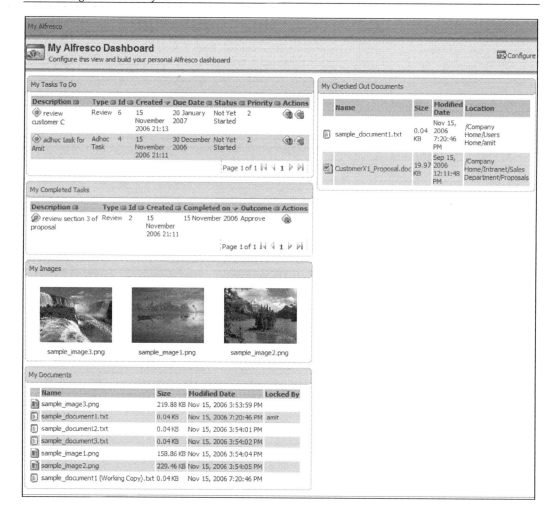

Writing Custom Dashlets

There are certain dashlets provided to you out of the box. Since the dashboard is going to be a place where you can see all the dynamic information, you might consider having custom dashlets to provide you with important information. For example, you might want to see the list of contracts approved in the last seven days. You might want to see the latest press releases.

Usually custom dashlets are written in a scripting language such as FreeMarker and called from a JSP (Java Server Page). The JSP can be configured in the web client so that the custom dashlet is visible for you to select in the dashboard.

The following steps are required to write and configure a custom dashlet:

1. Create a custom dashlet script.

2. Create a custom dashlet JSP (which internally uses the dashlet script).

3. Configure the custom dashlet JSP in the web client.

4. Restart Alfresco.

5. Use the custom dashlet in the My Alfresco dashboard.

Create a Custom Dashlet Script

As an example, write a custom dashlet script using FreeMarker template language to display the latest press releases from the **Company Home | Intranet | Press and Media | Press Releases** space.

The dashlet script could be plain HTML text, FreeMarker template, JavaScript, or a JSP page. For this example, let us use a FreeMarker template.

Using the following code, create a file with name `chapter11_press_releases.ftl` in your Alfresco configuration's templates folder. For a Tomcat installation the folder is `<install_folder>\tomcat\webapps\alfresco\WEB-INF\classes\alfresco\templates`.

```
<#------------------------------------------------------------------>
<#-- Name: chapter11_press_releases.ftl                        -->
<#--Displays a table of all the documents from a "Press Releases"-->
<#-- folder under Company Home/Intranet/Press and Media space   -->
<#-- NOTE: Obviously this folder needs to exist and            -->
<#--       the docs in it should have the title and content     -->
<#------------------------------------------------------------------>
<table>
  <#assign l_space = companyhome.childByNamePath["Intranet/Press and
                                      Media/Press Releases"]>
    <#list l_space.children as doc>
      <#if doc.isDocument>
      <tr>
        <td>
          <a class="title"href="/alfresco/${doc.url}">$
                                  {doc.properties.title}</a></td>
      </tr>
      <tr>
        <td style="padding-left:8px">
          <#if (doc.content?length > 500)>
            <small>${doc.content[0..500]}...</small>
```

```
        <#else>
          <small>${doc.content}</small>
         </#if>
       </td>
     </tr>
     <tr><td> <HR> </td></tr>
     </#if>
   </#list>
 </table>
```

Create a Custom Dashlet JSP

Once the custom dashlet script is created in the templates folder, the next step is to create a custom dashlet JSP, which uses the custom dashlet script.

Create a `chapter11_press_releases.jsp` file with the following code and place the file in the dashlets folder. For a Tomcat installation the folder is `<install_folder>\tomcat\webapps\alfresco\jsp\dashboards\dashlets`.

```
<%--
Name    : chapter11_press_releases.jsp
Purpose: Dashlet to display the latest press releases
--%>
<%@ taglib uri="/WEB-INF/repo.tld" prefix="r" %>
<%-- Note that this template is loaded from the classpath --%>
<r:template template="/alfresco/templates/chapter11_press_releases.
ftl" />
```

Configure the Custom Dashlet JSP in the Web Client

Now you need to configure the web client with the custom dashlet to make it visible in the dashboard wizard.

Add the following code in the `web-client-config-custom.xml` file before the last XML tag `</alfresco-config>`

```
<config evaluator="string-compare" condition="Dashboards">
<!-- Dashboard layouts and available dashlets for the My Alfresco
                                                      Pages -->
  <dashboards>
    <dashlets>
<!-- Add additional dashlet for press releases -->
      <dashlet id="press-releases" label="Press Releases"
                    description="Lists Press Releases with URL"
          jsp="/jsp/dashboards/dashlets/chapter11_press_releases.jsp"
```

```
                                                    allow-narrow="true" />
        </dashlets>
      </dashboards>
    </config>
```

The following table describes each dashlet element used in the XML configuration:

Dashlet element	Description
id	An ID string to uniquely identify the dashlet.
jsp	The JSP page to be used for the dashlet implementation.
label OR label-id	The label text or label i18n message ID for the dashlet. This label is shown in the list of available components presented to the user in the Dashboard Configuration Wizard.
description OR description-id	The description text or description i18n message ID for the layout. This description text is shown in the list of available components presented to the user in the Dashboard Configuration Wizard.

Restart Alfresco

To make the configuration changes effective, you need to restart Alfresco. The newly created custom dashlet example requires one or two press releases to be available in the **Company Home | Intranet | Press and Media | Press Releases** space. In Chapter 7, you created a few press releases in the **Company Home | Intranet | Press and Media | Press Releases** space.

Make sure you have at least two press releases created in the *Press Releases* space. Refer to the *Create a Press Release as HTML Content* section in Chapter 7.

Use the Custom Dashlet in the My Alfresco Dashboard

Click on the **My Alfresco** link provided in the tool bar menu to view the Dashboard. Click on the **Configure** icon given in the **My Alfresco Dashboard** and the **Configure Dashboard Wizard** will display the custom dashlet in the **Step Two – Select Components** screen as shown in the screenshot on the next page:

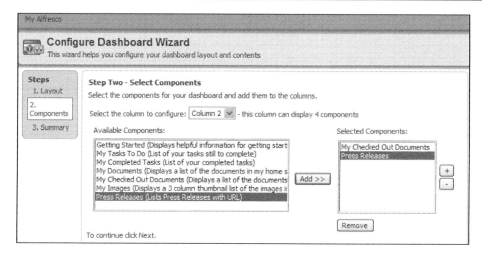

Select the **Press Releases** dashlet for **Column 2** as shown in the above screenshot. Once you finish the configuration, you will notice the custom dashlet in your dashboard as shown in the screenshot below:

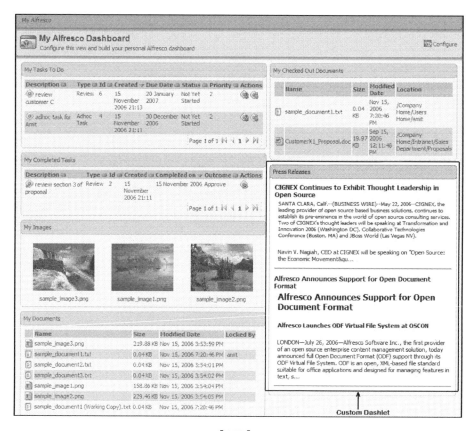

A FreeMarker Dashlet from the Repository

Dashlet components can contain any selection of JSF components, including the template component. This means it is possible to use the results of a FreeMarker template as the dashlet contents. In the previous example, you have used a FreeMarker template from the file system.

However you can also use a FreeMarker template from your web client's **Company Home | Data Dictionary | Presentation Templates** Space.

To display a template stored in the repository, copy the NodeRef of the template file and create the page by pasting your NodeRef value into the template attribute in the previous example:

```
<%@ taglib uri="/WEB-INF/repo.tld" prefix="r" %>
<r:template template="workspace://SpacesStore/
                        e4d1c727-e98b-11da-821a-936824f635fe" />
```

Presentation Templates

The space **Company Home | Data Dictionary | Presentation Templates** contains both built-in and custom presentation templates. Presentation templates can be used to preview the content and to provide look and feel for the content. An example of a presentation template is provided in Chapter 7, where a custom template is used to preview the press release content. Presentation templates are written in *FreeMarker template language* and will have the .ftl extension.

FreeMarker is an open-source template engine; a generic tool to generate text output (anything from HTML to auto-generated source code) based on templates. FreeMarker is designed to be practical for the generation of HTML web pages following the MVC (Model View Controller) pattern. The idea behind using the MVC pattern for dynamic web pages is that you separate the content authors from the programmers. This separation is useful even for projects where the programmer and the HMTL page author are the same person, since it helps to keep the application clear and easily maintainable.

In the figure on the next page, the content authors create document content in Alfresco. The programmers create the presentation template file with style sheets and HTML code, taking care of the look-and-feel requirements. The final content will be generated by the FreeMarker engine (which is embedded in Alfresco) by applying the presentation template on the document content as shown in the figure on the next page.

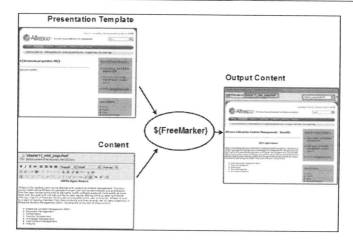

The FreeMarker Template Engine within Alfresco

The FreeMarker template engine is embedded within Alfresco. FreeMarker takes the Alfresco data model as input and generates text (HTML or XML) as output. FreeMarker also supports XSLT to translate XML content.

Alfresco Objects Available to FreeMarker

The default model provides a set of named objects that wrap Alfresco Node objects to provide a rich, object-oriented layer, suitable for scripting usage. If you are accessing the templates through the web-client UI, then the following named objects are provided by default.

Named object	Description
companyhome	The Company Home template node
userhome	Current user's Home Space template node
person	Node representing the current user's Person object
space	The current space template node (if you are accessing the templates through the Space Preview action)
document	The current document template node (if you are accessing the templates through the Document Preview action)
template	The node representing the template itself
args	A map of any URL parameters passed via the Template Content Servlet (only available if the template was executed via the servlet)
session	Session-related information (`session.ticket` for the authentication ticket)
classification	Read access to classifications and root categories

For example consider the following FreeMarker template:

```
<html>
<head>
<title>Welcome!</title>
</head>
<body>
<h1>Welcome ${person.properties.userName}!</h1>
</body>
</html>
```

At run time, the value of the variable `person.properties.userName` will be the name of the current user, who is accessing the system. Hence the template generates a dynamic greeting message.

 Alfresco Wiki website (`http://wiki.alfresco.com`) contains a complete reference guide to the FreeMarker template engine.

FreeMarker Template-Node Model API

These objects, and any child-node objects are called template-node objects, and they provide the following API:

Node method	Description
properties	A map of the properties of the node. For example userhome, properties, name. Properties may return several different types of object — this depends entirely on the underlying property type in the repository. If the property is multi-valued then the result will be a sequence, which can be indexed like any other sequence or array.
children	A sequence (list) of the child nodes. For example, a list of documents in a space.
url	The URL to the content stream for this node.
content	Returns the content of the node as a string.
size	The size in bytes of the content attached to this node.
isLocked	True if the node is locked, false otherwise.
name	Shortcut access to the name property.
parent	The parent node; can be null if this is the root node.

Node method	Description
childrenByXPath	Returns a map capable of executing an XPath query to find child nodes e.g. `companyhome.childrenByXPath["*[@cm: name='Data Dictionary']/*"]`.
childByNamePath	Returns a map capable of returning a single child node found by name path e.g. `companyhome.childByNamePath["Data Dictionary/Content Templates"]`.

FreeMarker Directives

Like any programming language, FreeMarker templating language also supports fundamental directives such as the following:

```
#if, #else, #elseif
#switch, #case
#list
#assign
#function
#include
<#-- comment -->
```

 For your reference, a complete guide is available at:
`http://FreeMarker.sourceforge.net/docs/`

Custom Template to Preview Web Pages

Let us develop a custom template to preview HTML documents.

Log in as *admin*, go to the **Company Home | Data Dictionary | Presentation Templates** space, and create a new template and name it appropriately (say *chapter11_web_template.ftl*). The template should display web-page layout as shown in the screenshot on the next page. The template can be applied on any text or HTML document in the Alfresco repository to generate a web page with layout as given in the screenshot on the next page:

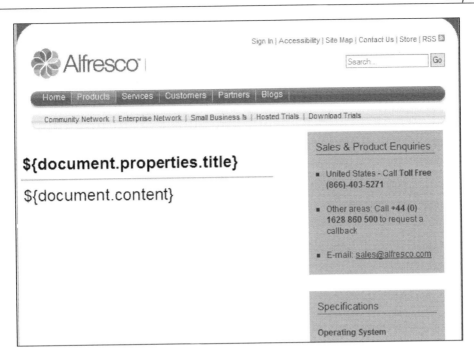

You can consider using the following code to create the custom template. The code uses images in the Alfresco repository to display the horizontal bar on the top and the vertical bar on the right side. Note that the image URLs may change in the code, based on the location of the actual images in your repository. You can use your own images or you can even create the HTML header and table structure as per your application.

The template extracts the document title and displays it as the page heading. Refer to the FreeMarker template code `${document.properties.title}`. Similarly, the template extracts the document content and displays it in the center portion of the page as shown in the above screenshot. Refer FreeMarker template code `${document.content}`.

```
<#------------------------------------------------------------------->
<#-- Extracts Title and Description from Content and            -->
<#--                  shows in web template                     -->
<#------------------------------------------------------------------->
<table width="100%" border="0" cellspacing="0" cellpadding="0">
  <tr>
    <td colspan="2" valign="top">
      <img src=
"http://localhost:8080/alfresco/download/direct/workspace/SpacesStore
                        /bfcc8130-4537-11db-972a953696db55bc/
                        chapter11_template_top_image.png" />
```

```
      </td>
    </tr>
    <tr>
      <td valign="top">
        <BR>
        <H4> ${document.properties.title} </H4>
        <HR>
        ${document.content}
      </td>
      <td valign="top">
        <img src=
            "http://localhost:8080/alfresco/download/direct/workspace/
                  SpacesStore/c87378c9-4537-11db-972a-953696db55bc/
                        chapter11_template_right_image.png" />
      </td>
    </tr>
  </table>
```

Create a new HTML document in one of the spaces in your Alfresco web client. Use the **Preview in Template** action button on the document and choose the custom template (in this example it is *chapter11_web_template.ftl*) to display the document content. The sample preview screen is shown in the screenshot on the next page:

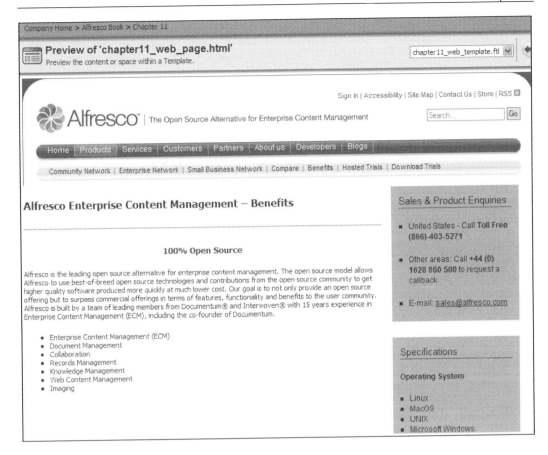

Custom Template for XML Content

The FreeMarker templating engine can be used for XSLT (XML transformations) to transform XML content to HTML with look-and-feel details.

This is a classic solution: to store the data in Alfresco's repository in native XML format and use FreeMarker custom templates to display the XML data in HTML format.

To test the XML transformation features, firstly you need to create an XML document in Alfresco. You can either create this as an XML file (say `book.xml`) on your desktop and upload it to the Alfresco web client or you can directly create this XML document in Alfresco. Create a document called `book.xml` in one of your spaces with the following content.

```
<?xml version="1.0" standalone="yes"?>
<book title="Book Title">
  <chapter>
    <title>Chapter 1</title>
```

```
      <para>p1.1</para>
      <para>p1.2</para>
      <para>p1.3</para>
    </chapter>
    <chapter>
      <title>Chapter 2</title>
      <para>p2.1</para>
      <para>p2.2</para>
    </chapter>
  </book>
```

Create a template in the **Company Home | Data Dictionary | Presentation Templates** space called xmlbook.ftl with the following code.

```
<#if document.mimetype = "text/xml">
  <#assign dom=document.xmlNodeModel>
    <h1>${dom.book.@title}</h1>
  <#list dom.book.chapter as c>
    <h2>${c.title}</2>
    <#list c.para as p>
    <p> ${p} </p>
    </#list>
  </#list>
</#if>
```

The template displays the title of the book and chapters using the HTML tags. When you apply the xmlbook.ftl template on the book.xml document, you will observe the output as shown in the screenshot below:

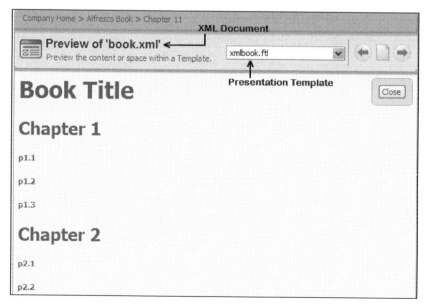

Custom Template for Space Custom View

A custom space view is a portal window, which appears at the top of each space when a **custom view** is selected. If you are implementing Alfresco for various departments and groups, you might consider having custom home pages for each department or group space.

As an example, let us build a custom view for all the department spaces. Let us say each department space contains two files `home_image.png` and `home_page.html`. Let us apply a presentation template as a custom view on the department space, which displays these two local files in that department as the department home page.

Create a template in the **Company Home | Data Dictionary | Presentation Templates** space called `chapter11_dept_home_template.ftl` with the following code:

```
<#---------------------------------------------------------------->
<#--      Displays Home Page for each department using     -->
<#-- (1) Home Page Image file home_image.png and                -->
<#-- (2) Home Page HTML file home_page.html                     -->
<#-- By Munwar Shariff, Nov 16, 2006                          -->
<#---------------------------------------------------------------->
<H4> Welcome to ${space.properties.title} </H4>
<#list space.children as child>
  <#if child.properties.name = 'home_image.png'>
    <img src="/alfresco${child.url}">
  </#if>
</#list>
  <#list space.children as child>
    <#if child.properties.name = 'home_page.html'>
      ${child.content}
    </#if>
  </#list>
```

Now create a sample space (say *Department A*) and within that space create two content files with the names `home_image.png` (department image) and `home_page.html` (department description). Now select the **chapter11_dept_home_template.ftl** template as custom view for your space (*Department A* space).

The steps to apply a presentation template as a **Custom View** are already explained in the *Applying a Custom View on a Space* section of this chapter. You will see the custom view of your space as shown in the screenshot on the next page.

This can be applied to each and every department and group within your organization. Consider having the department space as a space template, so that you could reuse the department space template to create spaces for many departments. More information about space templates is provided in Chapter 5.

Department members can update the image file and the HTML file as required to alter the home page information dynamically. Similarly, you can think of various presentation templates to display the information in a specific space.

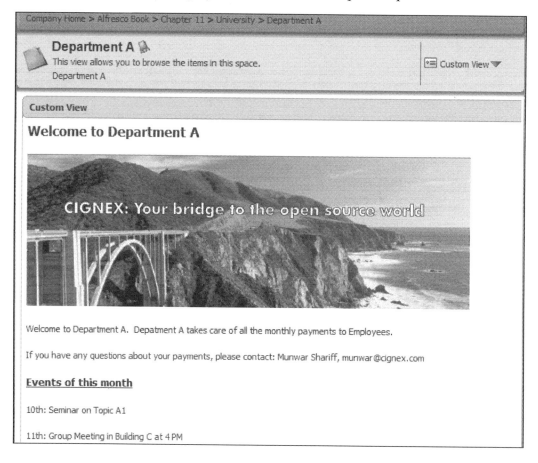

Summary

The web-client user interface can be customized to display your personal dashboard information such as the pending tasks, checked-out documents, and list of press releases. Presentation templates can be applied to spaces as well as content. Using a **Custom View** on a space you can consolidate all the important information at one place.

You can store content in the Alfresco repository in native XML format and use FreeMarker custom templates to display the XML data in various formats such as PDF and HTML. You have an option of separating the actual content from display information so that you get the leverage of having multiple views of the same content.

12
Maintaining the System

Once the system is built and in use, it is equally important to maintain it. A well-maintained system will give the highest return on investments. This chapter provides you with information about exporting data, upgrading your system to newer versions, and backing up important data at regular intervals. You will also find general maintenance tips about topics such as maintaining log files and resetting the admin password.

By the end of this chapter you will have learned how to:

- Export and import your personal or department information
- Export and import the complete repository
- Back up your data on a regular basis for storage and retrieval
- Perform general maintenance tasks such as examining log files
- Set up replication for high availability
- Upgrade your Alfresco application to newer versions

Exporting and Importing of Content

Export and import is useful to bulk extract and load personal, department, or team information from one location to another location, within the repository or to some other repository. It is also useful to back up and restore department or complete repository content.

In some situations, you can use this to integrate with third-party systems. For example, you can send the exported content from the Alfresco repository to another content management system, or internal system. Similarly, you can package the external content and import it into the Alfresco repository.

Alfresco Content Package (ACP)

The Alfresco web client has web-based utilities to export and import content using an **Alfresco Content Package**. An Alfresco content package (otherwise known as an ACP file) is a single file (with an extension of .acp) that bundles together the metadata, and content files, for the information to be transported.

The process for export and import is simple. Export produces one or more ACP files, which hold the exported information. As with all files, you can place them somewhere secure, or transfer them using transports such as email, FTP, etc. Security settings only allow export of those items that are readable by the user performing the export.

Import of an ACP file is the reverse of an export. The information held in the ACP file is placed into the repository location chosen at the import time. By default, the import process creates a copy of the ACP-held information.

An ACP file is simply a ZIP archive whose structure is as follows:

```
/<packagename>.xml
/<packagename>/
    contentNNN.pdf
    contentNNN.txt
    ...
```

The packagename is assigned on export. The XML conforms to the export and import view schema, which describes the transported nodes in terms of their types, aspects, properties, associations, and permissions. Content properties are handled, specifically where the binary content of the property is held in a separate file under the packagename directory of the ZIP archive and the XML contains a reference to the file.

Although the repository provides different ways to create an ACP file (i.e. export), it is also possible, to manually create one via any means. This is very useful for system-to-system integration.

Export and Import of Space Content

Any user of Alfresco may perform an export and import of folders and files they have access to. You can choose any space (personal or department) to export.

The scope of information to export is configurable, but typically involves specifying the location within the repository to export. For example, if you choose to export content in one specific space (say **Company Home | Intranet | Finance Department**), then the exported data includes:

- The current space and all the sub-spaces
- All documents (files, images, HTML/XML content, custom content, all versions) within the space and sub-spaces
- Complete metadata (aspects, audit, versions) associated with the documents
- Business rules set on spaces
- Invited users to a space or content item

Export of a Department Space using the Web Client

The process for export of a space within the web client is as follows.

1. Select a specific space to export (say Sales Department in your sample *Intranet* application).

2. Select the **More Actions | View Details** link to view the **Details** page of the space.

3. Select the **Export** action to launch the **Export** dialog as shown in the following screenshot:

4. Fill out the export options as follows: :
   - **Package name**: Name of the resulting export ACP file.
   - **Destination**: The location within the repository to place the ACP file.
   - **Include children**: If selected, will also export sub-folders.
   - **Include this space**: If selected, exports the selected folder, otherwise only exports the children.

- ○ **Run export in background**: If selected, the export will take place in the background eventually creating the export ACP file.

5. Select the **OK** button.

On success, the destination location will contain the ACP file. At this point the ACP file can be saved to a local file system for safe backup or transfer via email.

Import of a Department Space using the Web Client

The process for importing an ACP file within the web client is as follows:

1. Select a space to import information into.

2. Select the **More Actions | View Details** link to view the **Details** page of the space.

3. Select the **Import** action to launch the **Import** dialog as shown in the screenshot below:

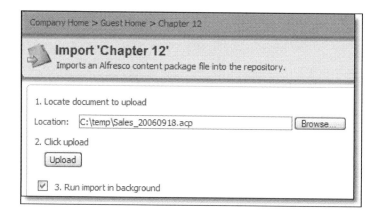

4. Fill out the import options as follows:

- ○ **Location**: Select an ACP file to import from the file system.
- ○ Select the **Upload** button.
- ○ **Run in background**: if selected, the import will take place in the background eventually creating all folders and files held in the ACP file.

5. Select **OK**.

On success, the information exported is extracted from the ACP file, and it will now reside in the destination space.

Export and Import of the Complete Repository

As an administrator of the Alfresco application, you may perform a full export and import. The exported data includes:

- Users' details including their name, email ID, passwords
- Groups and group users
- Categories and sub-categories
- Space templates, presentation templates, and email templates
- All scripts — JavaScripts files
- All spaces, sub-spaces
- All discussion forums
- All documents — files, images, XML files, custom content item
- Meta-data — aspects, audit information
- All business rules
- Security — invited users to a space or content
- Process — information about business process tasks pending and completed
- Saved searches — searches saved as reports for later use

Full export and import is used for backup purposes, or migrating from one installation to another. Migration may take place even if the source and destination repository databases are different, or the Alfresco versions are different (although some adjustment of the ACP-held information may be necessary). This is particularly useful for staging deployments.

Export via the Alfresco Web Client Administration Console

To export the full repository, click on the **Administration Console** button provided in the top menu, and click on the **Export** link. The export administration screen provides a **Complete Repository** option as shown in the screenshot on the next page:

It is recommended to use **Export** as the package name because the import scripts expect the package name **Export**.

This option creates several ACP files (plus one XML file) in the chosen repository location, where each ACP file represents a part of the repository storage. All file names are prefixed with the specified package name as listed in the screenshot below:

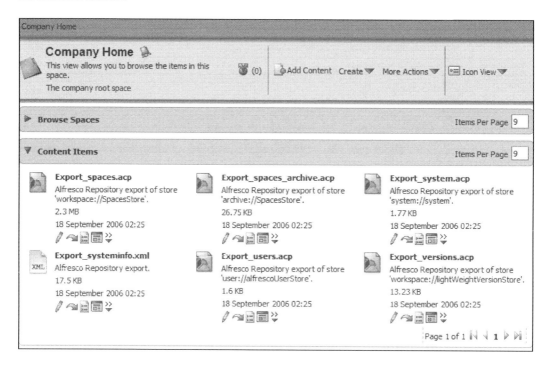

Full export may take some time. It is recommended that the usage of the repository is suspended while its export takes place.

Once export is complete, the next step is to extract the created files out of the repository. This is easiest via the CIFS, FTP, or WebDAV interfaces, where it is possible to copy many files at once. At this point, move all the created files to a secure place for backup purposes.

Bootstrap the Destination Repository from ACP Files Exported from Full Export

The Alfresco repository supports a bootstrap process, which is initiated whenever the repository is first started. The process populates the repository with information that is required upon the first login, such as system users, data dictionary definitions, and important root folders.

The bootstrap process is configurable allowing the population of any information during the first start of the repository. It is this configurability that allows the repository to be bootstrapped from an existing full repository export as described earlier. Upon startup of the repository, all the information exported from the source repository is imported, so that once started, the new repository will look just like the source repository.

 When exporting and importing from an older repository version to a newer repository version, all applicable patches are automatically applied.

Follow the steps given below for configuring the bootstrap process for a full restore.

1. Install Alfresco, but do not start (or ensure the existing Alfresco installation is configured against an empty database and file system).

2. Rename the existing `restore-context.xml.sample` to `restore-context.xml` in the configuration extension directory `/alfresco/extension`. For a Tomcat installation this is the `<install_folder>\tomcat\shared\classes\alfresco\extension` folder.

3. By default, `restore-context.xml` assumes a package name of `Export` was used. If this is not the case, replace all occurrences of `Export` with your package name.

4. Create a directory called `restore` within `/alfresco/extension`.

5. Place the exported files from the source repository into the /alfresco/ extension/restore folder.

6. Start Alfresco.

If all is configured correctly, log messages detailing the import of each back-up file are presented to the Alfresco server console.

Using Business Rules to Import Data

Using Alfresco rules and actions, it is possible to set up an automated import whereby an ACP file is automatically imported into the repository when placed into a designated space.

For example, the following rule (shown in the screenshot below) is defined against an *Import Drop Zone* space, which has a condition of *.acp and if met, has an action to import the ACP into the *Imported Content* space.

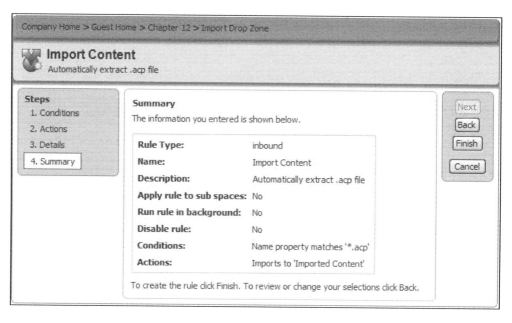

When an ACP file is placed into the *Import Drop Zone* space it automatically kicks off the import process and places the items held in the ACP file into the *Imported Content* space.

The important point to remember is that the import will be initiated regardless of how the ACP file was placed into the folder. For example, the import will initiate if the ACP file was placed there via CIFS, FTP, WebDAV, web client, or API. This is particularly powerful for system-to-system data integration.

Using Command-Line Tools

As of version 1.4, the Alfresco export and import tools are developed directly against the Alfresco repository foundation APIs. This means they execute stand-alone with an embedded repository. To perform an export and import via these tools requires configuration of the repository to ensure the appropriate storage locations (e.g. database and file system directory) are used.

Export Tool

The export tool is useful when you want to extract certain data from the Alfresco repository without using the Alfresco web client application. The Java class file for the export tool is located at `org.alfresco.tools.export`.

Since the Alfresco repository imposes a strict security policy, you need to provide your authentication credentials (user name and password) no matter how you access the repository.

The usage of the tool is as follows:

```
Usage: export -user <username> -pwd <password> -s[tore] <store>
[options] <packagename>
```

Where:

`<username>` is your log-in user ID.

`<password>` is your password.

`<store>` is the store to extract from, in the form of `scheme://store_name`.

`<packagename>` is the name of the file to export to (with or without extension).

Other important `[options]` include:

`-path`: the path within the store to extract from (the default is "/", which is the root directory).

`-nochildren`: do not extract children.

`-overwrite`: force overwrite of existing export package if it already exists.

`-quiet`: do not display any messages during export.

`-verbose`: report export progress.

For example to export the Intranet space from the repository, you would use the following command.

```
export -user admin -pwd admin -s workspace://SpacesStore -path /
companyhome -verbose Intranet.acp
```

Import Tool

The import tool is useful when you want to upload certain data into the Alfresco repository without using the Alfresco web client application. The Java class file for the import tool is located at org.alfresco.tools.Import.

The usage of the tool is as follows:

```
Usage: import -user <username> -pwd <password> -s[tore] <store>
[options] <packagename>
```

The [options] are as follows:

-path: the path within the store to import into (the default is "/" which is the root directory).

-verbose: report export progress.

-uuidBinding: CREATE_NEW, REMOVE_EXISTING, REPLACE_EXISTING, UPDATE_EXISTING, THROW_ON_COLLISION (default: CREATE_NEW).

For example to import the Intranet space into the repository, you would use the following command.

```
import -user admin -pwd admin -s workspace://SpacesStore -path /
companyhome -verbose -uuidBinding REPLACE_EXISTING Intranet.acp
```

It is possible to import from an ACP file or just a XML file. Importing just XML is useful if you want to import nodes without associated binary content e.g. People.

Data Backup

This is one of the most important, yet also one of the most neglected, areas of computing. Backing up your data should be at the top of your computer maintenance list, right next to virus protection. Without data backup, you are running the risk of losing your data. And it will happen; don't think that you don't have to worry about it.

Data loss can happen in many ways. One of the most common causes is the physical failure of the media the data is stored on. In some situations, users of the system might have deleted the content due to some error. No matter what, your data is your intellectual property and you have to protect it by taking proper backups regularly.

List of Items for Backup

Alfresco stores the content information in both database and file system. You need to back up both the file system and the relational database. As a part of implementation, you might have customized Alfresco, and hence you need to back up customization files. If you have used an external membership system such as Active Directory or OpenLDAP then you might have to back up the user and group data as well.

You can set up automated processes to back up data periodically. On Linux operating systems, you can write a **cronjob** to run a backup script on regular basis. Similarly, all other operating systems support back-up utilities, which you can use.

Most often, people tend to store the back-up data on the same server. This might create issues when the server crashes. Hence, it is recommended to move the back-up data on to some other external server to store.

In this section, let us examine various types of data that need to be backed up.

Content Stored in the File System

Typically the content in the file system is stored in your `<install_folder>\alf_data` folder as shown in the screenshot below. The folder `contentstore` contains the binary content with all the versions. The folders `lucene-indexes` and `backup-lucene-indexes` contain search information. The folder `audit.contentstore` contains audit trail details.

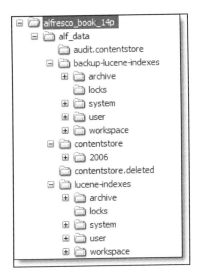

You need to back up the entire folder `alf_data` and the contents. Most operating systems provide back-up utilities.

If you are Windows user, you may use the back-up utility that comes with Windows XP (it is installed by default with the XP Home). You will find it from the **Start** menu under **All Programs | Accessories | System Tools | Backup**. When you start it, you are presented with the backup wizard.

Metadata Stored in the Relational Database

The relational database contains a bunch of tables defined as per the Alfresco schema. These tables hold information about users, security, audit, spaces, metadata, rules, scripts, and various business processes (jBPM).

Most of the database vendors (commercial or open source) provide utilities to take a database dump. Based on the database you have selected during installation (MySQL or Oracle or MS SQL Server) you can use an appropriate utility to take the database dump.

MySQL database provides a utility called `mysqldump` to back up both the database table definitions and contents. It can be used to dump a database or a collection of databases for backup or for transferring the data to another SQL server (not necessarily a MySQL server). The dump contains SQL statements to create the tables or populate them, or both.

The following is the command to take a database backup in MySQL.

```
Syntax: mysqldump [options] db_name [tables] [> output_file_name]
```

An example command is:

```
> mysqldump alfresco > alfresco_outfile.sql
```

Customization Files

You might be customizing your Alfresco application over a period of time. Typically you might have added or updated the following files:

- Logos, images, and style sheets
- JSP Files (dashboard)
- Presentation templates
- Configuration files, property files
- Files in the extension folder
- Custom application code (WAR File, source Java files, etc.)

The process you follow to maintain and back up your customization files depends upon the development process you follow within your organization. It is useful to maintain your customization files in some configuration management system such as CVS or SVN, which helps you to easily maintain and back them up.

Membership Data

If you have used the Alfresco out-of-the-box membership system, then the data is stored in the relational database. You don't have to do any special tasks to back up the data as you are already backing up the relational database tables.

If you have used an external membership system such as Active Directory or OpenLDAP to have single sign-on or centralized identity management system, then you must consider backup of your membership data.

You will have access to back-up tools based on the membership system you have used. Ensure that the data in the external membership system is backed up.

Log Files

The location of the log files depends upon the application server. For a Tomcat installation, the log files are located at `<install_folder>` itself. Tomcat application server creates a log file per day. The current log file is named `alfresco.log` and at the end of the day, the log file will be backed up as `alfresco.log.YYYY-MM-DD` (for example `alfresco.log.2006-09-18`).

Based on the usage of the system, and based on the logging level, the size of these log files might be pretty big. Hence it is a good practice to back up the older log files and remove them from the current location to save hard disk space.

Back-up Frequency

The frequency at which you take a back up really depends upon the nature of the application, your availability requirements, and the Alfresco deployment option you have chosen.

For example, you can consider only one time backup of customization files. You can back up the files whenever you enhance the application or upgrade the application to newer versions.

Since the content, metadata, and tasks change very frequently, the regular back up of Alfresco file system and relational database is required. You have to consider the business risk and system resources availability while deciding on the back-up frequency.

Backup is Based on Alfresco Deployment

If your application is highly accessed by thousands of users, then it is important for you to deploy Alfresco in a clustered environment. If it is a critical application such as finance, or insurance, then you should consider deploying Alfresco in hot back-up mode with master-slave configuration. The data backup policy and process might be different based on the way you have deployed Alfresco.

The typical process to back up the Alfresco repository is as follows:

1. Stop Alfresco to ensure that no one can make changes during the back up.
2. Export the MySQL (or other) database.
3. Back up the Alfresco `alf_data` directory.
4. Start Alfresco.

To restore the Alfresco repository:

1. Stop Alfresco.
2. Delete the `alf_data` folder and Restore the `alf_data` folder that you backed up earlier.
3. Drop the database and Import the database that you have exported.
4. Start Alfresco.

Alfresco Deployed as Repository Application Server

In this deployment (shown in the following figure) the web application becomes the host for an embedded repository and remote access is via the application i.e. HTTP. This is the default deployment option chosen by the Alfresco installer. This means the repository automatically benefits from any enhanced features provided by higher-end web application servers. For example, the repository can be embedded inside Apache Tomcat for the lightest weight deployment, but also embedded inside J2EE-compliant application servers from JBoss, Oracle, or IBM to take advantage of distributed transactions etc.

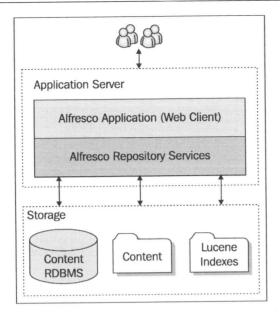

In this deployment option, you need to take a back up of the `alf_data` folder and the database. There will be one copy of the customization files.

Alfresco Deployed as Clustered Repository Server

A Clustered Repository Server, as shown in the following figure overleaf, supports large numbers of requests by employing multiple processes against a single Repository store. Each Embedded Repository is hosted in its own Web Server and the collection as a whole (i.e. the Cluster) acts as a single Repository.

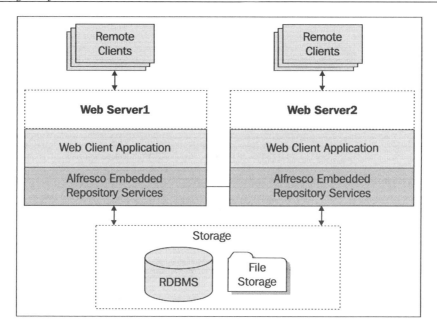

In this deployment option, you need to take a back up of the alf_data folder and the database. A set of customization files needs to be provided per web server box.

Alfresco Deployed in Hot Backup Mode

In this deployment, as shown in the figure on the next page, one Repository server is designated the master and another completely separate Repository server is designated the slave. The live application is hosted on the master and as it is used, synchronous and asynchronous replication updates are made to the slave, i.e. the backup. The backup remains in read-only mode. If for some reason the master breaks down, it is a relatively simple task to swap over to the slave to continue operation.

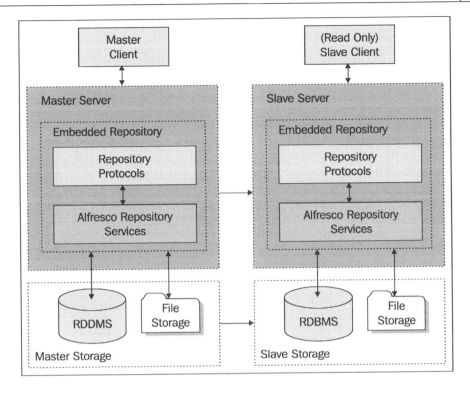

In this deployment option, you don't have to take a regular backup as the data is getting backed up automatically.

General Maintenance Tips

If you maintain the system regularly by cleaning up the database and by fixing the system errors, your system runs faster. Some of the tips are given in this section.

Regular Maintenance of Deleted Items

When you delete an item (content or space) in Alfresco, the item will not be deleted from the server, it will be moved to a temporary store called the archive space store. This gives an opportunity for you to recover the content that you have deleted earlier. More information about recovering the deleted content is provided in Chapter 5.

Deleted items will be in the temporary store for ever, consuming significant amount of storage space. It is the best practice to purge them periodically. Purged items are deleted forever, and can not be recovered. It is recommended to take regular backups of your data.

Examine Log Files

Your log files tell you very important issues and problems about your system. The level of details logged will be based on the level of logging (INFO, ERROR and DEBUG). Refer to Chapter 3, *Planning*, where you have set the level of logging to debug.

The log files are named `alfresco.log` (current one) or `alfresco.log.YYYY-MM-DD` (older ones). Examine one of the log files and you will notice the log entries made in the following categories.

- ERROR – Error occurred (requires FIX)
- WARN – Warning message (requires your attention)
- INFO – General information about the system

Sample messages are given below.

```
14:20:42,088 WARN  [org.hibernate.cache.EhCacheProvider] Could not
find configuration [org.jbpm.graph.def.Node]; using defaults.
14:21:45,056 ERROR [org.alfresco.repo.action.ActionServiceImpl] An
error was encountered whilst executing the action 'import'.
org.alfresco.service.cmr.view.ImporterException: Failed to import
package at line 8; column 19 due to error: A complete repository
package cannot be imported here...
15:03:19,308 INFO  [org.alfresco.repo.admin.patch.PatchExecuter] No
patches were required. .
```

You have to fix the errors listed in the log file and make sure there are no more ERROR messages in the log files. There are many utilities (based on the operating sytem), which examine the log file for ERRORs and send you notifications as required. Consider using such tool or developing such tool to be notified as soon as an ERROR occurs.

Reset the Administrator Password

Administrator has the highest powers in the Alfresco application. It is a good practice to periodically change the administrator password as a security process. You can change the password using the web client interface.

If for some reason you forgot the administrator password, you can reset the password as follows:

1. Configure the authentication component to accept all logins, using `org.alfresco.repo.security.authentication.SimpleAcceptOrRejectAllAuthenticationComponentImpl`.

2. Log in as anyone who has admin rights.

3. Reset the password.

4. Revert the configuration.

Reset the Complete Repository Data

If you are setting up an environment to test your Alfresco application, you might want to remove or reset the data once the testing is done. There might be other circumstances, where you want to remove the existing users, spaces, and rules from the repository, and start fresh. Before deleting or resetting the complete repository, you might want to back it up.

This is the process to reset the complete repository data:

1. Stop Alfresco.

2. Remove the `alf_data` folder.

3. Drop Alfresco database and create empty alfresco database.

4. Start Alfresco.

When you start Alfresco, the `alf_data` folder will be created and the default database tables will be created automatically.

Upgrading to New Versions of Alfresco

You can consider upgrading to a new version of Alfresco if you are expecting one of the following benefits:

- Security patches
- Bug fixes
- New features
- Compatibility with other systems

Even if you are not getting the benefits listed above, sometimes you might consider upgrading to newer version as you do not want to maintain a big gap between the Alfresco version on which your application is currently running and the latest Alfresco version. If this gap is too big, it might be very expensive for you to upgrade later on. This is the scenario with most enterprise software.

Alfresco has upgrade scripts, which help you to upgrade to newer versions automatically. However, it is essential to follow certain best practices while upgrading your system. Always try upgrading the test or staging server first before trying on the production server. It is essential that you back up your existing data before attempting an upgrade. Follow the information and instructions given in the *Data Backup* section.

Upgrading to a Minor Release

An Alfresco minor (or dot) release typically contains bug fixes and minor enhancements. There will not be any new features. An example is upgrading from Alfresco 1.3 to 1.3.1 release.

Since there are no new features, typically, the database schema remains the same. In this situation, you can replace only the web application (WAR) file to upgrade.

The WAR file (`alfresco.war`) for a Tomcat installation is located at the `<install_folder>\tomcat\webapps` folder.

Follow the following steps for minor upgrades:

1. Download the latest **alfresco.war** file from the Alfresco website.
2. Stop Alfresco.
3. Back up all the data including customization files (as explained in the earlier sections).
4. Delete the web application folder `<install_folder>\tomcat\webapps\alfresco`.
5. Replace the `alfresco.war` file in `<install_folder>\tomcat\webapps` folder with the latest one.
6. Restore the customization files.
7. Start Alfresco.

Test your application after upgrading it to ensure that the upgrade is successful.

Upgrading to a Major Release

An Alfresco major release typically contains new features, performance enhancements, and bug fixes. An example is upgrading from Alfresco 1.3 to 1.4 or from 1.4 to 2.0 releases.

As of 1.4.0, upgrade scripts will be executed automatically by the server, when starting up against an existing database. Scripts that support the various Hibernate dialects can be found in the `<configRoot>/alfresco/dbscripts/upgrade/*` folders. This means that you don't have to do manual upgrades any more.

For example, let us assume that you are using a Tomcat bundle of Alfresco 1.3.1 (installed in the `C:\alfresco1.3.1` folder) on Windows operating system, and you want to upgrade to Alfresco 1.4 release.

Follow the steps given below for major upgrades:

1. Stop Alfresco in your current installation folder `C:\alfresco1.3.1`.

2. Back up all the data including customization files (as explained in the earlier sections).

3. Download the complete Alfresco package, Tomcat bundle for Windows operating system.

4. Perform a new installation in different folder (say `C:\alfresco1.4`).

5. Copy the older Alfresco file content folder to the newer installation (Copy `C:\alfresco1.3.1\alf_data` folder to `C:\alfresco1.4\alf_data`)

6. Create a new database table and restore the relational database content from the older database. Update the Alfresco configuration file in the new installation to point to this new database.

7. Restore the customization files in the new installation.

8. Start Alfresco in the new installation.

Though most of the upgrade happens automatically, you might have to perform some manual steps to restore your customization files in the new installation.

There are some configuration files and a properties file in Alfresco's config folder (`\tomcat\webapps\alfresco\WEB-INF\classes\alfresco\`) that you might have updated, which requires manual updates.

While I was writing this book, I upgraded the example application from Alfresco 1.3.1 version to Alfresco 1.4 version. I used the following script to restore some of the customization files. I manually updated some of the configuration files. Refer to the batch file, which I used to restore the customization files on the Windows platform:

```
rem  --------------------------------------------------------------------
rem Replaces/Adds Alfresco Custom Files to new Alfresco installation
rem  --------------------------------------------------------------------
set L_LOCALDIR=%CD%
set L_SRCDIR=C:\J2EE\alfresco_book_131
set L_DESTDIR=C:\J2EE\alfresco_book_14p
rem ----------- Replace Logos ----------------
CD %L_DESTDIR%\tomcat\webapps\alfresco\images\logo
move AlfrescoLogo32.png AlfrescoLogo32.png-ORIGINAL
move AlfrescoLogo200.png AlfrescoLogo200.png-ORIGINAL
move AlfrescoFadedBG.png AlfrescoFadedBG.png-ORIGINAL
copy %L_SRCDIR%\tomcat\webapps\alfresco\images\logo\
                                   AlfrescoLogo32.png  .
copy %L_SRCDIR%\tomcat\webapps\alfresco\images\logo\
                                   AlfrescoLogo200.png  .
```

```
copy %L_SRCDIR%\tomcat\webapps\alfresco\images\logo\
                                      AlfrescoFadedBG.png .
rem ----------- Copy files in extension folder ---------------
CD %L_DESTDIR%\tomcat\shared\classes\alfresco\extension
copy %L_SRCDIR%\tomcat\shared\classes\alfresco\extension\
                                      custom-model-context.xml .
copy %L_SRCDIR%\tomcat\shared\classes\alfresco\extension\
                                      customModel.xml .
copy %L_SRCDIR%\tomcat\shared\classes\alfresco\extension\
                                      web-client-config-custom.xml .
CD %L_LOCALDIR%
echo I am done...
pause
```

You can create your own batch scripts to automatically restore your customization files. Typically most developers use tools such as Eclipse to build and deploy customization files to newer installations.

Test your application after upgrading it to ensure that the upgrade is successful.

Summary

The Alfresco web client has administrative utilities to export data from the Alfresco repository and import it within the repository or to another repository. It is also useful to back up and restore the department or complete repository content. It some situations, you can use this to integrate with third-party systems.

You must back up data at regular intervals to protect your data from hardware failures. Consider the hot backup-deployment option of Alfresco for high availability. If you need a high performance repository, you must consider deploying Alfresco in a clustered environment.

The upgrade scripts in Alfresco help you to upgrade to newer versions automatically. It is recommended that you try an upgrade on a test or staging server before going into the production server.

13

Implementing Imaging and Forms Processing

Alfresco is integrated with scanning and OCR (Optical Character Recognition) technologies. This chapter helps you to implement an end-to-end solution by collecting the paper documents and forms; transforming them into accurate, retrievable information; and delivering them into an organization's business applications. The information is then full-text searchable and goes through the various approval workflows, based on the organization's defined business process management.

By the end of this chapter you will have learned how to:

- Connect a scanner to a network drive and map it to the Alfresco's space
- Specify a business rule to automatically extract metadata from the scanned document
- Define and execute a workflow process for scanned documents
- Bulk upload scanned documents into the Alfresco repository
- Integrate OCR utilities into Alfresco
- Integrate and use Kofax Ascent Capture
- Integrate Alfresco with eCopy-enabled scanners

Introduction

You can extend the value of your ECM investment by implementing imaging and automated forms processing solutions, as per your organizational requirements. Increasingly, electronic document images have the same legal status as a paper document.

Alfresco integrates with various image capturing systems to provide flexible and intelligent form processing. This results in greater control and management of crucial information and documents, within and outside the firewall. These joint solutions enable you to include forms and the captured data as content types that can be version controlled, repurposed, integrated into workflows and managed by the ECM environment. This simplifies compliance with enhanced archiving, and audit capabilities. You can also reduce the costs of printing, storing, and distributing paper forms.

You can implement various solutions by leveraging the Alfresco's content management and business process management features. Some are listed below for your reference:

- Order fulfillment
- Claims processing
- Underwriting
- Loan origination
- Contracts management
- Accounts payable managing checks and invoices

Electronic Imaging and the Paperless Office

Managing paper documents is not easy. Distribution of paper documents is manual, and slow. The high cost of filing and retrieving them makes them expensive to manage. Eelectronic imaging technology offers an effective solution to these problems. The concept of "the paperless office" is up to scan and digitize business documents, and to process the images instead of the paper itself.

Electronic imaging produces the following benefits:

- Reduces shortage space
- Documents are stored as magnetic or optical images reducing the possibility of their deterioration due to age, adverse temperatures, or weather conditions
- Facilitates instant retrieval of the documents
- Document security by providing view, edit, and delete access only to the concerned people
- Simultaneous access to documents for multiple users
- Usage and tracking of documents
- Centralized database of documents belonging to various departments

- Helps speed-up business decisions, which requires approval processes
- File integrity, as the use of read-only files prevent document images from being altered

In early years of imaging, the absence of a workflow was the main barrier to customer acceptance. The development of robust workflow systems has driven widespread adoption of electronic imaging by allowing web-based approval processes.

Forms Processing

Automated forms processing is used to capture data on forms that are filled in by manual means using hand writing, machine printing, and checkboxes; and then returned to a centralized location for batch processing. Imaged hand writing or machine print is of little value until it is converted into computer-usable (ASCII) data.

Forms automation is ICR (Intelligent Character Recognition) intensive, and involves a process to convert bitmapped image data into ASCII data. Since over 80% of all business documents are forms, manual data entry to covert forms constitutes an enormous expense, which can be significantly diminished through the use of recognition-based automated forms processing.

The following is a typical process to convert and manage the forms in a content management system:

1. Scanning: Pages of forms are scanned, and converted into bitmapped (usually TIFF) images of forms, which are either compressed and stored for later batch processing, or are passed immediately in an uncompressed format to an ICR engine for recognition.

2. Image Enhancement: The document image is cleaned up and character images are enhanced, using image enhancement techniques.

3. Information Extraction: An information extraction template identifies which individual fields on the form image require recognition, and what is the nature of those fields. They can be barcode, signature, hand writing, machine print, numeric, alphabetic, and alphanumeric.

4. Electronic Content: The image with the converted ASCII data is then moved to a content management system as a content item. The information extracted from the form is stored as properties of the content item.

5. Workflow: The content goes through various workflow approval processes and is finally stored for future access.

Alfresco for Imaging and Forms Processing

Alfresco already has imaging solutions with Kofax and eCopy. You can also use the network drive features of Alfresco to automatically upload all the scanned documents to the repository without having a tight integration between your scanner and the Alfresco repository.

The figure below shows a sample architecture diagram using Alfresco for imaging and forms processing. A remote office can be connected to your central Alfresco repository to bulk upload the scanned documents. The documents could be forms, checks, invoices, engineering diagrams, legal contracts, or any kind of paper documents.

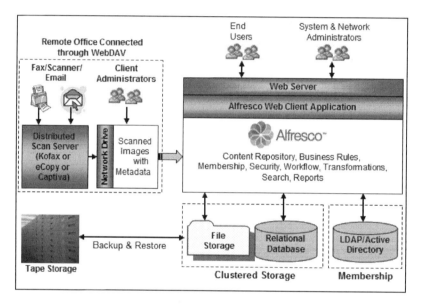

Once a document is uploaded to a space, business rules will be triggered, moving the document through a workflow process. The documents and the search indexes can be stored in high-end file storage, such as EMC Centera and the metadata can be stored in the relational database such as Oracle or MySQL. The storage can be clustered for high performance and heavy loads. You can even consider having single sign-on with an existing Active Directory or LDAP membership system.

Alfresco is highly scalable in terms of storage and performance. Alfresco is being used by a large French bank for loading all faxes of client trades into the repository. On a low-powered machine the bank was getting around 350 TIFF images loaded per minute (21,000 documents per hour), and the scalability tests showed that this could be scaled up pretty easily with more horsepower.

Example Imaging Solution with Workflow

Let us consider a sample imaging use case scenario. Let us say you have remote client offices, which scan all the checks, OCR them, extract metadata, and send them over to you for approval, payment, and storage.

The sample solution provided in this section uses all the features you have learned so far including business rules, transformations, security, and workflow. The solution will receive a scanned a paper document (such as check or claim form), OCRs it, extracts important data, transforms the document to a required format (such as a GIF image) and delivers it to your business application and database.

Refer to the architecture diagram shown in the previous figure. A remote office can be connected to your central Alfresco repository to bulk upload scanned documents. Once a document is uploaded to a space, business rules will be triggered transforming the document to a required format and moving it through a workflow process.

You are going to perform the following steps for a demo application:

1. Set up a space and security for your remote offices. You can create a separate space for each remote office to receive the scanned documents.

2. A remote office connects the scanner to a network folder, and maps it to Alfresco's space via WebDAV (HTTP protocol).

3. The scanned documents (checks, claims, and forms) will enter the Alfresco repository in TIFF format.

4. The Alfresco business rule extracts metadata and attaches it to the scanned image.

5. These documents will be automatically transformed from the TIFF format to a GIF format, and sent to the *Review* space. When a document gets into the Review space, the workflow kicks-off.

6. The reviewer can visit this space, and review the document. He or she can approve or reject the document.

7. The approved document will then be moved to the *Approved* space and then to the *Cut Check* space.

8. The rejected checks will be stored in the *Rejected* space and an email notification will be sent to the concerned people.

Set up Space and Security

Log in to the Alfresco web client, and go to the **Company Home | Intranet | Finance Department** space, and create a new space called *Office Accounts* for the imaging solution demo application.

Under the *Office Accounts* space, create the following sub-spaces:

- 01_Inbox
- 02_Under Review
- 03_Approved
- 04_Rejected
- 05_Cut Checks

Under *Offices*, create two office sub-spaces called *OFFICE1* and *OFFICE2*

- Offices
    - OFFICE1
    - OFFICE2

Set security for each office accordingly so that only the office personal have write access to that space. Go to the **Company Home | Intranet | Finance Department | Office Accounts | Offices | OFFICE1** space, and set the security. For example, you can add a user (say user1 from your remote Office1) and give the user the **Contributor** role so that he or she can add documents to the *OFFICE1* space. To ensure security, make sure nobody else has write access to this space, except some of the employees of Office1. For more information about securing spaces, refer to Chapter 4, *Implementing Membership and Security*.

Similarly, you can set security for the *OFFICE2* space.

Business Rule to Extract Important Metadata

Define a single business rule, which does the following three actions on all the incoming documents in the *Offices* space and all the sub-spaces.

1. Add the *Customer Details* aspect
2. Execute a script to extract important metadata, and fill the document properties
3. Move the document to the *01_Inbox* space

Refer to Chapter 7, where you have added a custom aspect called *Customer Details* to add customer-specific properties to documents. The properties include `CustomerName`, `CustomerContactName`, `CustomerContactPhone`, `CustomerProjectID`, and `NewCustomer`.

You can create your own script, using JavaScript language to automatically fill the document properties on all the incoming scanned documents. As an example, create a file called `chapter13_fill_metadata.js` in your personal computer with the following code. The following JavaScript fills three properties as shown. The `CustomerName` property is filled with the name of the office space, and the other two properties `CustomerContactName` and `CustomeContactPhone` are filled with some fixed values as shown below:

```
if (document.hasPermission("Write"))
{
    if (document.mimetype == "image/tiff")
      {
        var l_currentSpace = document.parent;
        document.properties["custom:CustomerName"]
                                        = l_currentSpace.name;
        document.properties["custom:CustomerContactName"]
                                            = "Office Admin";
        document.properties["custom:CustomerContactPhone"]
                                            = "111-222-3333";

        document.save();
      }
}
```

Go to the **Company Home | Data Dictionary | Scripts** space, and click on the **Add Content** button and upload the `chapter13_fill_metadata.js` file. Now you have your own custom script that can be used in the business rules.

Go to the **Company Home | Intranet | Finance Department | Office Accounts | Offices** space, and create a business rule on all the incoming documents with three actions as shown in the screenshot below:

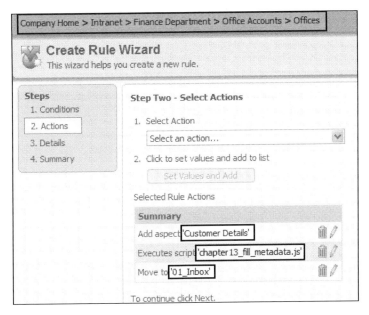

In the **Step Three—Enter Details** pane of the **Create Rule Wizard** provide appropriate **Title** and **Description**, and select the checkbox that says **Apply rule to sub spaces** as shown in the screenshot below:

Now, when a document gets into the *OFFICE1* space, additional properties will be added to the document (due to the *Customer Details* aspect), and some properties of the document will be pre-filled with data (due to the chapter9_fill_metadata. js script), and finally the document will be moved to the *01_Inbox* space for further workflow and approval.

Transform Documents to the Required Format

Create a new business rule on the *01_Inbox* space to transform the incoming TIFF file to a GIF image file and copy it to the *02_Under Review* space for the further workflow approval process.

Follow the steps provided below to add the business rule:

1. Ensure that you are in the **Company Home | Intranet | Finance Department | Office Accounts | 01_Inbox** space.

2. Click on **More Actions | Manage Content Rules**. Click on the **Create Rule** link, and you will see the **Create Rules Wizard**.

3. In the **Step One — Select Condition** drop-down list, select **Items with the specified mime type**, and click on the **Set Values and Add** button. In the **Set condition values** pop-up window, select the **TIFF Image** value as the **Type** and click on the **OK** button and then on the **Next** button.

4. In the **Step Two — Select Actions** drop-down list, select **Transform and Copy Image to a specific space** and click on the **Set Values and Add** button. In the **Set Action values** dialog window, select **GIF Image** as **Required Format** and the *02_Under Review* space as **Destination**. Leave the **Options** field empty to retain the size of the transformed image as it is. Click on the **OK** button and then on the **Next** button.

5. In **Step Three — Enter Details**, select **Inbound** as **Type**, and provide an appropriate **Title** and **Description** for this rule.

6. Finish the rule by clicking on the **Finish** button.

Define the Workflow Process

The next step is to define a workflow process for all the incoming documents, and set the option to send notifications to all concerned parties as shown in the figure below. For more information on defining the workflow and the email notifications, refer to Chapter 9.

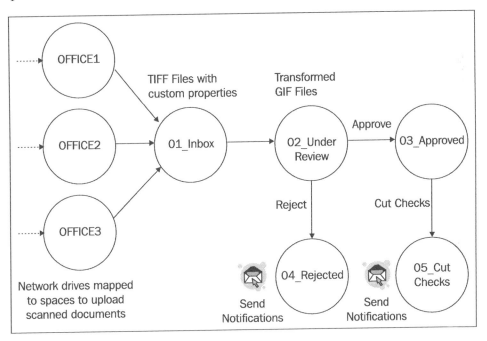

Add a simple workflow to all inbound items in the *02_Under Review* space. For the approve step, move the document to the *03_Approved* space and for the reject step, move the document to the *04_Rejected* space as shown in the previous figure.

Add simple workflow to all inbound items in the *03_Approved* space. For approve step, move the document to the *05_Cut Checks* space; and here there is no reject step.

Add a business rule to all inbound items in the *04_Rejected* space to send an email notification to the concerned people when a scanned document (check) is rejected.

Similarly, add a business rule to all inbound items in the *05_Cut Checks* space to send the email notifications to the concerned people, when a check is cut and released.

Connect a Scanner to a Network Folder

The scanner in your remote office can be connected to a local network folder (refer to the first figure of this chapter) and the network folder can be mapped to the Alfresco repository as a space via WebDAV or CIFS. More information about mapping a drive to Alfresco using CIFS or WebDAV is provided in Chapter 5.

You can map the network folder in your remote *Office1* to a secure space in Alfresco **(Intranet | Finance Department | Office Accounts | Offices | OFFICE1)**

To map the *OFFICE1* space in Alfresco as a network drive in the local Windows Explorer, follow the steps given below:

1. In the Windows Explorer, click on the **Tools | Map Network Drive** option. The **Map Network Drive** dialog appears.
2. Select an unused drive letter (say o for *OFFICE1* space).
3. In the folder text box, type \\<AlfrescoServer>_a\Alfresco\Intranet\ Finance Department\Office Accounts\Offices\OFFICE1. Replace <AlfrescoServer> with the actual server name.
4. Check the **Reconnect at logon** checkbox.
5. Click on the **Finish** button. As the space is secured the system will prompt for your authentication. Only users defined on the *OFFICE1* space will be able to connect to the *OFFICE1* space.
6. Type your Alfresco user name and password when prompted.

Bulk Upload Scanned Documents into the Repository

To test the network folder setup, drag-and-drop a few TIFF files from your personal computer to the o drive, which is mapped to the *OFFICE1* space. In the production environment, the scanner will be connected to the o drive to upload scanned images.

You will notice that as soon as the scanned documents (TIFF files) arrive in the *OFFICE1* space, additional properties are added to the documents, and the documents are moved to the *01_Inbox* space.

You will also notice that the original documents (TIFF format) are in the *01_Inbox* space and the transformed copies of the documents (in GIF format) are in the *02_Under Review* space for further workflow approval process.

If you examine the transformed documents in the *02_Under Review* space, you will notice a set of properties added and pre-filled due to business rules already applied on the documents. The screenshot below is the **Details View** of one of the documents in the *02_Under Review* space.

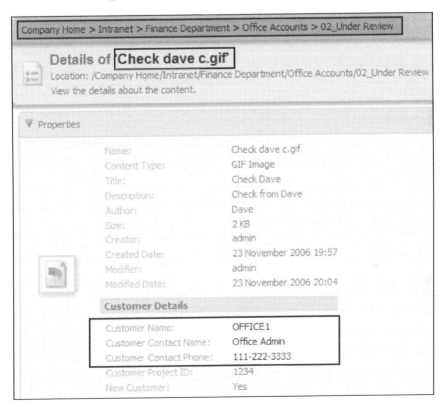

You can examine the documents in the *02_Under Review* space and either approve them or reject them. You can write a presentation template to have a custom view of all the documents in the *02_Under Review* space as shown in the screenshot below. More information about custom views is presented in Chapter 11.

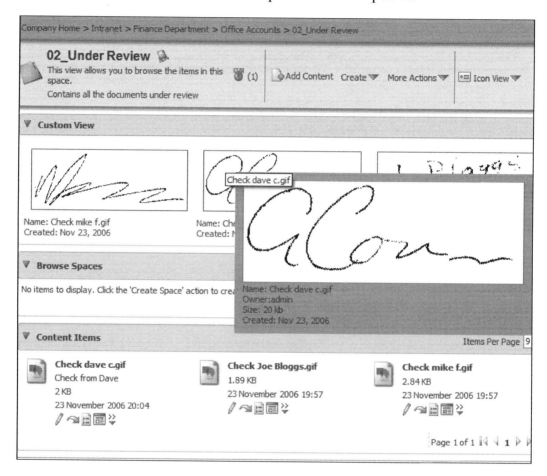

When you approve a document in the *02_Under Review* space, the document moves to the *03_Approved* space, and an email notification should be sent to the concerned people. When you reject a document in the *02_Under Review* space, the document moves to the *04_Rejected* space, and an email notification should be sent to the concerned people. Test the workflow by moving documents through various workflow spaces as shown in the figure defining the workflow.

Now that you have got an idea about implementing a solution, create a custom solution to solve your own business problem, and test it.

OCR Integration

Most of the OCR (Optical Character Recognition) utilities available in the market convert scanned archives into a PDF format, including both image and text in the same standard container. Alfresco supports a content transformation framework, where you can plug-in a third-party content transformation engine to convert a document from one format to another.

This gives you a great flexibility of converting your image document such as a TIFF file to a machine-readable format such as PDF, RTF, or Text.

The following figure illustrates the process of scanning a paper document using a network scanner and transferring the document in an image format into the Alfresco repository. Once the image document gets into the Alfresco repository, you can trigger a business rule, that converts it to a PDF document. You can still have the image document in the repository for future reference. The quality and the accuracy of the output PDF document will depend on the OCR utility you used for the transformation.

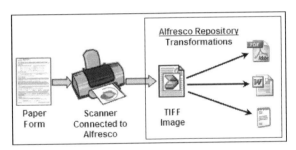

Intelliant OCR-Alfresco Bundle

Intelliant sells an OCR-Alfresco bundle, which can be downloaded from its web site. You can find more information about Intelliant's offerings from its website at, `http://www.intelliant.fr/en/alfresco-ocr-bundle.html`.

This OCR utility is integrated with the Alfresco repository as a content transformation. Intelliant's OCR utility converts TIFF images to PDF, RTF, and Text documents.

Follow the steps given below to enable OCR in Alfresco:

1. Download and install the Intelliant OCR utility.

2. Download and copy the Alfresco content transformations context file (`http://www.intelliant.fr/en/ocr-transformers-context.xml`) into Alfresco's `<extension>` folder.

3. Restart Alfresco.

4. Create a business rule on the space to automatically transform the incoming TIFF images to PDF documents.

This is the same process you need to follow to integrate any OCR utility into Alfresco.

Integration with Kofax Ascent Capture

Kofax is the world's leading provider of information capture solutions. Its product, Kofax Ascent Capture, is integrated with Alfresco offering customers access to a comprehensive production capture solution. The product includes automatic document classification, data extraction, and validation for both Internet-based distributed capture and centralized environments.

The integration was developed by Alfresco, Kofax, and a Kofax Certified Solution Provider—Aarden Ringcroft. The Kofax Ascent Capture integration module is available through the Alfresco Forge.

By leveraging the distributed features of Ascent Capture together with the power of the Alfresco web services API, integrators can easily deliver a scenario where documents are scanned in New York, validated in Bangalore, and then released to an Alfresco repository in London—all using standards based protocols.

Kofax Release Script Configuration

Alfresco Ascent Capture integration is built as release script. The release script connects to the Alfresco repository through web services, defines content types and aspects, maps indexing fields to content metadata, and transfers content as Image (TIFF), OCR Text, and PDF.

The following information will be captured via an Administration Dialog allowing configuration of the Release script:

- Alfresco Server Connection Details (username, password, repository instance)
- Destination Alfresco folder, where Kofax-captured information should be placed
- Mapping of Kofax-captured information (Metadata, TIFF, OCR, and PDF renditions) to the Alfresco Content Model
- Mapping of Kofax Document Class to the Alfresco Content Type
- Mapping of Kofax Index Value (as extracted from the document by Kofax) to an Alfresco property (of appropriate data type)
- Transferring Kofax Tiff, OCR, or PDF document to the Alfresco property (of binary data type)

The screenshot below shows the release script administration window's **Repository** tab. Notice that the connection to Alfresco is via URL over HTTP. There is no need to open special ports or use special protocols to communicate. All the files will be copied to the Alfresco space specified by the **Destination** field as shown in the following screenshot:

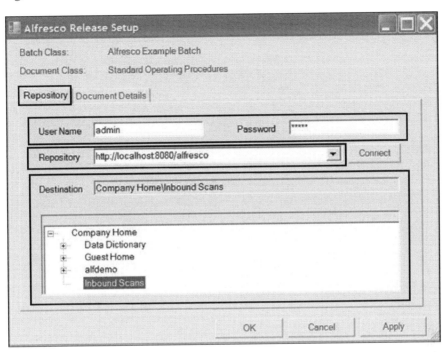

The screenshot on the next page shows the release script administration window's **Document Details** tab. Notice that the **Content Type** can be selected form the list of available types in the current Alfresco repository. Similarly, **Aspects** can be applied from the list of available aspects in the current repository.

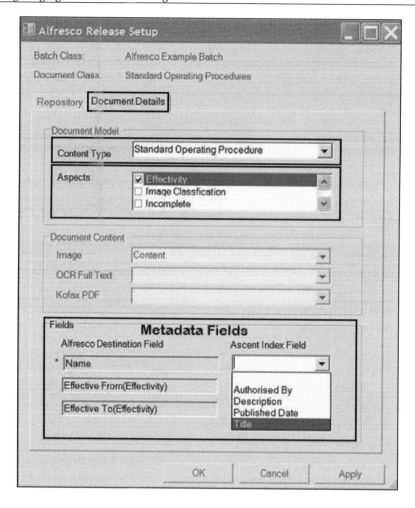

The **Document Content** section allows you to configure the formats that are released to the repository, which are Image (TIFF), OCR, Full Text, and PDF (Image/Image & Text). Multiple formats can be mapped to different content types. Text-based formats are full-text searchable within Alfresco.

Refer the above screenshot, where the metadata is listed dynamically, based on the content type selected. You can map the Kofax indexing fields to metadata so that when the document is scanned, the metadata is filled up automatically with values.

Release Script Functionality

The release script connects to Alfresco, using the connection details supplied. For each supplied Kofax document, release script does the following actions:

1. Starts a transaction

2. If the document does not already exist in the destination folder, creates one using the content type as defined in the **Administration** dialog, otherwise updates the existing document

3. Applies appropriate aspects (as defined in the **Administration** dialog)

4. Sets the property values (as supplied from Kofax, using mapping, as defined in the **Administration** dialog)

5. Sets the content (as supplied from Kofax, using mapping, as defined in the **Administration** dialog)

6. Returns the new content ID to Kofax providing a cross-reference between the systems

7. Commits or rolls back transaction based on success or error

If for some reason, a document could not be processed, then it reports the error back to Kofax so that some form of quality control can take place.

Integration with an eCopy-Enabled Scanner

eCopy provides products enabling anyone in an organization to transform paper documents into information that is easily integrated with all of their existing business workflows and applications. SIRA Systems Corporation (http://www.sirasystems.com) created a connector to integrate Alfresco into the eCopy suite, which allows users to scan in an image via eCopy and place it directly into Afresco.

Using the Alfresco connector, any documents can be scanned directly to a selected Alfresco repository using your eCopy-enabled digital copier or scanner. The Alfresco connector acts as an interface between your copier or scanner, and your Alfresco content management system. Once *eCopy ShareScan OP* is installed on your device, you can add the Alfresco connector, enabling your eCopy-enabled copier or scanner for adding the information directly into the selected Alfresco repository with user authentication.

Summary

Alfresco integrates with various image capturing systems. This adds to the flexibility, and provides intelligent forms processing that results in greater control and management of crucial information and documents, within and outside the firewall.

You can implement an OCR solution within Alfresco using the transformations framework. The Kofax Ascent integration also allows documents to be captured and stored in Alfresco, enabling customers to review and approve documents for long-term archival or records management purposes. Using the eCopy Alfresco connector, any documents can be scanned directly to a selected Alfresco repository using your eCopy-enabled digital copier or scanner.

Index

activities by assignee 236

RSS syndication
about 251
enabling 252, 253
RSS feeds, using 254, 255
RSS templates 256

S

scheduled actions
about 162
cron expression 167
example 163-166
XML configuration file 166-168

search engine, Alfresco
about 209
batch size, Lucene 212
Lucene, configuring 212, 213
max clauses, Lucene 212
max merge docs, Lucene 213
merge factor, Lucene 213
min merger docs, Lucene 213
properties, indexing 211
search results, limiting 210, 211

security model
choosing 85, 86
choosing, sample scenario 86
LDAP, configuring for centralized identity
    management 87
NTLM, configuring for single-sign-on 88
out-of-the-box security 86, 87

security permissions and roles
custom role, creating 79, 80
default permissions 78, 79
default roles 79

simple workflow
about 216
complex workflows, implementing 225
defining 217
email notification templates 224, 225
notification, sending to manager for ap-
    proval 221, 222
out of the box features 216, 217
spaces and security, identifying 217
testing 223
using 217
workflow, adding to items 219, 221

workflow process, defining 218, 219

space
business rules, using 129
copying, clipboard used 96
creating 67
custom icon, adding 262
custom view, applying on 259-261
default view, choosing 96
defining 83, 84
deleting 95
department space exporting, web client
    used 285, 286
department space importing, web client
    used 286
editing 94-96
exporting 284
hierarchy, importance 93
importing 284
managing 91-97
moving, clipboard used 96
properties, editing 94, 95
sample space structure for marketing
    project 97
securing 80-84
shortcut, creating 96
smart folder 92, 93
user roles 80, 81
users, inviting 81-83
views, configuring 258, 259

system users
existing users, searching 71
new user, creating 68-71
space, creating 67
user, deleting 72
user details, modifying 72

U

user access, individual
home page 73, 74
new user log in 73, 74
password, updating 74
personal details, updating 74

user groups
creating 75, 76
sub-groups, creating 75, 76
users, adding 76, 77

Thank you for buying
Alfresco

Packt Open Source Project Royalties

When we sell a book written on an Open Source project, we pay a royalty directly to that project. Therefore by purchasing Alfresco, Packt will have given some of the money received to the Alfresco project.

In the long term, we see ourselves and you—customers and readers of our books—as part of the Open Source ecosystem, providing sustainable revenue for the projects we publish on. Our aim at Packt is to establish publishing royalties as an essential part of the service and support a business model that sustains Open Source.

If you're working with an Open Source project that you would like us to publish on, and subsequently pay royalties to, please get in touch with us.

Writing for Packt

We welcome all inquiries from people who are interested in authoring. Book proposals should be sent to authors@packtpub.com. If your book idea is still at an early stage and you would like to discuss it first before writing a formal book proposal, contact us; one of our commissioning editors will get in touch with you.

We're not just looking for published authors; if you have strong technical skills but no writing experience, our experienced editors can help you develop a writing career, or simply get some additional reward for your expertise.

About Packt Publishing

Packt, pronounced 'packed', published its first book "Mastering phpMyAdmin for Effective MySQL Management" in April 2004 and subsequently continued to specialize in publishing highly focused books on specific technologies and solutions.

Our books and publications share the experiences of your fellow IT professionals in adapting and customizing today's systems, applications, and frameworks. Our solution-based books give you the knowledge and power to customize the software and technologies you're using to get the job done. Packt books are more specific and less general than the IT books you have seen in the past. Our unique business model allows us to bring you more focused information, giving you more of what you need to know, and less of what you don't.

Packt is a modern, yet unique publishing company, which focuses on producing quality, cutting-edge books for communities of developers, administrators, and newbies alike. For more information, please visit our website: www.PacktPub.com.

Implementing SugarCRM

ISBN: 1-904811-68-X   Paperback: 328 pages

A step-by-step guide to using this powerful Open Source application in your business.

1. Your complete guide to SugarCRM implementation – assess your needs, install the software, start using it, train users, integrate with existing systems

2. Covers both the free and commercial versions of SugarCRM – get maximum benefit from the free version before paying for add onst

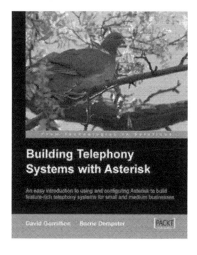

Building Telephony Systems With Asterisk

ISBN: 1-904811-15-9   Paperback: 180 pages

An easy introduction to using and configuring Asterisk to build feature-rich telephony systems for small and medium businesses.

1. Install, configure, deploy, secure, and maintain Asterisk

2. Build a fully-featured telephony system and create a dial plan that suits your needs

3. Learn from example configurations for different requirements

Please check **www.PacktPub.com** for information on our titles

Business Process Execution Language for Web Services 2nd Edition

ISBN: 1-904811-81-7 Paperback: 350 pages

An Architects and Developers Guide to BPEL and BPEL4WS.

1. Architecture, syntax, development and composition of Business Processes and Services using BPEL

2. Advanced BPEL features such as compensation, concurrency, links, scopes, events, dynamic partner links, and correlations

3. Oracle BPEL Process Manager and BPEL Designer Microsoft BizTalk Server as a BPEL server

Building Websites with OpenCms

ISBN: 1-904811-04-3 Paperback: 262 pages

A practical guide to understanding and working with this proven Java/JSP-based content management system.

1. Understand how OpenCms handles and publishes content to the Web

2. Learn how to create your own, complex, OpenCms website

3. Develop the skills to implement, customize, and maintain an OpenCms website

Please check **www.PacktPub.com** for information on our titles

17805156R00189

Made in the USA
Lexington, KY
28 September 2012